Exploring the Identity and Mission of Jesus

John Michael Perry

A Sheed & Ward Book

ROWMAN & LITTLEFIELD PUBLISHERS, INC.
Lanham • Boulder • New York • Toronto • Plymouth, UK

Other titles by John Michael Perry:

- *Exploring the Genesis and Creation and Fall Stories*
- *Exploring the Transfiguration Story*
- *Exploring the Resurrection of Jesus*
- *Exploring the Evolution of the Lord's Supper in the New Testament*

Sheed & Ward™ is a service of The National Catholic Reporter Publishing Company.

Library of Congress Cataloguing-in-Publication Data

Perry, John M., 1929-
Exploring the identity and mission of Jesus / John Michael Perry.
p. cm. — (Exploring scripture series)
ISBN: 1-55612-820-7 (pbk. : alk. paper)
1. Jesus Christ—Person and offices—Biblical teaching. 2. Bible N.T. Gospels—Criticism, interpretation, etc. I. Title. II. Series: Perry, John M., 1929- Exploring scripture series.
BT202.P447 1996
232'.8—dc20 95-45045
CIP

A SHEED & WARD BOOK

ROWMAN & LITTLEFIELD PUBLISHERS, INC.

Published in the United States of America
by Rowman & Littlefield Publishers, Inc.
A wholly owned subsidiary of The Rowman & Littlefield Publishing Group, Inc.
4501 Forbes Boulevard, Suite 200, Lanham, Maryland 20706
www.rowmanlittlefield.com

Contents

To Jeff Gierczak,
without whose prodding
this book might not have been written

Introduction

1

A NUMBER OF ASSUMPTIONS HELD BY CONSERVATIVE CHRISTIANS will be qualified or rejected in the course of this book. Although none of these assumptions belong to the *essential substance* of the Christian Message, they are usually thought to be essential by those who read sacred scripture literally. Such Christians might fear that the author of this book does not believe that the words of the Bible were inspired by God. This book's contents, therefore, will probably be more intelligible and less threatening if we begin with a brief reflection on the mystery of God's Self-revelation.

Traditional Christianity has assumed that God dictated the books of the Bible to their inspired authors. This view of revelation is found, for example, in the book of Exodus:

> Moses said to the LORD, "Oh, my Lord, I am not eloquent . . . but I am slow of speech and tongue." Then the LORD said to him, "Who has made man's mouth? Who makes him dumb, or deaf, or seeing, or blind. Is it not I, the LORD? Now therefore go, and I will be your mouth and teach you what you shall speak." (Ex 4:10-12)

> "Aaron, your brother . . . is coming out to meet you . . . . and you shall speak to him and put the words in his mouth; and I will be with your mouth and with his

> mouth, and will teach you what you shall do. He shall speak for you to the people; he shall be a mouth for you, and you shall be to him as God." (Ex 4:14b-16)

Contemporary biblical scholarship is convinced, however, that this ancient "mouth-to-ear" model must be deliteralized before it can be correctly understood by our scientifically advanced and critical age. The mouth-to-ear model of revelation (which assumes that God speaks directly into the physical or mental "ear" of the prophet) has long endured for three reasons:

First, it is employed explicitly in the Bible. Second, it is easily understood because visual. Finally, this model correctly recognizes that God can and does communicate with humans. (Most readers of this book have probably experienced some degree of God's subtle Self-communication in the depths of their being.)

God's Self-communication, however, is essentially *nonverbal* in nature. What God actually communicates to the prophets and evangelists is an experience of divine presence and love. Those prophets who are highly imaginative might spontaneously produce images or words which illustrate the meaning implicit in God's Self-communication. But these images and words come from the unconscious depths of their own minds and must be distinguished from God's Self-communication which stimulated them.

Under the impact of God's Self-communication, the prophets are inspired to use words they already possess in creative new ways when they speak for God. Love is the most inspiring experience a human can have, and God's love is the most inspiring of all. When empowered by love, we all see how to solve problems that previously seemed insuperable. And so it is with the prophets who are privileged to drink deeply of divine presence and love.

Because human understanding is always slowly evolving, God repeatedly communicates divine presence and love to the prophets in their changing historical circumstances. God's Self-communication encourages the prophets to recognize and express new insights into the mystery of God and the God-human relationship.

This view of God's revelatory activity enables us to see that throughout history God is continually revealing the same fundamental reality to humankind: the experience of divine presence and love. What is continually changing and slowly improving throughout history is our human ability to understand *the profound implications* of God's repeated Self-communication.

The contemporary model for God's Self-revelation enables us to explain the historical errors and contradictory statements found in the Bible. For example, the book of Daniel calls the Persian King Darius a Mede (instead of a Persian; Dan 5:31); it also confuses King Jehoiakim of Judah with his son Jehoiakin (Dan 1:1; cp. 2 Kgs 24:1-16). Such errors are inevitable if God has inspired fallible humans to speak for God to the best of their ability. But if God is dictating information to the prophets, the historical errors in the Bible are difficult to explain.

Also, when the law of Moses expresses its understanding of God's justice, it declares that God punishes children for the sins of their parents "to the third and fourth generation" (Ex 20:5). Nevertheless, when the prophet Ezekiel speaks for God centuries later, he insists that God *never* punishes children for the sins of their parents (Ez 18:1-20, esp. 20). These discrepant statements are intelligible if they represent inspired interpretations of God's justice spoken in differing historical circumstances. If, however, they are construed as spoken directly by God into the ear of the prophet, they become intolerable.

At the time when the view expressed in Ex 20:5 was taught, the Israelite concept of justice was still influenced by the ancient practice of blood feud. Those who pursued justice by the standards of blood feud punished a crime by executing not only the guilty person, but also every family member who shared the guilty person's tent or dwelling. And since three or four generations usually shared the same tent or dwelling, the justice sought through blood feud was usually collective, not individual. As long as a collective understanding of justice persisted in ancient Israel, the prophets naively assumed that God also would exercise collective justice.

Conversely, by the time that Ezekiel the prophet was inspired to speak for God, blood feud had largely been replaced, at least ideally, by the law of talion. The law of talion (*lex talionis*) required strict parity in matters of retribution for crime (an eye for an eye, a tooth for a tooth, and a person for a person; see Ex 21:23-25). Ezekiel, therefore, was inspired to teach that God's justice will only punish the offending *individual,* not the individual's family members.

God had to wait patiently for the historical consciousness of the ancient Israelites to evolve from collective vengeance seeking to individual responsibility. Once a more evolved understanding of justice had arrived, God encouraged Ezekiel to use it when teaching about divine justice. Analogously, God is always waiting patiently for us to improve our understanding of the Risen and Spirit-mediating Jesus so that we may proclaim the Good News from God more effectively and credibly at our time in history. (More will be said about the contemporary understanding of revelation in the answers to the first two questions in chapter fourteen.)

2

The Christian faith community considers the Risen Jesus to be the greatest of God's revelatory signs in human history. The teaching of the prophets before and after Jesus either prepares one to recognize God's conclusive Self-disclosure in Jesus or deepens and clarifies such recognition. None of the other great prophets in history were taken through tragic injustice and a hideous death into New Life and empowered to appear repeatedly to their disciples in manifest possession of this New Life.

Not only did Jesus manifest his New Life to his disciples, he was also empowered to communicate to them a *foretaste* of this New Life through the *experienced gift* of God's Spirit. The Risen Jesus, therefore, is peerless among the prophets because through him God has given humankind a mysterious yet experientially grounded assurance that we humans can transcend the terror of history and can reach Eternal Life and Joy.

Since the Risen Jesus embodies and mediates God's definitive answer to our ultimate questions, he does not merely speak a word for God like the other prophets. Rather, the very Word of God (i.e., God's conclusive Self-communication as saving knowledge and love) has become incarnate in Jesus:

> When time began, God's Word was already there, and the Word was face to face with God, and the Word was God. He was in the beginning with God; all things were made through him, and without him was not anything made that was made. In him was life, and the life was the light of humankind. (Jn 1:1-4)
>
> And the Word became flesh and Tabernacled among us, full of grace and truth; we have beheld his glory, glory as of the only Son from the Father. (Jn 1:14)

The Christian message tells us that God has joined the reality of God's own being to the human nature of Jesus in an unparalleled union of knowledge and love. God then acted conclusively in and through the Risen Jesus to assure humankind that we need not finally fear the evils in life which can tempt us to discouragement and despair. Tragedy, injustice, and repugnant death have no lasting power to harm us if we meet them with faith and trust in God's creative goodness as Jesus did. God has shown us through the crucified and Risen Jesus that we are able to reach Life Eternal, and can share unendingly in God's intoxicating Self-discovery and Joy.

Through faith in the Risen Jesus, God even now mediates to us the "foretaste" of the Holy Spirit (i.e., God's Self-communication as love, peace, and joy). Our experience of God's Self-gift, the Spirit, is a pledge from God (2 Cor 2:21-22: Rom 5:5) that our faith has empowered us to follow Jesus to the Great Marriage between heaven and earth where we will evermore taste the wine of God's love (1 Cor 12:13; Eph 5:18). The New Testament celebrates Jesus as the bridegroom-Word of God (Jn 1:14; 3:29) sent to wed us to himself through the marriage of grace (Jn 14:20-21). We are mystically joined thus to Jesus that he might take us with himself through death to the marriage feast of Eternal Life in the bridal chamber of our Creator's Bosom:

> Let us rejoice and exult . . . for the marriage of the Lamb has come, and his bride has made herself ready. (Rev 19:7)
>
> Blessed are those who are invited to the marriage supper of the Lamb. (Rev 19:9)
>
> And I saw the holy city, the New Jerusalem, coming down out of heaven from God, prepared as a bride adorned for her husband. (Rev 21:2)

Although our faith tells us that we encounter the revealing and saving presence of God "in Jesus" to an incomparable and unparalleled degree, we also know that our finite language is hard pressed to express this sublime mystery. Our only recourse is to engage periodically in flights of symbolic poetry. The problem of comprehensibility is compounded when we realize that the early Christians who wrote the New Testament were precritical thinkers who were unconsciously influenced by the "folk mentality" when they witnessed to Jesus.

The folk mentality characterizes the thinking of people who are still essentially "preliterate." With acquired instinct, folk historians adapt their message to the needs of precritical thinkers and the requirements of oral transmission. For economy's sake, therefore, they preserve only the bare essentials of an event. They also use "hyperbole" to insure that their listeners will "hear" the most important parts of a narrative.

Furthermore, folk historians will freely expand (and, on occasion, will even create) a narrative in order to defend or clarify an important memory or truth cherished by their community. They also draw on traditional ideas (including mythological assumptions about invisible causal power) to interpret their experience. Since such strategies and assumptions are part of their community's tradition, folk historians spontaneously reach for them when attempting to explain the meaning of significant happenings.

Legendary history produced by the folk mentality obviously differs from contemporary history in a number of ways. It is frequently difficult, therefore, for nonspecialists to decide if a statement about Jesus in the New Testament should be understood as *history* or as the early church's *theological interpretation* of Jesus' history. Equally difficult to determine is whether some of the things said about Jesus and his unparalleled relationship with God are meant to be taken literally or as symbolic poetry which points "hyperbolically" to God's incomparable revealing presence in Jesus (e.g., Jn 1:14; 14:6-10; 20:28).

The reader should understand that not all biblical scholars agree about how to interpret the ancient and precritical history of Jesus found in the Gospels. Opinions range from the far right to the extreme left. There is, however, a moderate consensus about most matters. It is the moderating views of the center which will be presented in this work. The naive literalism of the right and the arid skepticism of the left will be avoided.

Moreover, moderates also come in various shapes and sizes. They will not all agree with all the views put forth in this work. Since human opinion is so diverse, the matters we will be examining preclude unanimity. Readers, therefore, will have to weigh the interpretations of the data advanced in this book against their own experience and decide for themselves.

In the chapters which follow, we will begin by exploring the contemporary understanding of the Christian claim that Jesus is God's definitive Good News to the world. The apostolic witnessing which is secondary but essential to the historical mediation of this Good News will also be briefly examined.

We will then proceed to a contemporary reading of those portions of the New Testament which shed light on Jesus' parentage, birth, and place of origin. Next, we will consider Jesus' understanding of himself and his mission (as distinct from the church's post-Easter interpretation of these matters).

As Jesus' self-understanding is explored, the early church's *theological* assessment of Jesus will be differentiated and explained. We will discover that the church's interpretation of Jesus and his mission included a number of "precritical" assumptions and teaching devices which must be carefully qualified for our critical age. Unless we provide our contemporaries with reasonable and intelligible distinctions about the authentic meaning of the sacred history of Jesus, they will not be able to "hear" our witnessing to the Good News revealed by God through Jesus.

The apostolic church sincerely believed that God had fully informed Jesus in advance of everything the divine purpose intended to accomplish through him for humankind. However, contemporary scholarship prefers the view that Jesus did not learn of God's secret Messianic purpose at work in his mission until the time of his Resurrection. The contemporary view that Jesus' self-understanding underwent *development* can be disturbing to conservative Christians. But if we fully grasp the reasons which underlie the contemporary view, it is just as faith-filled and satisfying as the traditional view. It also has the advantage of being fully compatible with the scientific approach to history required by our age.

Some people are quite content with the traditional or *literal* understanding of the entire New Testament. Their right to prefer the literal reading should be sincerely respected. Increasing numbers of other people, however, are unwilling to accept such a reading. It is imperative, therefore, that we have available another option which explains the essentials of the Good News in a manner congruent with our present world view.

Contemporary biblical scholarship and official church teaching tell us that people who refuse to read everything in the Bible literally are fully justified. It is our duty as Christians to regularly update our interpretation of the New Testament by keeping it in harmony with sound advances in knowledge. Our sharing of the Good News should be as accessible and intelligible as possible to our generation and to future generations.

We will next turn our attention to the unparalleled relationship which God brought about in history between God's revealing "presence" and the human nature of Jesus (i.e., the mystery of the Incarnation). The pertinent texts in the New Testament which speak of this extraordinary union will be examined. And since the Incarnation of God's Word in Jesus is bound up with

Christian belief in the Holy Trinity, we will also discuss the relation between certain New Testament statements about Jesus and traditional Trinitarian doctrine.

When that stage of our task is completed, perceptive readers will have questions about the Incarnational and Trinitarian language in our traditional Christian profession of faith. Accordingly, we will briefly consider the contemporary reading of the symbolic language in the Nicene creed which derives from the New Testament.

The final chapter will be devoted to answering a number of questions which are usually raised by the material presented in the preceding chapters.

From this point forward, readers are urged to open their Bibles and relate the explanations being provided to the indicated biblical texts if they are not quoted. These texts will corroborate and clarify the material being presented. Readers who ignore this advice will fail to fully grasp much of what is being explained.

The scripture quotations in this book are taken ordinarily from the Revised Standard Version. Whenever they depart from that version, they are the author's own translation.

Questions for Review and Discussion

1. When God bestows revelatory knowledge on a human, what *is* happening and what *is not* happening?
2. Why do Christians consider Jesus the greatest of God's revelatory signs in history?
3. What kind of certainty is God communicating to Christians when we experience the "foretaste" of God's Spirit being mediated to us through our faith in the Risen Jesus?
4. Why is it difficult to talk about God's unparalleled revealing presence in Jesus?

5. What do biblical scholars mean by the "folk mentality," and why should we know about it if we hope to fully understand New Testament statements about Jesus?
6. For what reasons is it important for Christians to continually update their understanding of the New Testament?

Chapter One: Why Jesus Is God's Good News to the World.

1

THE CHRISTIAN MESSAGE ENSHRINED IN THE NEW TESTAMENT proclaims that the Risen Jesus is *God's definitive answer* to our ultimate questions. (Our ultimate questions are our questions about the ultimate meaning of our existence.) A definitive answer to such questions is one which provides a final solution which is essentially complete.) We humans, however, are not really able to "hear" an answer until we have truly "experienced" the question.

Unless we recognize that an answer is related in some vital way to the question of our own lives, we are not ready to grasp its full significance; the answer will roll off our minds like water from a duck's back. If we wish to proceed wisely, therefore, we should spend some time examining "the problem" which raises our ultimate questions before we reflect seriously on God's answer.

The fundamental problem confronting all humans is the riddle of our existence. Throughout history our greatest question has always been ourselves: Who are we? Where do we come from? What is our destiny? If the God who created us is good, why does God allow tragedy, suffering, and death in our world? Is death annihilating nothingness, or is it transition which can lead to ultimate fulfillment?

And if death can lead to ultimate fulfillment, will our past moral failures disqualify us? When death occurs, will God be for us or against us? Such questions are always expressions of ultimate concern for finite and fallible humans. To ask such questions and to seek their answers is a preliminary part of our destiny as self-transcending beings.

But what does it mean to be a self-transcending being? It means, first of all, that we possess a share of that astonishing power which philosophers call "spirit." Human spirit is the power of unlimited self-transcendence, the power to engage in creative discovery with mathematical infinity. Because of our self-transcending design, we humans can always see the possibility of surpassing any limits by which we presently find ourselves bound. We are never limited to what we presently know or have achieved; we can always learn and achieve more. Nor are we hopelessly held by habits we have acquired in the past; we can free ourselves from their grip by motivating ourselves to grow in new directions.

Our ability to transcend ourselves with the power of reason (which can always discover new possibilities) and freedom of choice (which can choose without absolute predetermination among recognized possibilities) is the basis of our singular human achievements. This power has enabled us to walk on the moon and return safely to earth. Yet, given the ambiguity which attends our "transempirical" (inferential) experience, even our reason can be profoundly uncertain about the question of our final destiny.

We predictably experience our existence as a problem because although we are finite and our physical being is temporal and mortal, we also have the spiritual power to think about *infinity* and *eternity,* and to yearn for *immortality.* As self-transcending beings, we inevitably aspire to transcend the limiting event of death and to participate in the infinity and eternity of our Ultimate Source.

Yet, is this aspiration empty and groundless dreaming on our part, as Freud would have it? Or is it an indication in our design which points to our true destiny, as Socrates maintained? The ultimate question before us is clearly urgent but also vexingly ambiguous since it admits of several possible answers. It is evidently part of our human task to weigh these various answers against our experience and to decide wisely among them.

2

As we reflect on the problem of our existence, the Chrisitian message claims to provide us with *God's answer* to our ultimate questions. This answer announces that the tragically crucified and Risen Jesus is God's guarantee that we humans do have a death-transcending destiny, and that none of the discouraging evils which threaten our lives have lasting power to harm us. We can finally transcend all evil through our faith in God's offer of love and forgiveness, and we can arrive at Eternal Life and Joy along with the Risen Jesus.

God knew from the outset that the best way to give us definitive assurance about the answers to our ultimate questions was through a human being who was truly one of us, i.e., a full participant in the "problem" of human existence. The Christian Message tells us that the human being God chose to work through was Jesus of Nazareth. God sent Jesus to us as God's "warranty" that we can defeat the powers of darkness which threaten our existence, and can attain Eternal Joy.

In order to become God's conclusive sign of salvation for humankind, Jesus had to submit to the painful and ambiguous conditions of existence with faith and trust in God's goodness. Jesus keenly experienced the tragedy, injustice, and cruelty of life, and the repugnance of premature and undeserved death. But he did not allow these discouraging evils to overwhelm and defeat him with hate-filled bitterness, self-pity, or despair. Rather, through the power of his faith in God's providential love and goodness, Jesus won the victory of the Resurrection and became God's confirmation that all other humans can do the same.

Through the Risen and Spirit-mediating Jesus, God has "shown" us that, despite its preliminary ambiguity, ours is truly a sublime destiny. We have also been shown "the Way" to live authentically in order to attain that destiny. God calls us *to follow Jesus* (Mk 8:34) by living lives of faith, trust, and love which serves (Jn 13:12-15; 15:12; Mt 25:31-46). If we do so, we also will be able to defeat the "powers of darkness" (i.e., the personal, social, and physical evils in life which can tempt us to despair).

The Risen and Spirit-mediating Jesus is the great negator of "the terror of history." He is God's great sign that destructive alienation and insane cruelty can be overcome through our faith in God's offer of reconciling love and healing forgiveness. The tragedy and absurdity which can suddenly engulf our lives can be transcended through our faith in God's promise of ultimate justice and Eternal Life and Joy. Our faith in Jesus reassures us that good finally triumphs over evil, life over death, and joy over tragic suffering:

> He will wipe away every tear from their eyes, and death shall be no more, neither shall there be mourning nor crying nor pain any more, for the former things have passed away. (Rev 21:4)

3

The world would never have heard the Good News spoken by God through Jesus without the cooperation of the "apostolic witnesses." God obviously did not want the appearances of the Risen Jesus which climaxed the Christ event to happen in the middle of an empty desert or aboard an abandoned ship at sea. The appearances were intended to occur in a social context which included witnesses who could testify to them as revelatory signs from God to the world. One of these witnesses, Paul the apostle, reminded King Agrippa while testifying to the

Christ event that, "the king knows about these things . . . for this was not done in a corner" (Acts 26:26).

God spent centuries preparing the ancient Jews to be the nation which would provide the necessary witnesses. The Jews were encouraged by God to understand and practice exclusive monotheism, and to believe in immortality for the righteous in the (visually accessible) form of resurrection. As members of the Jewish nation, the apostles of the Risen Jesus were able to grasp the revelatory significance of his Spirit-mediating appearances and proclaim them as Good News from God to the world in a manner that could be grasped by all.

The "apostles" were those men in the early church who (1) experienced the Risen Jesus *appearing* to them within a few years of his death, and who (2) were *called* by the Risen Jesus to witness to his Spirit-mediating appearances and their meaning. (For a contemporary explanation of Jesus' appearances to the apostles and their commission, see *Exploring the Resurrection of Jesus* in this series.)

This definition of an apostle differs from the narrower definition implied by Luke in Acts 1:21-22. (Luke is the name assigned by tradition to the author of the Gospel of that name and to the Acts of the Apostles.) Luke's definition intends (for *theological* reasons) to limit the number of apostles to *twelve* (Lk 6:13; Acts 1:2,26). Such a definition, however, would exclude Paul, who was certainly an apostle (1 Cor 9:1), but not one of "the Twelve" (Mk 3:13-19; see the distinction which Paul makes between these two terms in 1 Cor 15:5 and 7).

It is important to realize that the apostles did not derive their revelatory certainty about the Risen Jesus merely from his *appearances* to them. They knew that his appearances were revelatory signs from God because they were accompanied by an extraordinary communication of divine presence and love. When the apostles experienced Jesus appearing "externally," they *simultaneously* experienced God's Self-communication (the Spirit) being given to them "internally" (Jn 20:19,22).

This inner revelatory experience, with its mystical certainty, assured the apostles that God was there and that God's life-giving love (the Spirit) was the source of the power which had enabled Jesus to transcend death and appear to them. It was the indubitable "revelatory" nature of the appearances which assured the apostles that the appearances were signs from God.

The apostolic witnessing to the appearances was an essential part of God's revelatory purpose at work in the Christ Event. By the Christ Event we should understand the public mission and tragic death of Jesus which were followed by his momentous revelatory *appearances* to his disciples as Risen Lord of life and death:

> The Lord has truly risen and has appeared to Simon! (Lk 24:34)
>
> He was raised on the third day according to the scriptures, and . . . he appeared to Cephas, then to the twelve. Then he appeared to more than five hundred brethren at one time. . . . Then he appeared to James, then to all the apostles. Last of all, as to one untimely born, he appeared also to me. (1 Cor 15:5-8)

When the apostles reflected on the meaning of Jesus' appearances, they understood that God had assured them through these Spirit-mediating appearances that:

> "Death is swallowed up in victory." "O death, where is your victory? O death, where is your sting?" . . . But thanks be to God, who gives us the victory through our Lord Jesus Christ. (1 Cor 15:54-56)

4

When God raised Jesus as the Good News from God to the nations, a number of concurrent circumstances providentially expedited the success of the apostolic witnessing:

(1) The *Pax Romana* (the Roman Peace) had brought unprecedented freedom from the dangers of warfare, piracy, and banditry. This freedom enabled the apostles and disciples of Jesus to travel with relative safety by land and sea from the eastern to the western side of the Roman empire.

(2) The Greek language (which had been spread by Alexander the Great) was spoken in all of the cities and large towns of the Roman empire and well beyond. The apostles, therefore, could be understood in all of the larger communities of the empire to which they carried the Good News. (This circumstance explains why the New Testament was written in Greek.)

(3) In every city in the empire to which the apostles came, there was usually a community of monotheistic Jews who gathered every sabbath to study the law of Moses and the writings of the prophets. Gentiles who admired Jewish monotheism were allowed to become fully observant converts (proselytes), or to sit in the rear of the synagogue as worshipers (God-fearers) during the service.

(Before the Romans destroyed the Jerusalem temple in A.D. 70, the "synagogue" ordinarily gathered in a large room of a private residence. There are many written references to synagogues before the destruction of the second temple. But there is very little uncontested evidence for the existence of a building used exclusively for the synagogue service (and related community functions) until the middle of the second century. The ancient Jewish practice of gathering for worship in the houses of community members explains why the earliest Christians, who were Jews, established house-churches.)

(4) Belief in the resurrection of the dead was introduced to the Jews in the book of Daniel c. 165 B.C. (see Dan 12:2). Since the book of Daniel was read and explained at the sabbath-gatherings in Palestine and the diaspora (i.e., all the territory outside of Palestine where Jews had settled), its end-time teaching about the resurrection of the dead had become part of the theological tradition of the synagogues scattered throughout the empire and beyond.

As the apostles journeyed throughout the ancient world to proclaim the Good News, they always found the location of the Jewish synagogue in any given city. When the sabbath arrived, they attended the synagogue service and, after the readings from the law and the prophets, they would seek an opportunity to speak to the assembled community. Since the ancient synagogue service was basically egalitarian in spirit, their request was usually granted.

The apostles would then proclaim that the salvation promised by the law and the prophets had finally arrived. The Risen Jesus, they announced, is God's conclusive assurance that Israel and the nations can be saved from tragedy and death and can attain Eternal Life. The Jews and worshiping Gentiles who believed the testimony of the apostles then became the beginning of the Christian faith community in that region. In the Acts of the Apostles, we find the following summarized account of how the apostles carried out their task:

> Now Paul and his company . . . came to Antioch in Pisidia. And on the sabbath day they went into the synagogue and sat down. After the reading of the law and the prophets, the rulers of the synagogue sent to them, saying, "Brethren, if you have any word of exhortation for the people, say it." (Acts 13:13-15)
>
> So Paul stood up, and motioning with his hand said, "Men of Israel, and you that fear God, listen. The God of this people Israel . . . raised up David to be their king. . . . Of this man's posterity God has brought to Israel a Savior, Jesus, as he promised. . . . God raised him from the dead, and . . . he appeared to those . . . who are now his witnesses to the people. And we bring you the good news that what God promised to the fathers, this he has fulfilled to us their children by raising Jesus from the dead. (Acts 13:16-33)
>
> And when the meeting of the synagogue broke up, many Jews and devout converts to Judaism followed Paul and Barnabas, who spoke to them and urged them to continue in the grace of God. (Acts 13:43)

In his letter to the Romans, Paul the apostle explains that the process by which individuals are called to faith in the Risen Jesus through the apostolic testimony actually involves *two distinct* yet intimately related stages of "witnessing." The first and preliminary stage is the apostolic witnessing itself delivered *ex-*

ternally in history. (This stage is continued by the church's mission of preaching the Good News):

> But how are men to call upon him in whom they have not believed? And how are they to believe in him of whom they have never heard? And how are they to believe without a preacher? And how can men preach unless they are sent? As it is written, "How beautiful are the feet of those who preach good news." . . . So faith comes from what is heard, and what is heard comes by the preaching of Christ. (Rom 10:14-15,17)

The second and conclusive stage of witnessing is the internal testimony of God in which God "confirms" the truth of the external apostolic proclamation by pouring the experienceable gift of God's reassuring love (the Spirit) into our hearts:

> . . . and hope does not disappoint us, because God's love has been poured into our hearts through the Holy Spirit which has been given to us. (Rom 5:5)

We finally decide to believe in the Good News delivered by the apostles because of our experience of the inner witnessing of God's own Spirit (i.e., the transcendent peace, joy, and love that accompany, encourage, and corroborate a faith-filled hearing of God's word):

> When we cry "Abba! Father!" it is the Spirit himself bearing witness with our spirit that we are the children of God. (Rom 8:15-16)

The gift of God's Spirit, Paul tell us, is given to us as a foretaste and "guarantee" (*arrabōna*) of the joy and love which await us in Eternal Life:

> But it is God who . . . has . . . given us his Spirit in our hearts as a guarantee. (2 Cor 1:21-22)

Paul understands that the *preliminary preaching* of the Good News which prepares us for God's inner witnessing and the resulting gift of "confirmed" faith is an essential part of God's revelatory purpose in history. For God's confirming testimony is *nonverbal* and would be ambiguous without the external apostolic witnessing which precedes and supplies it with historical meaning. Paul emphasizes, accordingly, that the apostolic witnessing, although secondary and instrumental, is nevertheless essential to God's revealing and saving purpose for humankind.

God's wisdom fully comprehends that nothing can be consciously grasped by an inquiring mind without the mediation of a clarifying word. To insure that God's definitive Self-disclosure would be intelligible, God inspired the apostles (through the Risen Jesus and the gift of the Spirit) to bring into being a privileged constellation of words called the apostolic proclamation.

The substance of this historically privileged proclamation has been preserved in the New Testament. The inspired words and sacred symbols of the New Testament insure that throughout the remainder of history there will always be a faith community able to grasp and proclaim the meaning of God's conclusive Self-communication through the Risen Jesus and the foretaste of the Spirit.

5

The apostles could "record" their historically privileged witnessing to the Risen Jesus either in *writing* or in the *memories* of those who received their testimony. But since the apostles thought the world would end in their lifetime (1 Thess 4:17; 1 Cor 15:51-52), and knew that most of their contemporaries could not read, they chose to spend the "remaining time" (1 Cor 7:29) proclaiming the Good News to as many people as possible rather than formally committing it to writing.

It is for this reason that even the letters of Paul which antedate the four Gospels by twenty or more years are primarily pastoral directives dealing with problems currently faced by individual churches. Only secondarily do Paul's letters speak of doctrinal matters, and they tell us almost nothing about the words and deeds of the earthly Jesus.

When all the apostles had died, the Christian faith community realized that the apostles had been mistaken when they assumed the world would end in their lifetime. The community's leaders and teachers knew, moreover, that the substance of the apostolic witnessing recorded in their "memories" was historically privileged and essential to God's gracious purpose in history. They understood, accordingly, that it should be written down and preserved so that future generations could also "hear" the apostolic proclamation of the Good News.

Contemporary scholarship concludes that none of the Four Gospels was actually written by an apostle. All four are "subapostolic" in nature. After the turn of the first Christian century, folk teachers in the early church were eager to connect the Gospels directly to the apostles as a way of reassuring their preliterate communities that apostolic witnessing truly stands behind the Gospels.

It was then that two of the Gospels were attributed to the apostles Matthew and John. The other two Gospels were said to have been written by Mark and Luke, who were known to the early church as traveling companions of apostles (See Phm 1:24; Acts 12;12; 15;37; Col 4:10,14; 2 Tim 4:11; 1 Pet 5:13). Early Christian tradition assumed that Mark (the interpreter of Peter) and Luke (the fellow worker and physician of Paul) could easily recall and preserve in writing what they had often heard the apostles preach. The Gospels themselves do not tell us the names of their authors.

By now it should be apparent that the "apostolic age" must be divided into two periods, (1) the *apostolic period* when the apostles were still alive and witnessing, and (2) the *subapostolic period* when the apostles had died, but those who had been taught directly by them were still alive and witnessing. The "postapostolic" age arrived when early Christian leaders judged that all of the apostles and those who could remember their authentic teaching had died. After that transition, the official list of Christian scriptures (the New Testament canon) was closed, and no further additions were allowed.

6

Before we leave this chapter we should consider the view that Jesus was required by God to bring the Good News of salvation by atoning vicariously (substitutionally) for the sins of humankind. This explanation of the saving power of Jesus' death is stated or implied in a number of places in the New Testament (e.g., Rom 4:25; 5:19; 1 Cor 6:20; Mk 10:45; 14:24; Jn 1:29; Heb 9:11-12,15,24-26). Nevertheless, there are good reasons for concluding that this understanding of Jesus' death was foreign to the thinking of Jesus himself. Instead, it represents an interpretation of Jesus' tragic death that was created by the early church for "apologetic" reasons. (Apologetics is teaching designed to defend religious beliefs from attack.)

It is difficult for Christians living at our time in history to appreciate the enormous apologetic task which faced the early-church two thousand years ago. As members of a predominantly Christian culture, we have become accustomed to the idea that God's Messiah was a politically insignificant human being with no military or political power whatsoever. More importantly, we are no longer troubled by the fact that Jesus was rejected by the majority of the Jews, and suffered a shameful death at the hands of the Romans. It is difficult for us to appreciate that the first Christians were forced to view this matter far differently.

To the apostolic church it was painfully clear that Jesus was a shockingly unexpected kind of Messiah. He was not the majestic and invincible military conqueror of traditional Jewish expectations. The Jewish majority vigorously reminded the Jewish Christian minority that the ignominious fate of Jesus was utterly contrary to the Messianic ideal which Jews had been taught by their prophets and scribes.

The Jewish Christians had to defend their faith claims about the "spiritual" Messiahship of Jesus by creating an apologetic interpretation of his tragic history which was reconcilable with the Jewish scriptures. To accomplish this task, they searched the scriptures for proof texts which seemed to indicate that God's Messiah was mysteriously destined to suffer and be rejected. Accordingly, whenever a suffering righteous man was found in the scriptures, his tragic lot, if in any way similar, was seen as foreshadowing that of Jesus.

Teachers in the apostolic church soon discovered the idea of *vicarious* (substitutional) *atonement* in the fourth of the four "suffering servant poems" in the book of Isaiah (53:13-53:12). This poem describes the rejection and sufferings of a mysterious figure referred to as God's righteous servant (53:11). The sufferings of God's servant are interpreted in the fourth poem as *substitutional* atonement for the sins of Israel (53:1-12). The servant's faithful endurance is also seen as instrumental in bringing salvation to the nations (49:5-6).

A critical reading of the servant poems (Is 42:1-4; 49:1-6; 50:4-11; 52:13-53-12) indicates that the "servant" is probably a symbol for a "group" of devout Israelites among the exiles in Babylon. (A Babylonian context is inferred because the prophet who is encouraging this group has learned that Cyrus the Persian is marching to take Babylon and concludes that God will use Cyrus to free the Israelites from captivity; see Is 45:1-4; 44:27.)

The group designated as God's "servant" is struggling against harsh opposition to fulfill faithfully the requirements of God's law (Is 53:11) and is encouraging other Israelites to do the same (Is 49:5). The servant's mission to Israel *continues* (Is 53:10-12) even after a member of the group (possibly its leader) has suffered death (Is 53:9) at the hands of either hostile Jews or angry Babylonian officials. Such an ongoing mission indicates that God's "servant" is not an individual but a group. This group is presented in the servant poems as the "ideal" Israel.

Their experience of cruel opposition (Is 50:6; 53:7-8), however, has discouraged this devout group, and has led some of them to fear that God does not favor their mission (Is 53:2-3). They are nevertheless assured by God's prophet that their sufferings are *not* a sign of divine disfavor. Rather, God is allowing them to atone *substitutionally* for the sins of their nation (Is 53:4-12). And if they persevere in their courageous efforts to be faithful to God's law, they will be instrumental in Israel's restoration (Is 49:5; 53:11) and the eventual conversion of the nations (Is 42:4; 49:6) to worship of the one true God (Is 44:6; 45:5-6).

Jewish Christian teachers eagerly appropriated Isaiah's suffering "servant" figure and the idea of "vicarious atonement" to defend their faith in a suffering and rejected Messiah. These teachers believed that Jesus' tragic fate was foreshadowed in the sufferings of God's servant and was part of God's *secret Messianic purpose* (1 Cor 2:7-8). Consequently, they wove allusions to the servant and his atoning sufferings into their apologetic interpretation of Jesus' death.

The authentic parables and sayings of Jesus, however, contain no suggestion that Jesus thought he had to suffer vicariously for the sins of the Jews and all others before God would forgive them. Instead, Jesus assured those who believed in his prophetic message (Mk 2:5-7), even notorious sinners (Lk 7:47-49; 19:1-10), that their sins were forgiven from the moment they responded with faith and conversion. Jesus did not tell sinners, "Your sins *will* be forgiven after I die and satisfy the demands of God's justice." Rather, he assured them in the *present* tense, "Your sins *are* forgiven" (because God is graciously loving and merciful toward all, even disgraced prodigals; Lk 15:11-32).

Traditional exegetes will object that there are several Gospel sayings of Jesus in which Jesus speaks as though he knows that he, like Isaiah's suffering servant, must vicariously atone for the sins of others. The sayings which are usually adduced are Mk 10:45 ("The Son of Man also came not to be served but to serve, and to give his life as a ransom for many.") and Mk 14:24 ("This is my blood of the covenant, which is poured out for many.")

Less conservative exegetes respond, however, that both of these sayings have probably been expanded theologically to provide an apologetic rationale for the hideous and disgraceful death suffered by Jesus. These exegetes defend their view by reminding us that there are earlier forms of the sayings in Mk 10:45 and 14:24 in which the language which suggests that Jesus must pay for our sins is absent:

Lk 22:26 is clearly an earlier form of Mk 10:45. We know it is earlier because Jesus refers to himself without using the title Son of Man ("I am in the midst of you as one who serves."), and because Mark's "ransom" theology has not been added to the saying. We may be confident that the early church did not shorten but, instead, expanded Jesus' sayings over the decades.

In addition, about fifteen years before Mark wrote his Gospel, Paul the apostle (in 1 Cor 11:25) also quoted Jesus' cup saying at the Last Supper ("This cup is the new covenant in my blood."). There is, however, no reference to Mark's vicarious atonement thology in Paul's much earlier version of the saying. This indicates that the words in Mark's version which regard Jesus' death as atonement for others were probably added to an earlier form of the saying for apologetic reasons.

Moreover, the traditional vicarious atonement interpretation of Jesus' death presupposes that God would not love and forgive humankind until Jesus satisfied God's offended justice by paying for our sins. However, if God had sent Jesus to atone substitutionally for our sins, that would mean that it was love for us that moved God to send Jesus to suffer and die for us. But that would further imply that God already loved us *before* God sent Jesus to die for us, which logically cancels the necessity of sending Jesus to die for us so that we could be forgiven and loved.

These (and other) observations lead contemporary Christian exegetes and theologians and to the conclusion that God did not require the sufferings and death of Jesus as payment for our sins. That way of explaining Jesus' death was a later and *secondary* (i.e., nonessential) interpretation of his tragic history which met an urgent (but historically limited) apologetic need of the apostolic church.

Does this conclusion mean that it was not necessary for Jesus to die in order to assure us of salvation? Our answer must be a dialectical one which includes both "no" and "yes." God *did not* require Jesus to accept tragic and unjust death as substitutional payment for our sins. But God *did* encourage Jesus to accept his tragic and unjust death with a "yes" of faith and trust so that God could bring "Resurrection" out of that death. The appearances of the Risen Jesus to his disciples were intended by God as revelatory signs to the world that all who have faith and trust in God's creative goodness as Jesus did can defeat tragedy and death along with Jesus.

Jesus' acceptance of his death with faith and trust in God's creative wisdom and goodness was an essential part of God's saving purpose for the world. In that sense, therefore, Jesus' death was necessary and full of "saving power."

There is a way in which the Christian tradition has always been symbolically correct in viewing the death of Jesus as being, in some mysterious fashion, "the death of God." For God appropriated Jesus' death and made it peculiarly God's "death" in the following sense: God chose to be conclusively present in the death of Jesus and to suffer it with him in order to bring Resurrection out of that death as God's Good News to the world. God has assured the world through the sacred death of Jesus that God is present and suffering *in all other deaths* and will enable those who undergo them with faith and trust to participate in the victory of Jesus' Resurrection:

> Death is swallowed up in victory.
> O death, where is your victory?
> O death, where is your sting? . . .
> But thanks be to God, who gives us the
> victory through our Lord Jesus Christ.
> (1 Cor 15:54-55,57)

Questions for Review and Discussion

1. Why is it that we cannot truly hear an answer until we have experienced the question?
2. What is the basic problem which causes humans to ask ultimate questions? Explain your answer.
3. Why is it that we self-transcending humans inevitably experience our "design" as problematic?
4. What was the best way for God to give us humans a definitive answer to our ultimate questions?

5. What nation had God prepared so that the Good News could be understood when the time came for God to reveal it to the world through Jesus?
6. What is an "apostle"? (What two qualifying experiences were necessary for an apostle to claim that office?)
7. What is the *second* form of witnessing which Paul the apostle says must always accompany the apostolic witnessing before it can lead to "confirmed" faith in God's Good News?
8. What four historical developments were providentially present to expedite the apostolic witnessing to the Good News?
9. In what two ways could the apostles "record" their historically privileged witnessing to Jesus?
10. Which of these two ways of "recording" their witnessing were the apostles themselves far more inclined to use, and why was this so?
11. Into how many "periods" should the apostolic age be distinguished, and why is this distinction necessary?
12. What is "apologetics," and why is it frequently present in the Gospels?
13. What was the most serious apologetic problem faced by the apostolic church?
14. Why were many teachers in the apostolic church eager to interpret Jesus as the "suffering servant" of God spoken of in the book of Isaiah?

Chapter Two: Jesus' Parentage and Birth

1

MARK'S GOSPEL TELLS US THAT JESUS HAD BEEN A CARPENTER before he undertook his prophetic mission. The people in the synagogue at Nazareth reacted to Jesus' first visit after the beginning of his prophetic mission with the following query:

> Is not this the carpenter, the son of Mary? (Mk 6:3).

Jesus probably learned the carpenter's trade from his father Joseph (Mt 1:16; Lk 4:22; Jn 1:45), for Matthew's Gospel remembers that Joseph also was a carpenter:

> Is not this the carpenters son? Is not his mother called Mary? (Mt 13:53)

Since the early church derived no theological significance from her memory that Jesus and Joseph had both been carpenters, that memory is probably reliable history.

Along with Mary his mother, Jesus' brothers are mentioned several times during and after his public mission. His sisters are also mentioned on one occasion:

Mk 6:3

> Is this not the carpenter, the son of Mary and brother of James and Joses and Judas and Simon, and are not his sisters here with us?

Mk 3:31-32

> And his mother and his brothers came; and standing outside they sent to him and called him. And a crowd was sitting about him; and they said to him, "Your mother and your brothers are outside, asking for you."

Acts 1:12,14

> Then [after Jesus was taken up into heaven] they returned to Jerusalem from the mount called Olivet, which is near Jerusalem. . . . All these with one accord devoted themselves to prayer, together with the women and Mary the mother of Jesus, and with his brothers. (See also Jn 2:12; 7:3,5; 1 Cor 9:5; Gal 1:19)

Jesus' brothers are sometimes mentioned by name, but never his sisters. Moreover, Joseph is never mentioned as someone who is certainly alive during Jesus' public mission. It is generally assumed, therefore, that he had probably died earlier.

Traditional exegetes have maintained that the brothers and sisters of Jesus mentioned in the New Testament are either children of Joseph by a previous marriage or cousins of Jesus who are called his brothers and sisters because there is no word for cousin in Aramaic. In Aramaic, all of one's cousins are called one's brothers and sisters. However, most contemporary exegetes would respond to these traditional interpretations as follows:

There is no indication in the New Testament that Joseph had children from a prior union. To assume that Jesus had foster brothers and sisters is groundless speculation which results in a more complex solution when a much simpler one is available. Preferring a more difficult solution to a simpler one violates the law of parsimony (i.e., hypothetical constructs should never be multiplied beyond necessity; we should always prefer the solution which enables us to work with fewer assumptions rather than more).

In addition, these same exegetes would remind us that the New Testament was written in Greek, not Aramaic, and in Greek one's male cousins (*anepsioi*) and female cousins (*anepsiai*) are clearly distinguished from one's brothers (*adelphoi*) and sisters (*adelphai*). (Greek also permits one to refer to one's kinsmen or religious associates as "brothers." But the context of such references usually indicates that blood brothers are *not* meant.) The majority of contemporary exegetes concludes, therefore, that the brothers and sisters of Jesus spoken of in the New Testament were probably born of Mary and Joseph, and were truly Jesus' siblings.

Indirect support for this position is provided by Paul the apostle. Paul tells us that when he went to Jerusalem three years after his conversion to confer with Cephas (Peter), he also saw "James the Lord's brother" (Gal 1:18-19). James was certainly more than a passing acquaintance of Paul's, for Paul makes it clear that Paul and Barnabas later engaged in serious negotiations with "James and Cephas and John" (Gal 2:9). If Paul had known that James was Jesus' cousin instead of his brother, Paul would probably have used the Greek word for male cousin (*anepsios*) to identify James, rather than the word brother (*adelphos*).

One may certainly prefer the traditional interpretation of this matter. But would the contemporary view briefly explained above detract in any essential way from Jesus' ability to be God's definitive answer to humankind's ultimate questions? Would having brothers and sisters make Jesus less acceptable as a representative human in God's revelatory purpose? Since most humans do have brothers and sisters, the answer is obviously "no."

The view that Jesus probably had brothers and sisters can be disturbing to conservative Christians who believe that Mary remained a virgin even after she gave birth to Jesus. Belief in Mary's "perpetual" virginity, however, is based on later Christian folk tradition. This folk tradition intends to point with "hyperbolic" poetry to the unparalleled importance of Jesus for Christian faith and should not be taken literally. The perpetual virginity of Mary is nowhere taught in the New Testament. It is significant that Paul the apostle refers to the mother of Jesus as a "woman," not a virgin:

> But when the time had fully come, God sent forth his son, born of a woman. (Gal 4:4)

We may legitimately suspect that when Paul wrote his letter to the Galatians, the theological stories which speak of Jesus' "virgin birth" had probably not yet been created, or at least not widely circulated.

It is true that the Infancy Narratives in the Gospels of Matthew and Luke do tell us that Jesus was born miraculously of a "virgin" (Mt 1:18-23; Lk 1:26-38). Contemporary scholarship informs us, however, that these narratives were meant by their inspired authors to teach *theological* lessons about the birth of Jesus, not historical facts.

We will see below that an ancient literary form called "midrash" is employed apologetically in the infancy narratives to defend the early church's faith in the *disputed* Messiahship of Jesus. (Remember that apologetics is teaching intended to defend religious beliefs.) Before we consider the stories of Jesus' miraculous birth in the Infancy Narratives, we should reflect briefly on the nature of "midrash."

2

Midrash was a method of interpreting scripture created by the ancient Jewish scribes (biblical scholars) after the Exile to Babylon in 587 B.C. The scribes developed this new exegetical method in order to find contemporary meaning in the ancient and increasingly outmoded Jewish scriptures. Whenever some later development in religious belief required legitimation, a text in the law of Moses or the prophetic books which seemed to *foreshadow* it was sought as its authorization. Midrashic teaching could be either oral or written, and could take the form of *halakah* (interpretations of law) or *haggadah* (nonlegal religious lessons).

The midrashic method of teaching assumed that everything God intends to do in history is already mysteriously suggested in the law of Moses and the other sacred scriptures. Therefore, interpretations of law and other religious matters which could be shown to have a midrashic adumbration in scripture were regarded as divinely revealed.

Accordingly, the scribes searched the scriptures for texts that seemed to portend and corroborate their contemporary interpretations of religious belief and practice in ancient Israel. They then either *quoted* the text which they thought validated their teaching, or they *alluded* to it by weaving one or more of its "key" words into their presentation (which frequently took the more accessible form of a story). Either way, the confirming text was always indicated in a manner recognizable by those familiar with the scriptures and the midrashic method of theologizing.

Although midrashic teaching existed well before apocalyptic theology arrived in the book of Daniel (for example, Jer 23:5; 33:15; Zech 3:8 and 6:12 are all alluding midrashically to Is 11:1), midrash received an added measure of importance and meaning when it was used to validate the new "eschatological" hope introduced in that book. (Eschatology is the study of the things that will happen when God ends the world.)

The author of Daniel, for example, justified his novel teaching about the "resurrection of the dead" by appealing midrashically to the covenant promises made by God to Abraham in Gen 13:16; 15:5; 22:17; 26:4. (The ancient Jews did not believe in the resurrection of the dead until the book of Daniel was written c. 165 B.C.) In these verses God promised to give Abraham descendants more numerous than the *stars* in the sky, the *sand* on the seashore, and the *dust* that covers the earth:

> "I will make your descendants as the dust of the earth; so that if one can count the dust of the earth, your descendants also can be counted." (Gen 13:16)

> "Look toward heaven, and number the stars, if you are able to number them." Then he said to him, "So shall your descendants be." (Gen 15:5)

Daniel 12:2-3 allusively implies that Abraham's children are like the dust that covers the earth in this life, and are destined to become transformed like the stars in the sky when they are finally raised in radiant glory:

> And many of those who sleep in the dust of the earth shall awake, some to everlasting life, and some to everlasting shame and contempt. And those who are wise shall shine like the brightness of the firmament; and those who turn many to righteousness, like the stars for ever and ever. (Dan 12:2-3)

Contemporary scholarship assures us that the covenant promises found in Genesis do not intend to teach "eschatological" hope. But the midrashing author of Daniel sincerely believed that the promise of resurrection was already mysteriously foreintended in these promises given by God to Abraham.

The book of Daniel legitimizes its other eschatological "innovations" by means of similar midrashic allusions: The mysterious stone which becomes a mighty mountain and symbolizes God's Kingdom in Dan 2:34-35, 44-45 is based on Is 28:16 and 2:2. The "dominion" restored to one like a "son of man" in Dan 7:6,12-14, is based on Gen 1:26, Ps 8:3-6, Ps 80:17. The "seventy" weeks of years in Dan 9:24-27 is based on Jer 29:10-11 (see Dan 9:2). The eschatological "time of trouble" in Dan 12:1b is based on Is 33:2. The doomsday "book" in Dan 12:1c is based on Ex 32:32-33. The "awaking" from "sleep" in Dan 12:2 is based on Ps 3:5. The "time of the end" in Dan 12:4a is based on Zeph 1:18b.

During the period in the early church when the Gospels were being written, midrash had become the prevailing theological method among Palestinian Jews for teaching about God's purpose in history. We should bear in mind that the first Christians were Jews who had learned about midrash in the synagogue. These Jewish Christians also carried out the major part of their witnessing to the Jews while attending the synagogue (Acts 6:9; 13:13-43; 17:1-3). It was inevitable, therefore, that they would appeal to the authority of midrash in order to advance and defend their claims about the disputed Messiahship of the crucified and Risen Jesus.

For the Jewish Christians who constituted the earliest church, it was the Risen Jesus who had conclusively fulfilled all of the "promises" of salvation, both manifest and hidden, found in the scriptures. These Jewish Christians were utterly convinced that Jesus and his unexpected Messianic destiny were mysteriously presaged in the law and the prophets. We should not be surprised to learn, then, that the Gospels in general and the Passion and Resurrection narratives in particular are *filled* with midrashic teaching about Jesus.

Jewish Christian midrash, of course, has concerns and emphases peculiarly its own. Unlike purely Jewish midrash, Christian midrash is always engaged in teaching about Jesus in some way. Sometimes this teaching takes the form of explicit *quotations* from the Jewish scriptures (e.g., Mt. 1:22-23; 2:5-6; Jn 19:24,37). More frequently, however, midrashic *allusions* are woven into the stories being narrated about Jesus to avoid interrupting them (e.g., Lk 1:26-27; 32-33; Mk 14:20; 15:24; Jn 1:29,35; 20:13,15).

Theology done in the midrashic mode may strike us as strange. Nevertheless, to the earliest Christians it seemed to be the best way to successfully bring their faith claims about Jesus to the Jews, especially when witnessing in the synagogue. Unless we are well versed in the scriptures and informed about midrash, we will frequently fail to grasp what the Gospels truly intend to teach about Jesus. We also will fall into historical and theological error by taking *nonliteral* statements literally. If we make the effort to understand the viewpoint of Jewish-Christian midrash, we will discover that it is filled with theological meaning and beauty, and is often the key that unlocks the authentic meaning of the Gospel narratives.

3

We are now better prepared to understand the midrashic stories of Jesus' "miraculous" birth in the Gospels of Matthew and Luke. As we examine these stories, we should recall that the "folk history" in the Old Testament sometimes ascribes a miraculous birth to a "folk hero." Assigning someone a miraculous birth is meant to emphasize "hyperbolically" the crucial role played by that person in God's purpose for Israel. For example, the patriarch Isaac, through whom the Israelites traced their descent from Abraham, is described in Genesis as miraculously born to Abraham and Sara when they are exceedingly advanced in age:

> And God said to Abraham, "As for Sarai your wife, you shall not call her name Sarai, but Sara shall be her name. I will bless her, and moreover I will give you a son by her. . . . Then Abraham fell on his face and laughed, and said to himself, "Shall a son be born to a man who is a hundred years old? Shall Sara, who is ninety years old, bear a child?". . . . God said, . . . "Sara your wife shall bear you a son, and you shall call his name Isaac. I will establish my covenant with him as an everlasting covenant for his descendants after him." (Gen 17:15-17,19)

Again, we read in the book of Judges that Samson, the Israelite hero who was famous for his strength and his struggles with the Philistines, was conceived miraculously by his mother:

> And there was a certain man of Zorah, of the tribe of the Danites, whose name was Manoah, and his wife was barren and had no children. And the angel of the Lord appeared to the woman and said to her, "Behold, you are barren and have no children; but you shall conceive and bear a son. . . . and he shall begin to deliver Israel from the hand of the Philistines. (Judg 13:2-3,5)

At a later time in ancient Israel's history, the prophet Samuel, who helped save Israel from the Philistine threat by inaugurating the monarchy (1 Sam 9:15-10:25), is also assigned a miraculous birth:

> There was a certain man . . . whose name was Elkanah. . . . He had two wives; the name of the one was Hannah, and the name of the other Peninnah. And Peninnah had children, but Hannah had no children. . . . She was deeply distressed and prayed to the Lord, and wept bitterly. And she vowed a vow and said, "O Lord of hosts, if you will . . . give to your maidservant a son, I will give him to the Lord all the days of his life."
>
> And Elkanah knew Hannah his wife, and the Lord remembered her; and in due time Hannah conceived and bore a son, and she called his name Samuel, for she said, "I have asked him of the Lord." (1 Sam 1:1-2,10-11,19-20)

In like manner, the Gospel of Luke relates the birth of John the Baptizer as miraculous. It does so to stress John's important role as prophetic precursor of Jesus. We are told by Luke that John was born to Zechariah and Elizabeth in their old age (which parallels the miraculous birth of Isaac):

> But the angel said to him, Do not be afraid, Zechariah, for your prayer is heard, and your wife Elizabeth will bear you a son, and you shall call his name John. . . . And Zechariah said to the angel, "How shall I know this? for I am an old man, and my wife is advanced in years." (Lk 1:13,18)

The apostolic church believed that it was through the Risen Jesus that all of God's promises of salvation to Israel had been gloriously consummated (Jn 19:28-30). It seemed especially appropriate to early Christian folk teachers, therefore, to present the birth of Jesus as *miraculous* in order to emphasize his culminating role in the history of salvation. Knowledge of the miraculous-birth motif in the Bible alerts us that stories of this kind should not be taken as literal history. Instead, they should be understood as theological pronouncements which point dramatically and symbolically to the exceptional role played by certain persons in biblical history.

4

Matthew and Luke tell us that Jesus was descended from King David through his "putative" father Joseph (Mt 1:15,20; Lk 1:27; 2:4; 3:23). They both stress Jesus' Davidic ancestry to defend the apostolic church's belief that Jesus is the royal Messiah from David's line promised by the prophets. Israel's prophets expected a descendent of David as God's Messiah-King because of the solemn promise they believed God had made to David through Nathan the prophet:

> When your days are fulfilled and you lie down with your fathers, I will raise up your offspring after you, who shall come forth from your body. . . . and I will establish the throne of his kingdom forever. I will be his father, and he shall be my son. . . . And your house and your kingdom shall be made sure forever before me; your throne shall be established forever. (2 Sam 7:12-14,16)

When the house of David lost its power to rule at the time of the Exile to Babylon (587 B.C.), the prophets believed that God's promise was still binding, and that God would send a Messiah from David's line to be instrumental in restoring David's kingdom to Israel:

Ps 89:3-4

> You have said, "I have made a covenant with my chosen one, I have sworn to David my servant: 'I will establish your descendants forever, and your throne for all generations.' "

Ps 89:20,29

> I have found David, my servant; with my holy oil I have anointed him. . . . I will establish his line forever and his throne as the days of the heavens.

Ps 89:35-37

> I will not violate my covenant, or alter the word that went forth from my lips. Once for all I have sworn by my holiness; I will not lie to David. His line shall endure forever, his throne as long as the sun before me.

Jer 23:5-6

Behold, the days are coming, says the Lord, when I will raise up for David a righteous branch, and he shall reign as king and deal wisely, and shall execute justice and righteousness in the land. In his day Judah shall be saved, and Israel shall dwell securely.

Jer 30:9

But they shall serve the Lord their God and David their king, whom I will raise up for them.

Jer 33:15,17

In those days . . . I will cause a righteous branch to spring forth for David. . . . For thus says the Lord: David shall never lack a man to sit on the throne of the house of Israel.

Ez 34:23-24 (see also 37:24-25)

And I will set up over them one shepherd, my servant David, and he shall feed them and be their shepherd. And I, the Lord, will be their God, and my servant David shall be prince among them; I, the Lord, have spoken.

There is, of course, no way of "proving" that Jesus was descended from King David. The fact remains, however, that the apostolic church believed that he was:

Rom 1:1,3

Paul, a servant of Jesus Christ, called to be an apostle, set apart for the gospel of God . . . concerning his Son, who was descended from David according to the flesh.

Acts 13:22-23

And . . . he raised up David to be their king; of whom he testified and said, "I have found in David the son of Jesse a man after my own heart, who will do all my will." Of this man's posterity God has brought to Israel a Savior, Jesus, as he promised.

1 Tim 2:8

Remember Jesus Christ, risen from the dead, descended from David, as preached in my gospel.

Rev 22:16 (see also 5:5)

I Jesus have sent my angel to you with this testimony for the churches. I am the root and the offspring of David, the bright morning star.

The apostle Paul was convinced of Jesus' Davidic descent, and Paul was personally acquainted with Jesus' brother, James (Gal 1:18-19; see also Acts 21:18). We may reasonably assume, then, that Jesus' family believed that one of their ancestors was of David's lineage. This family tradition would not have been rare or highly unusual. There were probably dozens of Jewish families in Palestine who could make the same claim. For the harems of the kings of Judah produced many royal offspring who, although they never sat on David's throne, would nevertheless have been remembered with great pride by their descendants.

When the earliest Christians either remembered or discovered that the Risen Jesus was descended from King David, they concluded that Jesus is the promised Messiah from David's line. The Davidic Messiah was expected to bring definitive salvation to Israel and the nations, and that is what they believed Jesus had done. To identify Jesus as the Davidic Messiah, therefore, seemed justified and necessary.

However, when these Jewish Christians proclaimed Jesus as God's promised Messiah their witnessing was rejected by the majority of the Jews. The majority responded that the fate of Jesus was shockingly contrary to what they had been taught the Messiah would be like. Nothing in the writings of the prophets or the teaching of the scribes suggested that the promised Messiah would be rejected and shamefully executed as a criminal. Ancient Jewish tradition expected a Messiah who would be royal, majestic, and invincible in battle with Israel's foes.

The Jewish Christians answered that God had sent a "spiritual" Messiah to win the "spiritual" victory of the Resurrection, not a military Messiah to lead earthly armies. But most of the Jews could not accept this Jewish Christian claim. The Jewish refusal meant that Jewish Christians had to search the scriptures for midrashic signs that God had intended all along to send a suffering and rejected Messiah like Jesus. Accordingly, the sufferings of any righteous servant of God mentioned in the scriptures were pointed to as prefiguring Jesus and revealing the true nature of God's secret Messianic purpose.

It is for this reason that Matthew's infancy narrative suggests that just as Pharoah King of Egypt sought the life of Moses after he was born (Ex 1:16,22), so also Jesus was menaced by an evil king at the time of his birth. King Herod's desire to destroy the infant Jesus caused Joseph to take Jesus, the New Moses, down into Egypt. (We should also recall that the patriarch Joseph interpreted Pharoah's dream in Egypt.):

> Now . . . an angel of the Lord appeared to Joseph in a dream and said, "Rise, take the child and his mother and flee into Egypt, and remain there till I tell you; for Herod is about to search for the child to destroy him."
>
> And he arose and took the child and his mother by night, and departed into Egypt, and remained there until the death of Herod. This was to fulfill what The Lord had spoken by the prophet, "Out of Egypt have I called my son." (Mt 2:13-15)

Matthew's story suggests that the spiritual kingship of Jesus is far superior to military and political kingship. Evil King Herod represents the rulers of this world who actually did destroy Jesus. Therefore, those who prefer military kingship to the spiritual kingship of Jesus are foolish and blind to the true (midrashic) meaning of the scriptures.

5

Before Matthew relates his midrash on Jesus as the New Moses, however, he describes the miraculous birth of Jesus as that of the promised Davidic Messiah:

> Now the birth of Jesus Christ took place in this way. When his mother Mary had been betrothed to Joseph, before they came together she was found to be with child of

> the Holy Spirit; and her husband Joseph . . . resolved to divorce her quietly.
>
> But as he considered this, behold an angel of the Lord appeared to him in a dream, saying, "Joseph, son of David, do not fear to take Mary your wife, for that which is conceived in her is of the Holy Spirit; she will bear a son, and you shall call his name Jesus, for he will save his people from their sins."
>
> All this took place to fulfill what the Lord had spoken by the prophet:
>
> "Behold, a virgin shall conceive
> and bear a son,
> and his name shall be called Emmanuel"
> (which means God with us). (Mt 1:18-23)

Matthew's birth narrative concludes with a midrashic citation from the Old Greek translation of Is 7:14. He cites the Old Greek version (also called the Septuagint) because he is writing for a Greek-speaking church which uses the Old Greek Bible for study and worship. (The Old Greek version was begun c. 250 B.C. This translation was made by Greek-speaking Jews after Alexander's conquest spread the use of Greek throughout the Ancient Near East and the Mediterranean world.)

The famous passage from Isaiah quoted by Matthew is part of a promise made by Isaiah to King Ahaz of Judah at a time when David's dynasty was in danger of being destroyed by the kings of Israel and Syria (2 Kgs 16:5-9). These two kings had urged King Ahaz to join them in a revolt against Assyria. When King Ahaz refused, they tried to take Jerusalem by force in order to remove David's heir and appoint a new king (not of David's line) who would cooperate with them (Is 7:1-6).

Although the siege of Jerusalem had been lifted, the situation looked very grim for young King Ahaz. At that time he had no male heir, and his enemies planned to return and topple David's throne. It was in these precarious circumstances that Isaiah approached King Ahaz and reassured him that God was still with the house of David and the kingdom of Judah. Isaiah invited King Ahaz to ask God for a sign which would confirm

Isaiah's message, but the King refused. When Isaiah experienced the king's proud unwillingness, he delivered his famous "Immanuel" prophecy:

> And he said, "Hear then, O house of David! Is it too little for you to weary men, that you weary my God also? Therefore, the Lord himself will give you a sign. Behold, a young woman shall conceive and bear a son, and shall call his name Immanuel." (Is 7:13-14)

It is noteworthy that in the original Hebrew text Isaiah says that a "young woman" (*almah*) will give birth to Immanuel, *not a virgin.* There is a word in Hebrew for virgin, *bethulah,* but Isaiah chose not use it. Who is this young woman? If we remember that the "sign" was meant to reassure King Ahaz that God was still with David's threatened dynasty and the kingdom of Judah, then the young woman spoken of by Isaiah was probably one of the young king's wives in the royal harem.

Isaiah's words imply that the royal heir whom this young woman will soon bear will be a sign that God is still with the house of David and the kingdom of Judah. The house of David, therefore, will survive the danger in which it currently finds itself, and will not be destroyed.

The translators of the Old Greek version thought that the Greek word *"parthenos"* (virgin) was an acceptable translation for the Hebrew word *"almah"* (young woman). In Greek usage at the time of the Old Greek translation, if a very young woman was married but had not yet borne a child, she could still be called a virgin. Such a young woman would be in the situation of the young wife of King Ahaz before she conceived and bore "Immanuel." Historically, King Hezekiah was the promised "Immanuel" who succeeded King Ahaz and continued David's dynasty.

Matthew's midrashic story of Jesus' birth intends to teach that Jesus is "the true Immanuel." Jesus is the descendant of David through whom the promise made to the house of David has finally been fulfilled. In order to emphasize that Jesus is the true Immanuel, Matthew (following the Old Greek version of Is 7:14) relates that Jesus is born of a "virgin" who is married to a man of the "house of David" called Joseph (Mt 1:16-17,20). Jesus, therefore, is the promised Son of David who will reign "forever" over God's approaching Kingdom.

6

Luke's account of Jesus' miraculous birth is also designed to teach that Jesus is the true Immanuel, the *definitive* Messiah who insures the perpetuity of David's dynasty. In Luke's account, however, the Immanuel prophecy is not quoted. Instead, Jesus' mysterious fulfillment of the Immanuel prophecy is implied when Mary, his mother-to-be, is *twice* called a "virgin" (Is 7:14) who is joined to the "house of David" (Is 7:13):

> In the sixth month the angel Gabriel was sent from God to a city of Galilee named Nazareth, to a virgin betrothed to a man whose name was Joseph, of the house of David; and the virgin's name was Mary. (Lk 1:26-27)

The birth narrative which we find in Luke gives special emphasis to the promise of an everlasting dynasty made to David in 2 Sam 7:12-15 (quoted above). The words spoken by the angel to Mary are a paraphrase of that promise:

> And the angel said to her, "Do not be afraid, Mary, for you have found favor with God. And behold, you will conceive in your womb and bear a son, and you shall call his name Jesus.
>
> He will be great, and will be called
> the Son of the Most High;
> and the Lord God will give to him
> the throne of his father David,
> and he will reign over the house of
> David forever; and of his kingdom
> there will be no end." (Lk 1:30-33)

After Luke's account announces the imminent birth of Jesus-Immanuel, who is destined to fulfill God's promise made to David of old, the account indicates the conclusive role of Jesus in salvation history by describing his conception in appropriately "miraculous" terms:

> And Mary said to the angel, "How shall this be, since I have no husband?" And the angel said to her,
>
> "The Holy Spirit will come upon you
> and the power of the Most High
> will overshadow you;
> therefore the child to be born
> will be called holy,
> the Son of God." (Lk 1:34-35)

When the angel tells Mary that Jesus will be called the "Son of God," we should not conclude that Jesus is being described as a divine person who has a divine nature. The angel's statement has nothing to do with later Incarnational or Trinitarian theology. Instead, the angel is midrashically informing the "virgin" Mary that her son Jesus-Immanuel is destined to become God's "Messiah" from David's line. To correctly grasp this notion, we must return to the promise made by God to David through the prophet Nathan:

> When your days are fulfilled and you lie down with your fathers, I will raise up your offspring after you, who shall come forth from your body. . . . and I will establish the throne of his kingdom forever. *I will be his father, and he shall be my son.* . . . And your house and your kingdom shall be made sure forever before me; your throne shall be established forever. (2 Sam 7:12-14,16)

In this prophecy, God was understood to have promised David that God would adopt David's heir and would regard that heir as God's own Son. The title "Son of God," therefore, belonged preeminently to David's descendant who had been anointed as David's successor and God's Messiah, i.e., the earthly representative of God's Kingly Rule. The title "Son of God," therefore, was synonymous with the titles "Son of David" and "Messiah."

God's promise to adopt David's royal heir and make him God's own "Son" is *presupposed* in Psalm 2 (also in Ps 89:26-27) where the original promise made by God to David is recalled by the king who is David's reigning successor. (This psalm was sung on the day when a new king was anointed as David's successor, and probably also on the anniversary of that event throughout his reign.):

> I will tell of the decree of the Lord: He said to me, "You are my Son, today I have begotten you. Ask of me, and I will make the nations your heritage, and the ends of the earth your possession." (Ps 2:7-8)

7

Now that we are aware of the peculiar blend of folk history and midrashic theology in the miraculous stories of Jesus' birth, we should be able to understand why contemporary scholarship tells us that these stories are not "factual" history. Consider, for example, the serious contradiction which results if one takes Luke's story of the Annunciation literally and then reads about the noncomprehending and interfering response of Jesus' mother and brothers in the third chapter of Mark's Gospel.

Mark relates that Jesus' mother and brothers were alarmed when they learned that Jesus had undertaken a prophetic mission of preaching to crowds and healing the sick. They thought Jesus had lost his mind and tried to coax him to come out of Peter's house at Capernaum so they could force him to return with them to Nazareth. But Jesus understood their purpose and refused to go out to them. (Mark has separated the beginning of the story from its conclusion with his often noted "sandwich" technique.):

> And when his family heard of it, they went out to seize him, for they said, "He is out of his mind. . . . And his mother and his brothers came; and standing outside they sent to him and called him. And a crowd was sitting about him; and they said to him, "Your mother and your brothers are outside, asking for you."
>
> And he replied, "Who are my mother and my brothers?" And looking around on those who sat about him, he said, "Here are my mother and my brothers! Whoever does the

will of God is my brother, and sister, and mother." (Mk 3:21,31-35)

If the mother of Jesus had truly been visited by the angel Gabriel, had literally been informed by Gabriel of Jesus' exalted-Messianic destiny, and had truly consented to conceive Jesus miraculously, would she have been baffled and interfering when Jesus began to proclaim the nearness of God's coming Kingdom? Probably not.

It is easy to see why a folk teacher in the early church would have created the story of Jesus' miraculous birth to underscore Jesus' culminating role in salvation history. But it is difficult to imagine that the church would have created the story about Jesus' mother and brothers taking offense at him and attempting to take him home by force. The logical solution to this problem is to assume that the story of Jesus' miraculous birth is folk theology, whereas the story of his family's initial incomprehension is history.

Bearing all of this (and much more) in mind, the majority of contemporary exegetes conclude that Jesus was probably conceived in the same God-designed and God-intended way in which all other humans are conceived, i.e., from the seed of his father Joseph and the ovum of his mother Mary. This conclusion will be profoundly disturbing to conservative Christians who read the Infancy Narratives as literal history instead of ancient midrashic theology.

Increasing numbers of Christians, however, are unwilling to read the stories of Jesus' miraculous birth as literal history. These Christians should be allowed to bring their knowledge of folk history and ancient Jewish literary forms to the birth narratives. This knowledge will enable them to understand that the narratives were created to teach symbolic lessons about the exalted (and unexpected) "spiritual" Messiahship of Jesus.

In addition to the literary and historical reasons adduced above, there are also scientific and philosophic reasons for preferring a nonliteral reading of the wonder-filled and truly beautiful stories of Jesus' birth. It is essential to being human that one has a human nature which was provided biologically by both a mother *and* a father. If Jesus did not have a biological father, we may reasonably ask if he was truly human and therefore truly qualified to be God's definitive sign of assurance to all other humans.

Also, we know that God has so designed human nature (working indirectly through the evolutionary process) that the sex of a child is determined by a chromosome in the father's sperm. If Jesus did not have a father who supplied the Y chromosome which produces a male, he could not have been born a male able to fulfill God's promises to David, ancient Israel, and the world.

Conservative Christians usually reply to reasoning like that just expressed by asserting that the birth of Jesus was miraculous. A miracle, they would maintain, is something *contrary* to the laws of nature. And since the birth of Jesus was miraculous we should not be surprised to learn that it contradicted the laws of nature.

Contemporary scholarship responds to such assertions with observations like the following:

1. The birth of Jesus truly was sacred and miraculous, but so is every other human birth if one remembers that spirit-bearing humans are recycled stardust. If Jesus is a sign from God that all humans can transcend the terror of history and reach Eternal Life, then it is appropriate for Jesus to be a genuine human like all others, *all* of whom have fathers as well as mothers.

   Those who are offended by the idea that Jesus was not miraculously conceived should ask themselves why this possibility should disqualify Jesus from being the representative human through whom God answers our ultimate questions. Why would a normal conception prevent Jesus from becoming God's definitive assurance that all other humans can finally transcend tragedy, injustice, discouragement, and death? If Jesus is meant as God's guarantee to all other humans, is it unfitting for Jesus to have been conceived in the same way as all other humans?

2. Most contemporary exegetes reject the idea that God would interfere with or violate the laws of nature. Our God-given power of reason tells us it is *wrong* to act illogically, contradictorily, or uneconomically. We conclude, therefore, that God does not act in such ways. For if God were to violate the laws of nature, that would mean that God was acting illogically and contradictorily by destroying the very laws which God is everywhere creating and upholding as the Ground of all being.
3. When genuine miracles occur, therefore, they never violate the laws of nature. Rather, they accelerate or transcend the rate at which natural processes ordinarily operate. Genuine supernatural signs are divinely caused manifestations of a paranormal kind and *are not unnatural.* Paranormal happenings involve the actualization of latent and extraordinary possibilities within the realm of nature. They lie outside the expected range of the normal but are still within the range of the natural. Correctly understood, therefore, the miraculous involves the *divine* activation of some extraordinary capacity already latent in nature.
4. Divine action which respects and works through freedom is not the same as interference. If we humans are able to creatively influence and accelerate natural processes, so can God if human freedom opens itself to God with faith and trust. We humans, for example, can positively influence and accelerate the healing process with medication and psychotherapy. It is reasonable to infer, therefore, that God is also able to accelerate paranormal natural processes when a personal center freely opens itself to God's activity with faith and trust. Genuine miracles, therefore, never violate or contradict the laws of nature.

Questions for Review and Discussion

1. Before Jesus undertook his prophetic mission, what was his profession, and how did he probably learn that profession? How do we know our answer is probably true?
2. How would the majority of contemporary scholars respond to the *traditional* view that the brothers and sisters of Jesus mentioned in Mk 6:3 were either cousins of Jesus or children of Joseph by an earlier marriage (i.e., stepbrothers and stepsisters of Jesus)?
3. What is "midrash," and why should we know about it if we hope to fully understand the stories of Jesus' birth?
4. Why was the Messiahship of Jesus so difficult for the average Jew to accept when the apostolic church proclaimed it?
5. What is "apologetics," and why should we know about it when reading the Infancy Narratives in Matthew and Luke?
6. Why did the postexilic prophets assume that God would send a Messiah from David's line to restore the kingdom of Israel?
7. What traditional folk device does the Bible frequently use when describing the birth of a person who plays a crucial role in the history of salvation?
8. Mk 3:21,31-35 tells us that the mother and brothers of Jesus were alarmed when Jesus began his prophetic mission, and they tried to seize and take him home by force. But the message of the angel who spoke with Mary in Lk 1:26-35 should have prepared her for such a possibility. Which of the two accounts, therefore, is probably history and which is probably theology? Explain your answer.

Chapter Three: Jesus' Birthplace

1

WHEN WE ANALYZE THE DATA IN THE GOSPELS CRITICALLY, IT seems evident that Jesus was a Jew from the town of Nazareth in Galilee (Mt 2:23; Mk 1:9; 10:47; Lk 4:16; Jn 1:45-46; Acts 2:22). A New Testament concordance will show that Nazareth is mentioned twenty-five times as the place of Jesus' origin. Since the early church apparently attached no serious theological significance to Nazareth, the memory of Jesus' origin there is probably correct.

Matthew's Gospel contains the only clear attempt in the New Testament to assign "midrashic" meaning to Nazareth. We are told that Joseph, when returning from Egypt, was warned in a dream not to return to Bethlehem. After informing us that Joseph decided to take the child Jesus to Nazareth, Matthew concludes his narrative with the following observation:

> And he went and dwelt in a city called Nazareth, that what was spoken by the prophets might be fulfilled, "He shall be called a Nazarene." (Mt 2:23)

The citation from the "prophets" in this verse is problematic because it cannot be found anywhere in either the Hebrew or Greek canon of the Old Testament. The closest parallel to the text Matthew quotes is the occasional mention of the "Nazirite" in the Old Testament scriptures.

A Nazirite was a man whose life was vowed to God. He was not allowed to cut his hair or drink wine. Samson the judge, for example, whose hair was treacherously cut by Delilah (Judg 16), was a Nazirite (Judg 13). A Jewish Christian folk teacher in the early church would not have hesitated to see the word "Nazarene" cryptically foreshadowed in the biblical "Nazirite."

Nazirites are spoken of thirteen times in the Old Testament. Matthew, however, probably has in mind a specific text in the book of Judges which connects the term Nazirite with the "miraculous" birth of Samson, one of Israel's earlier saviors:

> And the angel of the Lord appeared to the woman and said to her, "Behold, you are barren and have no children; but you shall conceive and bear a son. . . . No razor shall come upon his head, for the boy shall be a Nazirite to God from birth; and he shall begin to deliver Israel from the hand of the Philistines." (Judg 13:3,5)

The memory that Jesus was born and raised in Nazareth had been securely embedded in early Christian tradition well before the later legendary stories of his birth at Bethlehem were created for theological reasons.

Similarly, since both of the genealogies provided for Jesus in the Gospels (Mt 1:1-17; Lk 3:23-38) originally stressed the importance of *Joseph* as Jesus' link with David (Mt 1:16; Lk 3:23,31), they were probably composed by folk historians in the early church *before* the stories of the "virgin" birth were created. By way of confirmation, the parenthetic denial of Joseph's paternity at the beginning of the genealogy in Luke interrupts the logical flow of the list and was probably added later:

> Jesus, when he began his ministry, was about thirty years of age, being the son (as was supposed) of Joseph, the son of Heli, the son of. . . . (Lk 3:23)

The parenthetical disclaimer was no doubt inserted in the genealogy by Luke to make the genealogy compatible with the miraculous conception of Jesus which Luke recounted in 1:26-38.

Contemporary historians judge that Jesus was born c. 3 B.C. This seemingly anachronous conclusion is the result of an error made by an ancient Christian scholar named Dionysius Exiguus (Denis the small). Dionysius was a Christian monk who died in Rome c. A.D. 550. By his time the barbarians had taken Rome repeatedly and had reduced its former glory to ruins.

Before Rome fell, Roman historians indicated the current year by estimating the total number of years since Rome's legendary founding. If, for example, they calculated that Rome had been founded seven hundred years ago, they referred to the current year as 700 A.U.C. (A.U.C. = Ab Urbe Condita = from the time when the city was founded).

Dionysius concluded that since the days of imperial Rome were finished, it no longer made sense to calculate the current year by connecting it to Rome's founding. As a Christian scholar, he decided that the most important event in history was not the founding of Rome, but the birth of Jesus, the Savior of the world: Rome was gone, whereas the Risen Jesus will reign forever. It seemed appropriate to Dionysius, therefore, to calculate the current year from the time of Jesus' birth.

Guided by the Gospel of Luke which says that John the Baptizer began to preach in "the fifteenth year of the reign of Tiberius Caesar" (Lk 3:1), when Jesus was "about thirty years old" (Lk 3:23), Dionysius determined the year in which he thought Jesus had been born. He then designated the year of Jesus' birth as A.D. 1 (A.D. = Anno Domini = in the year of the Lord), and numbered all subsequent years as additions to that beginning point.

Dionysius' new method of indicating the current year was eventually adopted by all Christian nations. Contemporary historians estimate, however, that he mistakenly placed the date of Jesus' birth a few years too late. And that explains why they think Jesus actually was born born c. 3 B.C.

Surprisingly, there was not much interest in the time "Before Christ" until the last half of the seventeenth century. It was then that the custom of referring to the period before Jesus as B.C. (Before Christ) was introduced. The French bishop Jacques

Benigne Bossuet is usually given credit for initiating this practice. He did so in a book he published in A.D. 1681 entitled, *Discours sur l'histoire universelle* (Discourse on Universal History). Many people in English-speaking societies mistakenly assume that because the abbreviation B.C. is based on English, the Latin abbreviation A.D. must be also and means "After Death."

2

The Infancy Narratives tell us that Jesus was born at "Bethlehem" for basically the same reason that they speak of his miraculous birth of a "virgin." They relate that Jesus was born at Bethlehem to remind us that Jesus is descended from King David. Since Bethlehem was the town where King David was born (1 Sam 17:12,14), a priest-editor of the book of Micah added (after the Exile in 587 B.C.) the promise that someday Bethlehem would produce an ideal king of David's line. This ideal king would then restore the kingdom of Israel to its former glory:

> But you, O Bethlehem Ephrathah,
> who are little to be among the clans of Judah,
> from you shall come forth for me
> one who is to be ruler in Israel,
> whose origin is from of old, from ancient days.
> (Mic 5:2)

Micah's Bethlehem text is freely quoted by Matthew in his account of Jesus' birth. Matthew cited the text to remind us that Jesus is descended from David and is the ideal king foretold in the book of Micah:

> Now when Jesus was born in Bethlehem of Judea in the days of Herod the King, behold, wise men from the East came to Jerusalem, saying, "Where is he who has been born king of the Jews? For we have seen his star in the East, and have come to worship him."
>
> When King herod heard this he was troubled, and all Jerusalem with him; and assembling all the chief priests and scribes of the people, he inquired of them where the

Messiah was to be born. They told him, "In Bethlehem of Judah; for so it is written by the prophet:

'And you, O Bethlehem,
in the land of Judah;
are by no means least
among the rulers of Judah;
for from you shall come a ruler
who will govern my people Israel.' "
(Mt 2:1-6)

In addition to the "Bethlehem" text quoted from Micah, Matthew's birth story alludes to another prophecy in the Old Testament which also connects the infant Jesus with the dynasty of David. That text is the passage from Balaam's prophecy in the book of Numbers which likens the rise of David's dynasty in Israel to the appearance of a portentous "star" in the heavens:

A star shall come forth out of Jacob,
and a scepter shall rise out of Israel;
it shall crush the forehead of Moab,
and shall break down all the sons of Sheth.
(Num 24:17)

The mysterious star that appears in Matthew's birth narrative is the star of David promised in the book of Numbers. It appears at the birth of Jesus to announce to Israel and the nations that their true light has come. Jesus, the Great Son of David, is the "Light" sent by God to free us from death's darkness:

The people who sat in darkness have seen a great light, and for those who sat in the region and shadow of death light has dawned. (Mt 4:15; see also 5:14-16)

3

Matthew's narrative implies that Joseph and Mary originally resided in "Bethlehem" (Mt 2:11), and that Joseph, in order to protect the child Jesus, moved to Nazareth after returning from from Egypt:

But when Herod died, behold, an angel of the Lord appeared in a dream to Joseph in Egypt, saying, "Rise, take

> the child and his mother, and go to the land of Israel, for those who sought the child's life are dead."
>
> And he rose and took the child and his mother, and went to the land of Israel. But when he heard that Archelaus ruled over Judea in place of his father Herod, he was afraid to go there, and being warned in a dream he withdrew to the district of Galilee. And he went and dwelt in a city called Nazareth. (Mt 2:19-23)

Luke, however, remembers correctly that Joseph and Mary resided at Nazareth before Jesus' birth:

> In the sixth month the angel Gabriel was sent from God to a city of Galilee named Nazareth, to a virgin betrothed to a man whose name was Joseph, of the house of David; and the virgin's name was Mary. (Lk 1:26-27)

The Lukan birth narative explains that Joseph and Mary were required to journey to "Bethlehem" to register for a tax census ordered by the Roman emperor. And while they were there the time came for Mary to deliver her child. It was for that providential reason, the Lukan narrative informs us, that Jesus was born in Bethlehem. (Luke implies that Caesar Augustus rules the world, but Caesar, nevertheless, is subject to God's hidden Messianic purpose):

> In those days a decree went forth from Caesar Augustus that all the world should be enrolled. . . . And all went to be enrolled, each to his own city, and Joseph also went up from Galilee, from the city of Nazareth, to Judea, to the city of David which is called Bethlehem, because he was of the house and lineage of David, to be enrolled with Mary, his betrothed, who was with child.
>
> And while they were there, the time came for her to be delivered. And she gave birth to her first-born son and wrapped him in swaddling cloths, and laid him in a manger, because there was no place for them in the inn. (Lk 2:1-7)

Historians tell us that although the Romans required people to register periodically for the purpose of taxation, there is no record of a census at the time of Jesus' birth. Moreover, if there had been such a census, the Romans (renowned for their practicality), would not have required people to register in the place where their distant ancestors had resided. Instead, people were enrolled in the town or city where they currently lived so they could be found and taxed *there*.

This journey to Bethlehem, therefore, is a folk strategem employed by Luke. His strategem reminds us midrashically of Jesus' Davidic lineage by connecting Jesus with David's birth place. There are two other midrashic "signs" in the Lukan birth story cited above. Again, the first of these signs intends to point to Jesus' descent from King David:

When we are told that Jesus was wrapped in "swaddling cloths," we are meant to recall that Solomon, the first of David's royal sons to succeed him, describes himself in the *Wisdom of Solomon* as wrapped in "swaddling cloths" at his birth. (Because this book was written in Greek, it was not included in the Hebrew Bible. It was, however, an integral part of the Old Greek Bible which was used for worship and study by the Greek-speaking majority in the early church):

> And when I was born I began to breathe the common air . . . and my first sound was a cry, like that of all. I was nursed with *swaddling cloths*. For no king has had a different beginning of existence. (Wis 7:3-5)

The Lukan birth story quoted above relates that after Jesus was born and wrapped in "swaddling cloths," he was laid in a "manger" (*phatnē*). The mention of a "manger" is a midrashic allusion to a prophecy in Isaiah which laments Israel's refusal to *understand* and *obey* God's word. Luke intends Isaiah's lament as a midrashic allusion to Israel's absence at the birth of her promised Messiah. This absence, Luke suggests, presages the eventual rejection of Jesus by Israel and her leaders:

> The ox knows its owner, and the ass its master's manger [Old Greek = *phatnē*); but Israel does not know, my people does not understand.
>
> Ah, sinful nation, a people laden with iniquity, offspring of evildoers, sons who deal corruptly! They have for-

> saken the Lord, they have despised the Holy One of Israel, they are utterly estranged. (Is 1:3-4)

To compensate for the absence of Israel (God's flock) and her blind leaders (unworthy "shepherds;" see Ez 34:1-16) at Jesus' birth, Luke's story says that God sent angels to notify poor "shepherds" near Bethlehem of the birth of Israel's promised Shepherd-King from David's line (Ez 34:23; cp. 2 Sam 7:8):

> And in that region there were shepherds out in the field, keeping watch over their flocks by night. And an angel of the Lord appeared to them, and the glory of the Lord shone around them, and they were filled with fear.
>
> And the angel of the Lord said to them, "Be not afraid; for behold; I bring you good news of great joy which will come to all the people; For to you is born this day in the city of David a Savior, who is Messiah and Lord." (Lk 2:8-11)

The shepherds (and we) are assured that this royal child (Immanuel) can be recognized with the aid of midrashic "signs":

> "And this will be a sign for you, you will find an *infant* wrapped in *swaddling cloths* and lying in a *manger.*" And suddenly there was with the angel a multitude of the heavenly host praising God and saying,
>
> "Glory to God in the highest,
> and on earth peace among men
> with whom he is pleased!"

The joyful song of the angels after their revelation to the shepherds is a midrahsic reference to a passage of sacred poetry in Job. The passage in Job is taken by Luke to presage the joy in heaven at the birth of Jesus who, as Risen Lord, is destined to be the "foundation" and "cornerstone" of God's glorious New Creation. The arrival of the New Creation is guaranteed because it has already mysteriously begun with the birth (and Resurrection) of Jesus:

> Where were you when I laid the *foundation* of the earth? Tell me, if you have understanding. Who determined its measurements—surely you know! Or who stretched the

> line upon it? On what were its bases sunk, or who laid its *cornerstone,* when *the morning stars sang together,* and all *the sons of God sang for joy?* (Job 38:4-7)

To fully appreciate Luke's midrash on the passage from Job, we must recall that in that book the expressions "sons of God" and the parallel "morning stars" both indicate the angelic beings who serve God in the heavens (Job 1:6-12; 2:1-6).

When we search carefully behind the midrashic theology and folk motifs in the Matthean and Lukan stories of Jesus' birth, reason guides our faith to conclude that Jesus was probably born of Mary and Joseph at Nazareth in Galilee. Also, Jesus' family probably remembered (with great pride) that one of their forebears was descended from King David.

After the revelatory "appearances" of the Risen and Spirit-mediating Jesus, this connection with the house of David was assigned enormous theological significance for all the reasons indicated above. It was to call attention apologetically to Jesus' possession of the Davidic descent requisite for Messiahship that the early church eventually created the stories of Jesus' "virgin" birth at "Bethlehem."

4

At this point in our considerations, it will be helpful if we pause to reflect on the important difference between "exegesis" and "eisegesis." Exegesis means taking out of an ancient biblical text the meaning that its author actually intended. Eisegesis, on the other hand, means reading into an ancient biblical text a later meaning which its author did not intend. It is obvious that we should always strive to practice exegesis and avoid eisegesis when reading the sacred scriptures.

When reading the Infancy Narratives, therefore, we should remember that their ancient authors were writing midrashic theology for apologetic reasons. These narratives were never meant to be read as "factual" history. If we do so, we are unwittingly acting contrary to the intention of their authors and are practicing eisegesis instead of exegesis.

Those who read the Infancy Narratives as literal biography are usually doing so sincerely. They have been taught by their precritical tradition to understand these stories as historical fact. But once we rediscover the theological function of the ancient literary forms in these stories, it becomes clear that it is mistaken to insist that everyone must understand them literally.

Contemporary scholarship does not wish to suggest that the Infancy Narratives are totally devoid of historical content. The stories correctly recall that (1) Jesus was a Jew who was born in Palestine, that (2) the early church believed he was descended through Joseph from the house of David, and that (3) after his death, his disciples claimed that God had raised him up as the promised Messiah from David's line.

These correct historical memories, however, were intertwined with their midrashic-apologetic interpretation by the early church. It is important, therefore, to distinguish the underlying history of Jesus in the infancy stories from that history's later theological interpretation by the church. If we fail to make this important distinction we are practicing eisegesis rather than exegesis.

A literal reading of the infancy stories will also be cognizant of the genuine history which underlies them. Likewise, a literal reading will recognize the theological lessons joined to those historical memories by the early church. Such a reading, however, will mistakenly identify the theological lessons in the stories with the history underlying them. This mistaken identification does not usually harm those who make it. The harm will arise when they try to share their faith understanding of Jesus with educated people outside the Christian faith community or with increasingly better informed young people within the community.

Many of those to whom they witness will be acquainted with the scientific way of doing history as well as ancient literary forms. These listeners will be repelled by what they perceive as naively unfounded claims about Jesus. Such disaffected listeners will predictably reject the Christian Message as "mythological" nonsense. Misunderstandings of this kind exemplify what Paul Tillich called the tragic ambiguity which plagues religion under the conditions of existence.

Questions for Discussion and Review

1. Why do historians tell us that Jesus was probably born c. 3 B.C.? How do they explain this seemingly contradictory conclusion?
2. Do contemporary historians think that the Romans would truly have required Joseph to register for a tax census at a distant place where his remote ancestors had once lived? Explain your answer.
3. Why do the Infancy Narratives in Matthew and Luke state that Jesus was born at "Bethlehem"? Is this statement intended as factual history or midrashic theology? Explain your answer.
4. Why does Matthew say that a "star" guided the wise Men to Bethlehem? Should the star be understood literally or symbolically? Explain your answer.
5. Why does Matthew tell us that Joseph took the infant Jesus down to "Egypt"? Was that journey historical or theological? Explain your answer.
6. What other evil king mentioned in the Old Testament is King Herod intended to recall in Matthew's story of the flight into Egypt? Why does Matthew want us to remember that other evil king, and what midrashic reference in the story assures us that this was truly Matthew's intention?
7. Why does Luke say that the infant Jesus was wrapped in "swaddling cloths" when he was born? Is Luke's statement intended as history or theology? Explain your answer.
8. Why does Luke tell us that the infant Jesus was laid in a "manger" after his birth? Is Luke's statement historical memory or apologetic theology? Explain your answer.

9. Why does Luke tell us that angels sang joyfully on the night when Jesus was born? Should we understand Luke's words as historical memory or midrashic theology? Explain your answer.
10. Where would the majority of contemporary biblical scholars say that Jesus was probably born? Why do they think this?
11. What is the difference between "exegesis" and "eisegesis"?
12. What are some of the undesirable consequences of practicing eisegesis instead of exegesis?

Chapter Four: Jesus' Sense of Identity and Mission

1

THIS CHAPTER WILL UNDERTAKE TO ANSWER THE QUESTION, "How did Jesus understand himself and the mission to which God had called him?" In the following chapters this question will be sharply distinguished from the related question, "How did the early church understand Jesus and the mission to which God had called him?" Although these questions are closely related, we will see below that the answer to the first is significantly different from the answer to the second.

When attempting to distinguish Jesus' self-understanding from the theological convictions of the evangelists, we must frequently engage in hypothesizing. Such hypothesizing is legitimate (1) if it is honestly acknowledged as such, and (2) if it leads to conclusions which are reasonably supported by a critical reading of the New Testament data.

There is always a danger that our hypothetical search for underlying signs and motives might drift beyond an interpretation reasonably compatible with the question-raising data. If that were to happen, we would wander off into groundless speculation or special pleading. The reader should be alert to this real possibility and should weigh all interpretations of the Gospels suggested in this book against experience and common sense.

2

When we read the Gospels with critical eyes, we are led to conclude that Jesus probably did not apply to himself most of the titles which the apostolic church bestowed on him (e.g., Messiah, Son of God, Son of David, Son of Man, Savior). After Easter, the church *assumed* that Jesus must have secretly known that all these titles belonged to him. She did not hesitate, therefore, to place them on his lips when she explained her memory of his words and deeds.

As we proceed, we will learn why and how the church decided that she should confer titles on Jesus which he himself did not claim or covet during his public mission. The reader should be forewarned that verifying this conclusion is a complex procedure. Not until the end of the process will the full range of reasons which justify such a conclusion become apparent. The reader will then be able to decide if the conclusion suggested just above is reasonable and convincing.

In order to achieve our goal we will have to reflect critically on a number of Jesus' sayings found in the Synoptic Gospels (Mark, Matthew, and Luke). The highly theological sayings of Jesus in the Gospel of John will not ordinarily be considered. Moreover, the reader should understand that there is wide disagreement among scholars as to which of Jesus' reported sayings are substantially authentic.

Some extremely conservative exegetes favor the view that all, or almost all, of the sayings found on Jesus' lips are authentic. On the other side, there are skeptical exegetes who assume that the apostolic church created all, or almost all, of Jesus' sayings. Common sense tells us that truth stands somewhere between these two extremes. (A good example of biblical scholarship which avoids extremes is John P. Meir's *A Marginal*

Jew, 3 vols.) Scholarly views which search carefully for this middle ground will guide our undertaking. Only sayings of Jesus considered authentic by moderate scholarship in general will be used in our exploration of Jesus' self-understanding.

We will see below that the folk mentality operating in the apostolic church certainly led the church to interpret and expand the sayings of Jesus. But even when the early church created new sayings, she was always guided by her memory of something Jesus actually did or said. It would be absurd to conclude that the early church did not remember the substance of Jesus' words and deeds, or that she arbitrarily created sayings of Jesus apart from such memories. On the contrary, new sayings were usually created to defend or explain something which Jesus had actually done or said (or the church's understanding of something Jesus had done or said).

3

A critical reading of the evidence in the Gospels indicates that Jesus did not think of himself as God's "Messiah" during his earthly mission. He did not know that he had been chosen by God to be Israel's promised Messiah until he was carried through death into Risen life. Learning to understand and accept this limitation on the earthly Jesus' knowledge is comparable to a "Copernican Revolution" in our reading of the Gospels. Once we grasp the reasons for this critical conclusion, a host of mistaken assumptions and groundless problems is eliminated, and elegant simplicity emerges from daunting complexity. We are then free to understand Jesus and God's saving purpose at work in him with new clarity, economy, and consistency.

Some people are understandably upset by the idea that Jesus did not know he was God's Messiah before his Resurrection. If we find ourselves among their number (and the author of this work once did), we should ask ourselves what difference it truly makes if Jesus did not learn about his exalted Messianic destiny until *after* he had fulfilled its unexpected requirements with faith and trust in God.

Does accepting this view of Jesus' knowledge truly make the Risen Jesus any less acceptable as the conclusive revelatory sign through whom God assures us of Eternal Life? On the contrary, it is easier to identify with Jesus as a divinely provided example of faith and trust in God if we assume that he did not have definite foreknowledge about the future events in his life and their glorious outcome. Uncertainty about the future and the need for faith and trust in God's goodness are essential characteristics of the human condition, and Jesus was truly human.

It is true that on several occasions Jesus is depicted in the Gospels as claiming to be (or implying that he is) God's promised Messiah:

> Mk 14:61-62
>
> Again the high priest asked him, "Are you the Messiah, the son of the Blessed One?" And Jesus said, "I am."
>
> Jn 4:25-26
>
> The [Samaritan] woman said, "I know that Messiah is coming (he who is called Christ); when he comes, he will show us all things." Jesus said to her, "I who speak with you am he."
>
> Jn 18:33,36-7
>
> Pilate entered the praetorium again and called Jesus and said to him, "Are you the King of the Jews?". . . . Jesus answered, "My kingship is not of this world; if my kingship were of this world, my servants would fight, that I might not be handed over to the Jews; but my kingship is not from the world.

We will see in later chapters, however, that these instances probably represent the early church's theological *interpretations* of Jesus worked out in the light of her historically conditioned "Resurrection" faith. These interpretations were retrojected onto her memory of Jesus' words and deeds and were meant to express her belief that Jesus knew from the start of his mission that he was God's Messiah. The early church assumed without any doubt that God had revealed God's secret Messianic purpose to Jesus *beforehand:*

> Surely the Lord God does nothing, without revealing his secret to his servants the prophets. (Amos 3:7)

The few occasions when Jesus is described as accepting the title Messiah must be carefully weighed against other occasions when he reacted to it differently. We will see, for example, in a later chapter that when Peter gave Jesus the title Messiah at Caesarea Philippi, Jesus, in the original form of the story, probably rejected the title vigorously (Mk 8:27-29,33). It was very likely Mark the evangelist who later modified the story with his Messianic Secret theology (Mk 8:30-32). He did so to render the story compatible with the church's belief in the spiritual Messiahship of the Risen Jesus.

In addition, Mark, Matthew, and Luke are probably correct when they relate that Jesus laconically refused to discuss the title Messiah when questioned about it by the Roman prefect Pontius Pilate (Mk 15:2; Mt 26:63-64; Lk 22:67,70). Conversely, when John relates that Jesus claimed the title before Pilate in a qualified (i.e., spiritual, nonmilitary) sense (18:33,36-37), John probably does so in pursuit of his characteristic theological goals.

It is easy to see why John would have created Jesus' positive (but qualified) response to Pilate as part of the Johannine interpretation of Jesus' exalted Messiahship. But it is very difficult to conceive that Mark, Matthew and Luke would have created Jesus' noncommital response for any theological purpose. (The synoptic accounts of Jesus' interrogations by the high priest and the Roman prefect will be examined in chapter nine.)

In actuality, Jesus probably rejected the title Messiah as theologically unacceptable because of its traditional association with military violence and bloodshed. He did not think that God's coming Reign over the restored Kingdom of creation would be established by military conquest. Rather, its arrival would be accomplished by the irresistible power of God (as indicated in Dan 2:44; 7:23-27).

4

The title which Jesus preferred when speaking of the king to come as the earthly representative of God's Reign was "Son of Man." The Hebrew word for "man" in the inclusive sense is *"adam."* And this word was eventually treated as the personal name of the first man, Adam. The title "Son of Man," therefore, really means "Son of Adam," i.e., the "New Adam" who will reign over the "New Creation." We will also see below that, before Jesus' Resurrection, Jesus probably did not identify himself with the exalted Son of Man whose coming he expected.

It has recently been advanced that Jesus never used the title Son of Man or taught an eschatological message. (Eschatology is the study of the things that will happen when God ends the world.) This view is sometimes recommended on the basis of the "number of ballots" cast at a seminar. It seems wiser, however, not to make serious scholarly judgments on the basis of anonymous ballots cast for ambiguous reasons. Instead, we should always ask "who" has said "what" and for what "carefully weighed reasons." Unwarranted skepticism, subtle contradictions, and the need for critical distinctions are easily overlooked by a ballot box.

The view that Jesus never spoke of the Son of Man or looked forward to the end-time Judgment which inaugurates God's coming Kingdom is unconvincing for a variety of reasons. To begin with, the title Son of Man is found on Jesus' lips 69 times in the Synoptic Gospels (this sum includes the repetition by Matthew and Luke of sayings which they found in Mark and the Q sayings) and 13 times in the Fourth Gospel.

Only once in the entire New Testament does someone other than Jesus (Stephen) give Jesus this title (Acts 7:56; in Rev 1:13 and 14:14 Jesus is *alluded to* as the Son of Man with language reminiscent of Dan 7:13). Considering the frequency of the title's almost exclusive use by Jesus, it is not likely that the title's presence in sayings of Jesus is due entirely to the editorial activity of the early church.

There is no denying that in her efforts to understand, explain, and honor Jesus the church eventually inserted the Son of Man title into some of his noneschatological sayings, i.e., into sayings that did not address the end-time (which is the only context in which Jesus himself had used the title). But if the church had gone to the trouble to create every instance of this title spoken by Jesus, she probably also would have used the title apart from sayings of Jesus.

It agrees better with our experience of social and pedagogical reality to conclude that the early church placed the title almost exclusively on Jesus' lips because she remembered that he had actually spoken of the Son of Man destined to come as God's regent at the end-time. The church wished to be essentially faithful to her memory of Jesus' end-time teaching, but, in folk fashion, she felt free to interpret and expand that teaching to meet her pressing theological needs.

In reality, the Greek-speaking church soon decided to avoid the Son of Man title, apart from the sayings of Jesus, because the title proved to be problematic. When the title was translated from Hebrew (*ben adam*) or Aramaic (*bar nasha*) into Greek (*ho huios tou anthropou*), it lost its royal Adamic connotation and suggested nothing more than a pedestrian reference to some human being's son. To Gentile converts, therefore, the title suggested nothing majestic or titular, and its exalted end-time import was difficult to grasp. Consequently, the title quickly disappeared from theological discourse in the Greek-speaking church. The title was nevertheless retained in sayings of Jesus because of the authority of his remembered way of speaking.

It was because the title Son of Man proved unsatisfactory in Greek that Paul never used it his letters. Paul preferred to translate the title into an intelligible equivalent. Accordingly, he spoke of the Risen Jesus as the "second" or "last Adam" who has freed us from the curse of sin and death inflicted on us by the "first Adam" (1 Cor 15:21-22, 45-47; see also Rom 5:14-19).

Also, in several of his *eschatological* sayings Jesus clearly distinguishes the Son of Man from himself. In these sayings Jesus speaks of himself in the *first* person and the *present* tense, whereas he speaks of the Son of Man in the *third* person and the *future* tense:

> And I tell you, everyone who acknowledges me before men, the Son of Man also will acknowledge before the angels of God; but he who denies me before men will be denied before the angels of God. (Lk 12:8; see also Mk 8:38)

It is difficult to believe that the early church invented this distinction which Jesus makes between himself and the Son of Man, for she quickly identified the Risen Jesus as the exalted Son of Man. It seems far more likely that the early church preserved the sayings in which this *unexpected* distinction is made because she remembered that Jesus himself had spoken that way.

5

In defense of the view that Jesus truly preached an eschatological message (like that of John the Baptizer whose mission he continued), we may point to the authentic parables and sayings in which Jesus speaks of, implies, or metaphorically alludes to the end-time Judgment: the coming harvest (Mk 4:3b-8; Mt 13:24-30); the separated fish (Mt 47-48); coming retribution, positive (Mt 20:1-15) and negative (Mk 12:1-9a); the unexpected thief (Mt 24:43-44; Lk 12:39-40); the wise and foolish maidens (Mt 25:1-12); the watchful servants (Lk 12:35-36); the rejected invitation (Lk 14:16b-23); the fate of the selfish rich man (Lk 16:19-25); the buried talent (Mt 25:14-29); the woes upon faithless cities (Lk 10:12-14; Mt 10:15); the positive fates of the Queen of the South and the men of Nineveh at the Final Judgment (Lk 11:31-32; Mt 12:41-42). And finally, the angelic condition of the resurrected (Mk 12:25).

Moreover, Jesus' choice of "the Twelve" to assist him with his mission probably had eschatological significance. By choosing "the Twelve" Jesus signified that his mission was preparing for the restoration of "the twelve tribes" of Israel (Mt 10:6-7) which was expected historically when God's Reign was fully established on earth (Is 49:5-6; Jer 31:1; Ez 31:10; 37:19-22; Ez

47:13-14; Sir 36:11). After the emergence of apocalyptic eschatology, many devout Jews expected the ingathering of the twelve tribes to follow the end-time Judgment (Dan 12:2-3; Sir 36:11; 48:10; Ps Sol 17:44,50; *Psalms of Solomon* is an extrabiblical work found among the pseudepigrapha):

> And he appointed twelve, to be with him, and he sent them out to preach and have authority to cast out demons: Simon whom he surnamed Peter; James the son of Zebedee and John the brother of James, whom he surnamed Bo-anerges, that is, sons of thunder; Andrew, and Philip, and Bartholomew, and Matthew, and Thomas, and James the son of Alpheus, and Thaddaeus, and Simon the Cananaean, and Judas Iscariot, who betrayed him. (Mk 3:14-19; see also Mt 10: 1-4; Lk 6:12-16).

Some have asserted that the statements about the Twelve in the Gospels are theological creations by which the early church sought to justify her existence as the New Covenant people of God. It is certain, however, that Jesus himself chose the Twelve, for Jesus' choice of Judas Iscariot as one of the Twelve proved to be a serious embarrassment to the apostolic church. The Jews, understandably, asked how Jesus could have made such a bad choice if he truly was the greatest of God's prophets and God's Messiah.

The church defended Jesus' tragic choice by teaching that his betrayal by Judas was foreordained in the scriptures as part of God's secret Messianic purpose (cp. Ps 49:1 and Mk 14:20-21; also cp. Zech 11:12-13 and Mt 27:3-4). Jesus' choice of Judas, the church explained, was something Jesus understood as divinely mandated in the scriptures:

> For the Son of man goes *as it is written of him,* but woe to that man by whom the Son of Man is betrayed! (Mk 14:21)

Furthermore, Jesus assured the Twelve that they would eat at his table at the Great Supper in God's coming Kingdom (Lk 22:30; in this saying Luke has changed God's Kingdom into Jesus' Kingdom; Jesus himself never spoke of the Kingdom as his; see Lk 11:2; 13:29; 14:15; also Mt 6:10a). The joyful Supper which Jesus celebrated regularly with his disciples was intended as an anticipation of the Great Supper in God's Kingdom. Jesus also taught that Abraham, Isaac, and Jacob would be guests of honor at this Supper which will celebrate the final ingathering of their faithful descendants (Mt 8:11; Lk 13:28-29).

The authentic promise of fellowship at Jesus' table in the Kingdom is presupposed by the ugly attempt of James and John to obtain seats of honor at Jesus' right and left hand (Mk 10:35-40). Parts of this account were certainly added by the early church (e.g., 10:38-39), but she would never have invented the underlying substance of such an unflattering story about two of the Twelve. She remembered the incident because it truly happened, and it was the context necessary for understanding Jesus' admonition about the importance of "service" in his Kingdom-anticipating community.

Moreover, the same promise of privileged table fellowship with Jesus in the Kingdom is presupposed by the eschatological saying of Jesus to the Twelve which probably followed his cup-saying at the Last Supper:

> Truly I say to you, I shall not drink again of the fruit of the vine until that day when I drink it new in the Kingdom of God. (Mk 14:25)

It was his anticipation of *being separated* from his disciples by impending betrayal and death that prompted Jesus to say sadly that he would not drink wine again until he drank it (with them) at the Great Supper when God's Kingdom arrived. (The reasons for concluding that the substance of this saying is authentic will be presented in the next chapter.)

Finally, we should also recall that Paul the apostle claimed to possess eschatological teaching which *derived from Jesus.* Paul imparted the following instruction to assure the Thessalonian Christians that those who die before the second coming of Jesus will not be forgotten or left behind:

> For this we declare to you *by the word of the Lord,* that those who are alive, who are left until the coming of the Lord, shall not precede those who have fallen asleep.

> For the Lord himself will descend from heaven with a cry of command, with the archangel's call, and with the sound of the trumpet of God.
>
> And the dead in Christ will rise first; then we who are alive, who are left, shall be caught up together with them in the clouds to meet the Lord in the air; and so we shall always be with the Lord. (1 Thess 4:15-17)

Paul's attribution of this eschatological instruction to Jesus is intriguing. Such *detailed* teaching about the end-time is manifestly lacking in the Gospels. Paul's statement, however, indicates that the early church believed she possessed end-time teaching which derived from Jesus himself. How should we assess Paul's claim? It is conceivable that Jesus truly did impart detailed instruction about the raising of the dead when the Son of Man arrives, but this instruction was not included in the Gospels. It seems far more likely, however, that the much briefer end-time teaching of Jesus about the Son of Man's role as final judge (e.g., Lk 12:8; Mk 8:38) has been theologically expanded by the apostolic church.

It is evident that the early church quickly decided that the Risen Jesus is that glorious Son of Man to come of whom the earthly Jesus had spoken. Christian prophets and teachers then concluded that Jesus would soon return on the clouds of heaven to exercise the end-time role of the Son of Man. Guided by their faith in Jesus' end-time teaching, these prophets and teachers probably supplied details for the end-time events of which Jesus had briefly spoken. They would have assumed in folk fashion that their additions to Jesus' teaching were essentially correct and certainly known to Jesus.

Eschatological teaching which derives ultimately from Jesus, therefore, probably does underlie the end-time tradition which Paul says he received from the Lord (by way of the church). But the teaching of Jesus which Paul received had probably been reflected on and amplified before Paul received it. We have no way of knowing if Paul knew that the "word of the Lord" which was passed on to him had been augmented along the way. But if he did, he still would probably have regarded it as the "word of the Lord" since it derived ultimately from Jesus. Why may we assume this?

In chapter seven of 1 Corinthians, Paul cites a teaching which he attributes to Jesus:

> [10]To the married I give charge, *not I but the Lord,* that the wife should not separate from the husband [11](but if she does, let her remain single or else be reconciled to her husband)—and that the husband should not divorce his wife. (1 Cor 7:10-11)

The teaching, however, which Paul describes as the word of the Lord in 7:10 is very likely an adaptation of Jesus' actual teaching about divorce in 7:11b (compare these two verses to the similar adaptation of Mk 10:11 in Mk 10:10). The apostolic church probably added the adapted verse (7:10) in order to instruct Gentile converts who, contrary to Jewish custom, assumed that women could divorce their husbands. (We may suspect that divorce initiated by women was a problem for the early church because in both Paul and Mark the adaptation for women of Jesus' teaching is placed *before* the original form of Jesus teaching which addressed only men.)

Since Jesus was a Palestinian Jew, he would have presumed, with the Law of Moses (Deut 24:1-4), that men sometimes divorce their wives (Mt 19:3,9), but not the reverse. However, as a diaspora Jew (i.e., a Jew who was born and raised outside of Palestine), Paul probably understood that an original saying of Jesus had to be qualified and expanded by the Jewish Christian mission for the sake of Gentile converts. Yet Paul seems to regard the expansion (1 Cor 7:10) of Jesus' original saying (1 Cor 7:11b) as "the word of the Lord," i.e., a legitimate and necessary interpretation of the mind of Jesus.

6

The only title which Jesus seems to have been willing to accept for himself during his mission is the title "prophet." Jesus never explicitly claims this title in the Gospels. Nevertheless, since Jesus decided to continue proclaiming the Baptizer's eschatological message, and because God confirmed Jesus' message with astonishing miraculous healings, Jesus was widely regarded by his contemporaries as a prophet:

(Mk 3:7-8,10)

> Jesus withdrew with his disciples to the sea, and a great multitude from Galilee followed; also from Judea and Jerusalem and Idumea and from beyond the Jordan . . . a great multitude, hearing all that he did, came to him. . . . for he healed many, so that all who had diseases pressed upon him to touch him.

(Lk 7:16)

> Fear seized them all [when Jesus raised the widow's son]; and they glorified God, saying, "A great prophet has arisen among us!"

(Mt 21:10-11)

> And when he entered Jerusalem, all the city was stirred, saying, "Who is this?" And the crowds said, "This is the prophet Jesus from Galilee."

(Mt 21:46)

> But when they [the chief priests] tried to arrest him [Jesus], they feared the multitudes, because they held him to be a prophet.

There is no indication in the Gospels that Jesus objected when he was revered by the crowds or spoken of by his disciples as a prophet:

> And on the way he asked his disciples, "Who do men say that I am?" And they told him, "John the baptist [come back from the dead]; and others say, Elijah; and others one of the prophets." (Mk 8:27b-28)

Moreover, we read in Mark that when the majority at Nazareth responded to Jesus and his mission of preaching and healing with skepticism, Jesus, with obvious reference to himself, quoted a traditional saying about a prophet:

> And Jesus said to them, "A prophet is not without honor, except in his own country, and among his own kin, and in his own house." And he could do no mighty work there, except that he laid his hands on a few sick people and healed them. And he marveled at their unbelief. (Mk 6:4-6)

Although the earthly Jesus probably did not think that he was the mysterious Son of Man destined to come at the end-time, he, nevertheless, understood his own prophetic message as inseparably related to the Final Judgment over which the Son of Man was expected to preside (with angelic assistance). Accordingly, when Jesus' special concern for social outcasts caused some in his society to scornfully reject him and his message, Jesus admonished them as follows:

> And I tell you, every one who acknowledges me before men, the Son of Man also will acknowledge before the angels of God; but he who denies me before men will be denied before the angels of God. (Lk 12:8-9; see also Mk 8:38)

The substantially authentic words and deeds of Jesus make good sense only if Jesus believed that he was truly a prophet sent by God to herald God's approaching Kingdom. Jesus solemnly warned his contemporaries that those who rejected his message were in danger of eternal loss. For there is an inseparable connection between the way they have responded to his message and the judgment they will receive when the Son of Man finally comes to search their hearts as God's end-time designate.

7

Before we discuss Jesus' prophetic activity, we should reflect briefly on the circumstances that probably preceded and contributed to his mission. Mark's Gospel indicates that Jesus practiced the carpenter's trade before he received his prophetic call. Jesus, therefore, was probably working as a carpenter when he learned about the prophetic activity of John the Baptizer. John's appearance would have roused excitement among many devout Jews because public prophecy had largely lain dormant for several centuries. It is likely that Jesus also experienced the excitement caused by John's mission. For the Gospels tell us that he travelled to Judea to hear John preach, and that he received John's baptism:

> In those days Jesus came from Nazareth and was baptized by John in the Jordan. (Mk 1:9)

The authentic words and deeds of Jesus suggest that he was a deeply religious Jew who had habitually experienced God's presence and love well before he heard John's preaching and received John's baptism. When Jesus began his own prophetic mission a short time later, he was serenely and unshakably certain that God is gracious and forgiving love. He was also utterly confident that God wanted him to proclaim the offer of God's *love* and *forgiveness* to all, even notorious sinners, in return for their faith, trust, and conversion.

Some of Jesus' Jewish contemporaries criticized him harshly and rejected his message because of his efforts to assure social outcasts that they too were invited to the Great Supper in God's Kingdom. When faced with such criticism, Jesus serenely continued to carry his message to the lost sheep of the house of Israel. We will see below that it was Jesus' practice of allowing such questionable people to join his disciples at his Kingdom-anticipating Supper, *even before their conversion,* that especially offended his critics.

Jesus' behavior implies that long-standing communion with God was the source of the unshakable certainty that underlay both his promise of God's forgiveness and his mission of healing. To confidently believe that God would heal and forgive others through his mission presupposes long established communion with God which had generated profound faith and trust. It is reasonable to conclude that God healed people through Jesus not only to encourage people to accept Jesus' Kingdom message as divinely authorized, but also to encourage Jesus to continue his frequently misunderstood and bitterly criticized mission. (Jesus' miraculous healing of the sick will be examined in the next chapter.)

It seems very likely, therefore, that the manifest ability of Jesus to surmount the hostility of those who rejected his prophetic message presupposes an extraordinary and *habitual* experience of God's reassuring presence. The Gospels suggest that Jesus was in the habit of communing with God's indwelling presence:

> And in the morning, a great while before it was day, he rose and went out to a lonely place, and there he prayed. (Mk 1:35)

So certain was Jesus of his profound experience of God's presence that he presumed he could ignore narrow interpretations of the law of Moses which were incompatible with his experience of God's love. The Gospels indicate that Jesus faithfully observed the written law of Moses. But whenever oral traditions meant to interpret or supplement the law were unreasonable or interfered with kindness and love, Jesus rejected them. When Jesus was accused of disrespect for God's law by those who were narrowly traditional or harshly legalistic, he remained unperturbed and appealed to the common sense of his critics:

> Now he was teaching in one of the synagogues on the sabbath. And there was a woman who had had a spirit of infirmity for eighteen years; she was bent over and could not fully straighten herself. And when Jesus saw her, he said to her, "Woman, you are freed from your infirmity." And he laid his hands upon her, and immediately she was made straight, and she praised God.
>
> But the ruler of the synagogue, indignant because Jesus had healed on the sabbath, said to the people, "There are six days on which work ought to be done; come on those days and be healed, and not on the sabbath day.
>
> Then the Lord answered him, . . . "Does not each of you on the sabbath untie his ox and his ass from the manger, and lead it away to water it? And ought not this daughter of Abraham whom Satan bound for eighteen years, be

loosed from this bond on the sabbath day?" (Lk 13:10-16)

8

It was probably Jesus' habitual experience of God's indwelling presence that motivated him to go and listen to John the Baptizer's prophetic message. We may surmise that when Jesus heard John's words about the coming end-time Judgment, God caused divine love to well up mightily within Jesus thereby confirming the substance of John's message. Jesus, therefore, would have experienced John's words as divinely inspired because they were *Spirit-mediating*. Consequently, Jesus "knew" that John was truly God's prophet and that God endorsed (the substance of) John's message. Prompted by God's grace, therefore, Jesus received John's baptism and became John's disciple:

> [9]In those days Jesus came from Nazareth of Galilee and was baptized by John in the Jordan. [10]And when he came up out of the water, immediately he saw the heavens torn open and the Spirit descending upon him like a dove; [11]and a voice came from heaven, "You are my beloved Son; with you I am well pleased." (Mk 1:9-11)

Verse 9 in Mark's baptismal account contains reliable historical memory. But the tearing open of the heavens and the descent of the Spirit upon Jesus as a dove in verse 10, as well as the words of God addressed to Jesus in verse 11 are midrashic theology added later to v. 9; they should not be mistaken as history. Mark created verses 10 and 11 as parts of his *Messianic Secret* theology. This theology was created by Mark and the early church to defend and explain the shockingly unexpected nature of Jesus' Messiahship.

The heavens are described as torn open in verse 10 to suggest that revelation is flowing from God above to Jesus below. God's Spirit is immediately sent down upon Jesus to anoint him as God's hidden Messiah. (The anointing Spirit is assigned the form of a dove to suggest that Jesus is destined to be the New Adam foreshadowed by Noah who was likewise a second Adam;

see Gen 8:8-12.) God then speaks to Jesus in verse 11 and reveals to him the secret and unexpected nature of the Messianic office which God is conferring on him: "You are my beloved Son; with you I am well pleased."

God's message addressed to Jesus is a combination of words taken from various places in the Old Testament: As God's secret (Wis 2:17-22) Messiah-Son (Ps 2:7), Jesus is destined to suffer an atoning death like God's suffering servant spoken of in Is 42:1-2; 53:4-6 (see Mk 10:45; 14:24). For Jesus is the "true" Isaac (Isaac is called Abraham's "beloved" son in the Old Greek version of God's request for Isaac's sacrificial death; Gen 22:2).

Since Christian theological concern has certainly colored the language which describes the baptism conferred by John, we are unable to say with certainty what John intended by his baptism. Nevertheless, the description of John's baptism by Mark (1:4) and Luke (3:3a) as "a baptism of repentance for the forgiveness of sins" is probably reliable. For it is difficult to imagine that the early church would have invented this problematic description ("for the forgiveness of sins") of the baptism which Jesus submitted to.

Although Matthew used Mark's Gospel, he could not bring himself to describe the baptism which Jesus received from John as "a baptism of repentance for the forgiveness of sins" as Mark (and Luke) did. Instead, when Matthew described Jesus' baptism by John, he prefaced it with a "theological" conversation between John and Jesus in which John insists that it is he who ought to be baptized by Jesus. Matthew thereby suggested that Jesus had asked for baptism not to acknowledge his own sinfulness, but to signify his intention to suffer substitutionally for the sins of all others (to satisfy God's righteous demand; see Mt 20:28; 26:28):

> Then Jesus came from Galilee to the Jordan to John, to be baptized by him. John would have prevented him, saying, "I need to be baptized by you, and do you come to me?" But Jesus answered him, "Let it be so for now, for thus it is fitting for us to fulfill all righteousness." And then he consented. (Mt 3:13-15)

We are reminded by Matthew's defensive theological stance that Jesus' baptism by John raises a difficult question. When Jesus asked for John's baptism, was Jesus thereby acknowledging that he experienced himself as guilty of sin? The early church decided that the answer to this question had to be an emphatic "no." For she had early begun teaching for apologetic reasons that Jesus' death was *vicarious atonement* for the sins of the world (Mk 10:45; 14:24; Jn 1:29; 4:42).

And if Jesus had to die to pay for the sins of all others, then he himself had to be sinless. Otherwise his death would have been punishment deserved for his own sins and could not have satisfied substitutionally for the sin of the world. Once the church became committed to this apologetic explanation of Jesus' shocking and disgraceful death, she had to be consistent and declare him sinless.

We have already seen in earlier chapters, however, that God did not actually require Jesus to suffer and die substitutionally for the sins of all other humans. Therefore, it was not really essential to God's saving purpose at work in Jesus that Jesus had to be sinless. Furthermore, if Jesus did not have to learn how to exercise his freedom responsibly like all other humans, and did not make mistakes which made him feel anxious and guilty, was he truly human? Is Jesus able to be God's conclusive assurance that we humans can be forgiven for our many moral failures if Jesus himself never experienced God's forgiveness with faith and trust?

(In this context, we should understand "sin" as any failure, minor or major, against truth, justice, and love. Our faith in God's word tells us that we must habitually strive to practice truth, justice, and love if our lives are to be truly oriented toward the attainment of Eternal Life with God. When we fail against this fundamental recognition, we appropriately experience guilt and shame which goad us to return to our commitment. As we grow older and wiser, major failures should disappear. However, to experience periodic moral failure, appropriate guilt, and the recognition that we should return to life's fundamental task with renewed commitment is an essential part of what it means to be human.)

In reality, Jesus is a more fitting guide for sinful and anxious humans if he himself had sinned as all others do but learned to turn away from sin and experienced God's amazing love and forgiveness with faith and trust. We may reasonably believe that God graciously encouraged him to do so for our sake. It is precisely Jesus' profound certainty that God will forgive sinful humans which lies at the heart of God's saving purpose in the Christ Event. Jesus could assure us of God's forgiveness with profound certainty because Jesus had probably experienced God's forgiveness himself.

Jesus courageously believed in God's love and forgiveness while submitting to a hideous death which many in his society would have construed as punishment for sin (Deut 21:23). God encouraged Jesus to accept death with faith and trust to show all other humans how to transcend our fear that personal tragedy might be God's wrathful response to our past mistakes. Reason tells us that Jesus probably learned from his own experience that God is gracious and forgiving toward frail humans.

It seems likely, therefore, that by receiving John's baptism, Jesus was publicly signifying his commitment to turn away from anything that might interfere with doing God's will or hinder the coming of God's Reign on earth. Both of these concerns appear regularly in the teaching of Jesus. (There is no indication that the Baptizer spoke of a coming Kingdom; Kingdom language was probably added by Jesus to John's end-time message.)

Jesus probably remained John's disciple until John was seized by Herod Antipas and imprisoned. When John's mission was abruptly halted by his arrest, Jesus probably anticipated that someone would step forward and continue proclaiming John's end-time message for God. When no one did so, the possibility of personally taking up John's prophetic mantle must have occurred to Jesus.

It is reasonable to assume that Jesus prayed over this matter, and that when he did he experienced divine encouragement (in the form of the silent language of God's love) welling up within him mightily. After prayer and reflection, Jesus probably understood that his extraordinary experience of God's Self-communication was affirmation of the idea that he should continue John's mission to Israel. When Jesus decided to do so, God further reinforced that decision by healing people with astonishing frequency through Jesus' touch or word.

9

We are told by Matthew (and Luke in 7:19-20) that when John learned from prison of Jesus' prophetic activity he sent some of his disciples to question Jesus:

> Now when John learned in prison about the deeds of the Messiah, he sent word by his disciples and said to him, "Are you he who is to come, or should we look for another?" (Mt 11:2-3)

It is, of course, Matthew who has inserted the title Messiah into this otherwise reliable memory; the title represents the church's post Easter theological understanding of Jesus and is absent in Luke's account of the same incident (Lk 7:18). In reality, Jesus was not proclaimed as God's Messiah before he began appearing as Risen Lord of life and death.

The story of the delegation sent to Jesus by the imprisoned Baptizer is probably reliable because, among other things, it correctly remembers that John did not really know who Jesus was. This doubtlessly correct memory, however, flies in the face of Matthew's theologically expanded account of Jesus' baptism by John in which John clearly knows who Jesus is. Such a memory also contradicts the highly theological baptismal account in the Fourth Gospel:

> And John bore witness, "I saw the Spirit descend from heaven, and it remained on him. I myself did not know him; but he who sent me to baptize with water said to me, 'He on whom you see the Spirit descend and remain, this is he who baptizes with the Holy Spirit.' And I have seen and have borne witness that this is the Son of God." (Jn 1:32-34)

In Matthew's account of the baptism John *also* knows with revelatory certainty that Jesus is the coming one. For Matthew allows John to participate in God's revelation to Jesus of the Messianic Secret. The voice of God is addressed (in the third person) *to the Baptizer* in Matthew's account (3:17), whereas in Mark's version God's voice is addressed *to Jesus alone* (1:11). But if the Baptizer had literally received such revelatory information about Jesus, he would have known who Jesus was and would not have had to inquire through his emissaries.

When John was told by his disciples that Jesus was preaching an eschatological message essentially like his own and that God was confirming the Message with miraculous signs, he was probably perplexed. Jesus clearly seemed to be someone who enjoyed God's approval, or God would not have miraculously healed people through him. And yet, Jesus was not the eschatological figure that John had anticipated:

> I baptize you with water for repentance, but he who is coming after me is mightier than I, whose sandals I am not worthy to carry; he will baptize you with the Holy Spirit and with fire. His winnowing fork is in his hand, and he will clear his threshing floor and gather his wheat into the granary, but the chaff he will burn with unquenchable fire. (Mt 3:11-12)

John evidently expected the advent of an eschatological figure who would preside at a fiery end-time Judgment. Since the coming one spoken of by John is wearing sandals, he is probably not God, but an exalted human who is God's end-time designate. John's description of this coming one in the passage cited just above is probably reliable. For since the early church believed that Jesus was the one of whom John spoke, she, had she created the description, would probably have described John's ambiguous coming one with one of the titles she had bestowed on the Risen Jesus (e.g., Son of Man, Son of God, or Messiah).

The early church probably did, however, modify John's description of the baptism to be administered by the coming one. Matthew and Luke, following the Sayings Source instead of Mk 1:8, relate that the coming one will baptize "with the Holy Spirit and with fire" (Mt 3:11c; Lk 3:16c). Their additional reference to fire is probably original, whereas mention of the Holy Spirit is probably secondary and theological. The mention of the Spirit was probably added (or substituted in the case of Mark) as a more accurate description of the Spirit-conferring Baptism of Jesus.

By adding "the Spirit" to John's description of the coming one's baptism, the evangelists intended that the coming one spoken of by John would be recognized as the Spirit-mediating Jesus. In addition, there are several literary indications that the coming one's baptism was originally "with fire." First, baptism "with fire" contrasts and balances more logically "with water" in John's total description. Second, a fiery baptism or cleansing accords better with the coming one's role as judge, his winnowing fan, and his burning of the separated chaff "with unquenchable fire."

Who did John think this mysterious "coming" one would be? We cannot say with any degree of certainty. But a possible candidate is the mysterious eschatological figure described as "coming" with the clouds of heaven in the book of Daniel. This exalted human is invested by God with authority to preside over the expected end-time Reign of God:

> I saw in the night visions, and behold coming with the clouds of heaven was one like a son of man; he came to the ancient of days and was presented before him.
>
> And to him was given dominion and glory and kingdom, that all peoples, nations, and languages should serve him; his dominion is an everlasting dominion which shall not pass away, and his kingdom one which shall not be destroyed. (Dan 7:13-14)

This passage in Daniel is the source of the end-time speculation which eventually produced the explicit title "Son of Man" (i.e., the Son of Adam or New Adam who will be king of the New Creation). But Daniel's midrashic *allusion* to an exalted one who is like a son of Adam (see Gen 1:26, Ps 8:3-8, and Ps 80:170) is deliberately imprecise and mysterious; it has not yet become the eschatological title "Son of Man." Nevertheless, since the mysterious figure spoken of in Daniel bears a family resemblance to the mysterious coming one spoken of by the Baptizer, the end-time prophecy in Daniel 7 is quite possibly the direct or indirect source of John's end-time expectation.

It was evidently because Jesus did not manifest the traits of the fiery and exalted end-time Judge expected by John that John sent his disciples to Jesus seeking clarification:

> And Jesus answered them, "Go and tell John what you hear and see: the blind receive their sight and the lame walk, lepers are cleansed and the deaf hear, and the dead are raised up, and the poor have good news preached to them. And blessed is he who takes no offense at me." (Mt 11:2-6)

The substance of Jesus' response to John's disciples is probably reliable even though it was very likely amplified by the early church. It is reasonable to suspect that Jesus' original reply lacked the catalogue of confirming signs which it now includes. If John's emissaries had observed such signs prior to their question (as Jesus' response indicates), there would have been no need for Jesus to list them. Moreover, the catalogue sounds like a "midrashic" review of the signs which occurred *throughout* Jesus' public ministry. This list of signs was probably appended to Jesus' original response to remind the church that Jesus' astonishing end-time ministry of healing was foreshadowed in the book of Isaiah:

Is 61:1

> The Spirit of the Lord is upon me, because the Lord has anointed me to bring good news to the poor; he has sent me to bind up the brokenhearted, to proclaim liberty to the captives, and the opening of the prison to those who are bound.

Is 35:5-6a

> Then the eyes of the blind shall be opened, and the ears of the deaf unstopped; then shall the lame man leap like a hart, and the tongue of the dumb shall sing for joy.

Is 29:18-19

In that day the deaf shall hear the words of a book, and out of their gloom and darkness the eyes of the blind shall see. The meek shall obtain fresh joy from the Lord, and the poor among men shall exult in the Holy One of Israel.

Is 26:19

Your dead shall live, their bodies shall rise. O dwellers in the dust, awake and sing for joy.

It is not likely that Jesus appealed midrashically to *the scriptures* to justify himself and his mission. Instead, it was the apostolic church who carefully searched the scriptures and habitually appealed to their authority to justify her faith in Jesus' disputed Messiahship. Jesus himself seems to have appealed directly to his successful combat with the powers of darkness to vindicate his mission and his Kingdom Message:

But if it is by the finger of God that I cast out demons, then the kingdom of God has come upon you. (Lk 11:20)

Therefore, Jesus' original response to the question put by John's disciples was probably as follows:

And Jesus answered them, "Go and tell John what you hear and see. And blessed is he who takes no offense at me." (Mt 11:2-6):

Jesus' answer implies that John should be able to recognize that the end-time message proclaimed by Jesus is in essential agreement with John's own message. In addition, the exorcisms and miraculous healings which God is manifesting through Jesus are divine authorization of Jesus' decision to continue John's mission. Therefore, those who accept Jesus and his Message will be blessed when God's Kingdom, which has already begun to arrive through Jesus' words and deeds, finally comes in all its fullness.

Questions for Review and Discussion

1. Why did Jesus probably reject the title Messiah?
2. What title for the end-time King and Judge did Jesus evidently prefer?
3. What evidence do moderate scholars point to in defense of their conviction that Jesus truly did speak of the end-time Judge called the Son of Man?
4. Why did the Greek-speaking church eventually stop using the Son of Man title when she taught about Jesus?
5. Into what other equivalent title did Paul the apostle transpose the Son of Man title?
6. What evidence do moderate scholars point to in defense of their conviction that Jesus truly did anticipate the end-time judgment?
7. What evidence indicates that Jesus himself probably did choose the Twelve?
8. Explain why Jesus' choice of the Twelve indicates that he had undertaken an "end-time" mission.
9. What is the only title which Jesus seems to have been willing to accept for himself during his mission?
10. Whose mission did Jesus decide to continue, and why did he probably do so?

Chapter Five: The Kingdom of God in Jesus' Message

1

JESUS BEGAN HIS PROPHETIC MISSION BY PROCLAIMING THAT the "Kingdom of God" was near at hand (Mk 1:14-15). By the Kingdom of God, Jesus meant the final and everlasting restoration of God's Reign over the Kingdom of creation. Ancient Israel thought that God's Reign over creation had been disrupted by the sin of Adam, the first king appointed by God to represent God's Reign on earth.

But ancient Israel's understanding of God's Kingly Reign on earth underwent a number of significant changes in the course of her long history. It would be wise for us, therefore, to briefly review all of the major steps in that development in order to better comprehend the end-time Kingdom proclaimed by Jesus.

Not surprisingly, Israel's understanding of God's Reign over creation begins with the two creation stories located at the beginning of Genesis. The Genesis creation stories tell us that Adam was the first king appointed by God to rule over the Kingdom of creation. The oldest of the two stories (Gen 2:4b-3:24) *implies* that Adam was given authority over creation when God authorized him to name all the animals which God had created:

> So out of the ground the Lord God formed every beast of the field and every bird of the air, and brought them to the *man* [Heb = *adam*] to see what he would call them; and whatever the man called every living creature, that was its name. (Gen 2:19)

However, the newest of the creation stories (Gen 1:1-2:4a) states *explicitly* that Adam was given universal dominion as the human representative of God's Kingly Rule:

> So God created *man* [Heb = *adam*] in his own image, in the image of God he created him; male and female he created them. And God blessed them, and God said to them, "Be fruitful and multiply, and fill the earth and subdue it; and have *dominion* over the fish of the sea and over the birds of the air and over every living thing that moves over the face of the earth." (Gen 1:27-28)

Adam, however, proved to be a foolish and disobedient king, and his dominion over creation was taken from him (Gen 3:1-24). By the time of the early monarchy (c. 1000 B.C.), the Israelites believed that God had begun to restore God's Reign over creation through *the kingdom of David.*

In the first book of Chronicles, King David is described as praising Israel's God as the King of creation. In the second of the two passages we are about to read, David also speaks of the kingdom of Israel as "the kingdom of the Lord":

1 Chr 29:11

> Yours, O Lord, is the greatness, and the power, and the greatness, and the victory, and the majesty; for all that is in the heavens and in the earth is yours; yours is the kingdom, O Lord, and you are exalted as head above all.

1 Chr 28:4a,5

> The Lord God of Israel chose me from all my father's house to be king over Israel. . . . And of all my sons . . . he has chosen Solomon my son to sit upon the throne of the kingdom of the Lord over Israel.

Eventually, Nathan the prophet promised David in God's name that David's dynasty would be everlasting and that God would evermore regard David's reigning son as God's own "Son":

> When your days are fulfilled and you lie down with your fathers, I will raise up your offspring after you, who shall come forth from your body, and I will establish his kingdom. . . .
>
> *I will be his father and he shall be my son.* . . . And your house and your kingdom shall be made sure for ever before me; your throne shall be established for ever. (2 Sam 7:12,14a,16)

In 922 B.C., the kingdom of David and Solomon was split by internal rivalry into the sister kingdoms of Israel and Judah. Nevertheless, the Israelites in the kingdom of Judah continued to believe that one of David's worthier sons would one day be instrumental in establishing God's Kingly Reign (and obedience to God's holy law) over all the nations on earth.

This hope was expressed in the royal psalm sung on the day when David's successor was anointed and installed on David's throne. The king thus anointed was believed to have become the privileged sign of God's Kingly Reign on earth. (The anointed Son of David is speaking throughout the psalm we are about to read; notice that he adverts explicitly to Nathan's promise that God would adopt David's successor as God's own Son.):

> Why do the nations conspire, and the peoples plot in vain? The kings of the earth . . . take council together against the Lord and his anointed [representative] saying, "Let us burst their bonds asunder and cast their cords from us,"
>
> He who sits in heaven laughs; the Lord has them in derision. Then he will speak to them in his wrath, and terrify them in his fury, saying, "I have set my king on Zion, my holy hill."
>
> I will tell of the decree of the Lord: He said to me, "You are my son, today I have begotten you. Ask of me, and I will make the nations your heritage, and the ends of the

> earth your possession. You shall break them with a rod of iron, and dash them in pieces like a potter's vessel." (Ps 2:1-8)

Under the influence of the royal Davidic ideology, the prophets in the kingdom of Judah began to teach that when the ideal son of David finally comes and extends God's Reign over all the nations, the Golden Age will arrive. The Golden Age was to be a time of unprecedented longevity, fertility, and security. There would be no more injustice or warfare on earth, and all the nations would come to know and serve the God of Israel:

> It shall come to pass in the latter days that the mountain of the house of the Lord shall be established as the highest of the mountains, and shall be raised above the hills; and all the nations shall flow to it, and many people shall come and say, "Come, let us go up to the mountain of the Lord, to the house of the God of Jacob; that he may teach us his ways and that we may walk in his paths."
>
> For out of Zion shall go forth the law, and the word of the Lord from Jerusalem. He shall judge between the nations, and shall decide for many peoples; and they shall beat their swords into plowshares, and their spears into pruning hooks; nation shall not lift up sword against nation, neither shall they learn war any more. (Is 2:2-4; see also Mic 4:1-4)

We find another early expression of this hope in Is 9:2-7. Isaiah's lyrical prophecy was probably prompted by the birth of King Ahaz's son and heir, Hezekiah. This royal heir was born after a period of crisis which threatened David's dynasty with extinction. Isaiah clearly hoped that the child Hezekiah would become the righteous king who would establish the Golden Age:

> The people who walked in darkness have seen a great light; those who dwelt in a land of deep darkness, on them has light shined. You have multiplied the nation, you have increased its joy. They rejoice before you as with joy at the harvest, as men rejoice when they divide the spoil. (Is 9:2-3)
>
> For every boot of the tramping warrior in battle tumult and every garment rolled in blood will be burned as fuel

> for the fire. For to us a child is born, to us a son is given; and the government will be upon his shoulder, and his name shall be called "Wonderful Counselor, Mighty God, Everlasting Father, Prince of Peace."
>
> Of the increase of his government and of peace there will be no end, and upon the throne of David, and over his kingdom, to establish it and to uphold it with justice and with righteousness from this time forth and for evermore. The zeal of the Lord of hosts will do this. (Is 9:5-7)

At a later time, the prophets became even more exuberant in their descriptions of the Golden Age. They likened it to the original innocence and freedom from violence that characterized Paradise before the Fall. Everything would then be restored except immortality:

> The wolf shall dwell with the lamb, and the leopard shall lie down with the kid, and the calf and the lion and the fatling together, and a little child shall lead them. The cow and the bear shall feed; their young shall lie down together; and the lion shall eat straw like the ox.
>
> The sucking child shall play over the hole of the asp, and the weaned child shall put his hand in the adder's den. They shall not hurt or destroy in all my holy mountain; for the earth shall be full of the knowledge of the Lord as the waters cover the sea. (Is 11:6-9).

2

We learn from the books of Kings, however, that David's sons proved to be unworthy of their high calling. They were swept from power at the time of the exile to Babylon (587 B.C.), and could no longer claim to be the earthly representatives of God's Kingly Reign. Nevertheless, many of the prophets during the period of the exile and thereafter continued to promise that God would raise up a descendant of David to be God's instrument in restoring the kingdom to Israel:

Ps 89:3

You have said, "I have made a covenant with my chosen one, I have sworn to David my servant: 'I will establish your descendants, and build your throne for all generations.' "

Ps 89:34-37

I will not violate my covenant, or alter the word that went forth from my lips. Once for all I have sworn by my holiness; I will not lie to David. His line shall endure for ever, his throne as long as the sun before me. Like the moon it shall be established forever; it shall stand firm while the skies endure.

Is 11:1

There shall come forth a shoot from the stump of Jesse, and a Branch shall grow out of his roots.

Jer 23:5

Behold, the days are coming, says the Lord, when I will raise up for David a righteous Branch, and he shall reign as king and deal wisely, and shall execute justice and righteousness in the land.

Jer 33:20

Thus says the Lord, "If you can break my covenant with the day and my covenant with the night, so that day and the night will not come at the appointed time, then also my covenant with David my servant may be broken, so that he shall not have a son to reign on his throne.

Ez 34:23-24

And I shall set over them one shepherd, my servant David, and he shall feed them; he shall feed them and be their shepherd. And I, the Lord, will be their God, and my servant David shall be prince among them; I, the Lord, have spoken.

Hos 3:5

Afterward the children of Israel shall return and seek the Lord their God and David their king; and they shall come in fear to the Lord and to his goodness in the latter days.

Amos 9:11

In that day, I will raise up the booth of David that is fallen and repair its breaches, and raise up its ruins, and rebuild it as in the days of old.

Zech 12:8-9

On that day the Lord shall put a shield about the inhabitants of Jerusalem so that the feeblest among them on that day shall be like David, and David shall be like God, like the angel of the Lord, at their head. And on that day I will seek to destroy all the nations that come against Jerusalem.

3

During the late postexilic period, Jewish thinking about the restoration of God's Kingly Reign underwent a dramatic change. This change was precipitated by the cruel persecution inflicted on the Jews by Antiochus IV, the Hellenizing king of Syria. (To Hellenize is to encourage or impose Hellenistic [i.e., Greek] culture.) Antiochus tried to force the Jews to abandon their monotheism, and to worship the gods of Greece. When the majority of the Jews refused to submit to his demands, he persecuted them ruthlessly. In 167 B.C. they rebelled against Antiochus under the leadership of the Maccabees.

In addition to triggering the Maccabean uprising, the Syrian persecution caused a major "faith crisis" for devout Jews. Traditional Jewish religious belief had always assumed that those who faithfully served God would be rewarded unfailingly by a long and happy life *in this world.* Blessing from God was expected during one's life on earth. After death one had to go to sheol, the subterranean abode of the dead. In the silent gloom of sheol, one experienced *unending* deprivation of life and joy as punishment for Adam's sin.

As the Syrian persecution raged on, however, it became painfully evident to suffering Jews that their traditional assumption that the righteous would be blessed in this life was being contradicted. Large numbers of Jews who were determined to remain faithful to their belief in one God were put to death. Jews who embraced polytheism, on the other hand, were spared and even rewarded. Suddenly, devout Jews were confronted by massive amounts of evidence that undermined an important part of their traditional belief-system: The good, they realized, do not unfailingly enjoy a long life, and the wicked are not quickly sent to sheol.

An anonymous Jewish prophet was inspired to resolve the resulting faith crisis by creating the "apocalyptic" theology which we find in the book of Daniel. This anonymous prophet, however, was faced with an additional problem. Jewish tradition held that the canon (official list) of prophetic writings had been "closed" at the time of Ezra's death (traditionally assumed to be c. 400 B.C.; in reality, Ezra probably died c. 380 B.C.). Consequently, the anonymous prophet had to write his teaching *pseudonymously* by using the name of a famous wise man, Daniel (Ezek 28:3; 14:14), who antedated the death of Ezra. Only by means of this strategem could the anonymous prophet's teaching be lawfully read at worship services to instruct and comfort the discouraged Jews.

The apocalyptic theology in the book of Daniel (written c. 165 B.C.) offered "eschatological" hope to faithful Jews who had experienced the contradictions of the Syrian persecution. Apocalyptic eschatology assured these Jews that the world will soon end (Dan 12:4-13). On that day the dead will be raised and judged along with the living (Dan 12:2). After the Final Judgment, the righteous will enjoy Everlasting Life and Joy in the restored Kingdom of God's creation. The wicked, however, will receive unending punishment as recompense for their deeds:

> And many of those who sleep in the dust of the earth shall awake; some to everlasting life, and some to shame and everlasting contempt. And those who are wise shall shine like the brightness of the firmament; and those who turn many to righteousness, like the stars for ever and ever. (Dan 12:2-3)

The New Creation promised by the Book of Daniel was eagerly anticipated as the final and permanent establishment of God's Kingly Reign over creation. God's victorious "end-time" Kingdom is mentioned for the first time in Daniel:

> The God of Heaven will set up a kingdom which shall never be destroyed, nor shall its sovereignty be left to another people. It shall break in pieces all these kingdoms and bring them to an end, and it shall stand forever. (Dan 2:44)

It is probably this everlasting kingdom which Jesus had in mind when he announced that the Kingdom (or Reign) of God is near (Mk 1:14). The actual expression, "Kingdom of God" does not occur in the Hebrew scriptures. It is mentioned in the Greek version of the Old Testament only in Wis 10:10. The pseudepigraphal book called the *Psalms of Solomon* (written c. 50 B.C.) also speaks of the "Kingdom of God" in 17:1.

(The pseudepigrapha are ancient Jewish religious books which were not accepted into either the Hebrew or the Old Greek versions of the Old Testament. The formidable word "pseudepigrapha" means "pseudonymous writings;" these writings are all pseudonymous for essentially the same reason given above for the book of Daniel: They were attributed to some ancient worthy who antedated Ezra's death in the hope that they would be accorded prophetic authority.)

4

The book of Daniel discloses that God's end-time Kingdom will be presided over by a mysterious king who is presented as the New Adam. After creation has been freed from all the evils inflicted on it by the old Adam, especially the persecuting Syrians, the New Adam will reign forever over the New Creation as God's regent. The New Adam is not explicitly assigned the role of end-time Judge in the book of Daniel. He is, however, a king (Dan 7:14), and in ancient Israel the reigning king was always understood to be the chief judge who upheld God's law in the kingdom (2 Sam 8:15; 15:2).

In Dan 7:13, the New Adam is alluded to midrashically as a "son" or descendant of the old Adam. In order to grasp this allusion, we must remember that the Hebrew word for human being (or "man" in the inclusive sense) is *adam*. By the time the book of Genesis was translated into Greek (c. 250 B.C.), Jewish scribes had begun treating this common noun as the personal name of the first human, "Adam."

The passage we are about to read indicates that The New Adam is a mysterious human who is authorized by God to be the end-time representative of God's victorious Reign over creation. God confers upon him, therefore, the "dominion" taken from the old Adam after his fall:

> I saw in the night visions, and behold, coming with the clouds of heaven was one like a *son of man;* he came to the Ancient of Days and was presented before him.
>
> And to him was given *dominion* and glory and *kingdom,* that all peoples, nations, and languages should serve him; his *dominion* is an everlasting *dominion,* and his *kingdom* one that shall not be destroyed. (Dan 7:13-14)

Daniel's reference to "one like a son of man" (or son of Adam) who receives "dominion" from God over the "kingdom" of creation assumes that we are familiar with the traditional Israelite theme of Adam as the divinely appointed king of creation. We have already found this royal Adamic theme in Gen 1:26-28 where Adam is given "dominion" by God and told to "rule" over creation. The royal Adamic theme is also found in one of the psalms of ancient Israel based on the same passage in Genesis (and possibly also on the Adam myth that underlies Ez 28:11-16):

> When I look at the heavens, the work of your fingers, the moon and the stars which you have established; what is *man* that you are mindful of him, and *the son of man* that you care for him?
>
> You have made him little less than God, and crowned him with glory and honor.
>
> You have given him *dominion* over the works of your hands; you have put all things under his feet, all sheep

> and oxen, and also the beasts of the field, the birds of the air, and the fish of the sea. (Ps 8:3-8)

The author of Daniel also believed that ancient Israel, because of the promises God had made to her through the prophets, would be associated with the Son of Adam in a privileged way in ruling over the nations gathered into God's end-time Kingdom.

> And the *kingdom* and the *dominion* and the greatness of the kingdoms under the whole heaven shall be given to the people of the saints of the Most High; their *kingdom* shall be an *everlasting kingdom* and all dominions shall serve and obey them. (Dan 7:27)

It is sometimes suggested that the "one like a son of man" who comes "with the clouds of heaven" and receives "everlasting dominion" in Dan 7:13-14 is an "angel" rather than the mysterious descendant of Adam elected by God to be the New Adam. This claim is advanced because the "interpreting angel" who periodically instructs Daniel is said to have the "appearance of a man" (Dan 8:15b; see also 9:21; 10:5,18; 12:6,7).

However, likening angels to humans was an established literary convention well before Daniel was written (see Ez 9:1-11; Zec 1:8-2:5). Furthermore, the same book also calls the prophet Daniel a "son of man" (8:17) and a "man" (10:19) in recognition of his humanity.

The claim that the "one like a son of man" is an angel fails to recognize the deliberate midrashic allusions in Dan 7 meant to contrast the original Adam with the New Adam appointed by God as king of the New Creation. As the original king of creation, Adam of old received "dominion" over the "beasts" (Gen 1:26-28). It is for that reason, therefore, that the Gentile kings and kingdoms which have subjugated Israel since the exile are likened in Dan 7 to "beasts." These Gentile "beasts" are destined to be ruled over by the New Adam when God's Reign over creation is finally restored.

These four Gentile kingdoms are also said to have received temporarily the "dominion" (Dan 7:6,12) taken from the old

Adam and, later, from David's sons at the time of the exile. We saw above that Daniel believed this dominion would finally be taken from the "beasts" and restored to the Son of Adam (7:13-14) and to faithful Israel (7:27). Since there were no descendants of David on the horizon who possessed political or military power when Daniel was written, it probably seemed more realistic to its author to base Israel's hope for final salvation on a "Son of Adam" rather than a "Son of David."

In addition, it seems reasonable to conclude that since the "four great beasts" spoken of in Dan 7:3-7 represent "four kings" (Dan 7:17) who rule over four successive Gentile kingdoms, then the "one like a son of man" also represents a human (i.e., a son of Adam) who is destined to rule as king over God's end-time Kingdom. The ancient Jews could not envision an earthly kingdom, even an *everlasting* kingdom, without a king who was appointed by God as the representative of God's Reign on earth.

So true is this observation that even after the exile when the house of David lost its dominion over Israel, it was assumed by Daniel that God gave that forfeited dominion to the four successive kings (Dan 7:17) who subjugated Israel. An earlier prophecy in Is 45:1-4 had already announced that Israel's God had appointed King Cyrus of Persia to conquer Babylonia and rule over Israel:

> Thus says the Lord to his anointed, to Cyrus, whose right hand I have grasped, to subdue nations before him and ungird the loins of kings, to open doors before him that gates may not be closed:
>
> "I will go before you and level the mountains, I will break in pieces the doors of bronze and cut asunder the bars of iron, I will give you the treasures of darkness and the hoards in secret places, that you man know that it is I, the Lord, the God of Israel, who call you by your name.
>
> For the sake of my servant Jacob, and Israel my chosen, I call you by your name, I surname you, though you do not know me." (Is 45:1-4)

For ancient Israel, God was the Lord of history before whose invincible might all earthly kings must finally bow down. It is true that Daniel envisions Israel as being protected by angelic beings who serve God (Dan 12:1). This tradition, however, is as old as Ex 14:19. As Israel understood history, therefore, God would not need to call upon an angel to establish or represent God's Kingly Reign *on earth.* When the midrashic associations in Daniel 7 are read in tandem with ancient Israel's traditional theology of kingship, they fully justify the reading given above.

5

After the Jews had succeeded in throwing off the Syrian yoke, many of them decided that they could not completely abandon their traditional national hope for a Davidic Messiah. These Jews believed that the prophetic promises of a Davidic king who would fully restore God's Reign over Israel and the nations had to be fulfilled. Some of these Jews, accordingly, joined their traditional Messianic hope to the eschatological hope they had recently acquired from the book of Daniel. They eventually gave expression to these combined hopes by creating a variant form of apocalyptic literature called the "two-stage apocalypse."

By way of illustration, one of these two-stage apocalypses, *2 Esdras,* teaches that God's Messiah will come and win a decisive victory over all the nations. He will then reign gloriously for 400 years. During this 400 year reign, there will be no suffering or death. All who have shared in the Messiah's victory will enjoy miraculous longevity and prosperity (7:28). This *modified* Messianic Golden Age will conclude with the end of the world; it will be followed by the resurrection of the dead, the General Judgment (7:31-35), and, finally, the New Creation (7:75). In the Talmud, some of the rabbis refer to the first of these two stages as "the days of the Messiah," and to the second or permanent stage as "the world to come."

2 Esdras is one of the apocrypha. (The apocrypha are the books from the Old Greek version of the Old Testament which

were not included in the Hebrew Old Testament.) It can be found in the rear of those Protestant Bibles which include the apocrypha.

Because of the development of two-stage apocalyptic, many of the Jews at the time of Jesus believed the Messiah would come as a military leader who would triumphantly establish the Reign of God within history as a *preamble* to the New Creation. We will see in a later chapter, however, that Jesus rejected two-stage apocalyptic theology and its hope for a military Messiah. With the author of Daniel, Jesus believed that the Kingdom of God would come, not by military violence and bloodshed, but by the irresistible power of God.

It was probably for that reason that Jesus rejected the title "Messiah" and preferred to speak of the King who would preside over God's end-time Kingdom as the "Son of Man." The midrashic reference in Daniel 7:13-14 to "one like a son of man" is not yet an explicit eschatological title. It is evident that by the time of Jesus, however, Daniel's allusion to one like a son of Adam had become such a title. We do not know if apocalyptic circles in Palestine had already transformed the Adamic allusion in Daniel into a title, or if Jesus was the first to do so. There is no reliable evidence either way.

Questions for Review and Discussion

1. Who did Ancient Israel believe that God had appointed as the first king of creation? Where in the Old Testament could we find the answer to this question?
2. What royal family did Ancient Israel believe that God had chosen as the means by which God's Reign over creation would eventually be restored? Indicate two places in the Old Testament where this belief is expressed.
3. What extraordinary promise did Nathan the prophet make to David about David's dynasty? Where in the Old Testament can we find this promise?

4. What extraordinary honor did David's heirs believe God had conferred upon them when they were anointed as David's successors? Where in the Old Testament did they themselves tell us about this belief?
5. After the exile to Babylon in 587 B.C., why did the prophets continue to expect that God would raise up a son of David to restore the kingdom to Israel?
6. Why did the Syrian persecution of the Jews in 168 B.C. cause a faith crisis of the first magnitude for devout Jews?
7. What prophetic book was written to help the Jews resolve the faith crisis caused by the Syrian persecution? What is unusual about this book's authorship?
8. Why was the apocalyptic theology in the book of Daniel of great importance to the Jews at the time when it was written?
9. What mysterious figure does Dan 7:13 say will preside over God's end-time Kingdom? Why would this expected figure's arrival seem appropriate?
10. Give several reasons why the "one like a son of man" in Dan 7:13 is probably a human and not an angel. Why do some scholars think this mysterious figure might be an angel?
11. What is a two-stage apocalypse, and why was such an unusual form of religious literature created? Name one of the ancient two-stage apocalypses, and explain where one would be able to find it.
12. What did Jesus probably think about two-stage apocalyptic theology? On what evidence is your answer based?

Chapter Six: The Miracles of Jesus

1

ALL THE STRANDS OF TRADITION GATHERED INTO THE FOUR gospels affirm that Jesus enjoyed extraordinary success at healing people in God's name. Granted that Mark is prone to hyperbole, he is probably an essentially reliable witness when he reports that Jesus was renowned for having healed many people from various physical and psychological infirmities:

> And they brought to him all who were sick or possessed with demons. . . . And he healed many who were sick with various diseases, and cast out many demons. (Mk 2:32a,34a)

Even those who rejected Jesus' prophetic authority could not deny his astonishing ability to cure people and free them from demonic torment. They maintained, however, that Jesus derived his power over demons from one of the rulers of the demons who assisted Jesus in order to lead the multitudes astray:

> And the scribes who came down from Jerusalem said, "He is possessed by Beelzebul, and by the prince of demons he casts out the demons." (Mk 3:22)

The apostolic church would never have invented such an ugly accusation; she only preserved it for the sake of Jesus' canny response:

> How can Satan cast out Satan? If a Kingdom is divided against itself it cannot stand. . . . And if Satan has risen up against himself and is divided, he cannot stand, but is coming to an end. (Mk 3:23b-24,26)

This authentic saying of Jesus recalls another saying cited earlier but deserving of repetition because of its congruence with the foregoing:

> But if it is by the finger of God that I cast out demons, then the kingdom of God has come upon you. (Lk 11:20)

The hostile charge brought against Jesus by his critics and his response to that charge remind us that in Jesus' day illness, physical and psychological, was explained *mythologically,* not scientifically. Jesus and his contemporaries, because of their historically limited knowledge, would have assumed that all mental illness and many physical infirmities were caused by demons (fallen angels). We should recall, for example, the "loathsome sores" which "Satan" inflicted on Job's body:

> So Satan went forth from the presence of the Lord and afflicted Job with loathsome sores from the sole of his foot to the crown of his head. (Job 2:7)

Guided by the same tradition, one of the Gospel stories relates that Jesus healed an autistic boy who was thought to be afflicted by an evil spirit. However, when the boys' father describes his son's symptoms, it is apparent that the boy was probably suffering from epilepsy:

> Teacher, I brought my son to you, for he has a dumb spirit; and wherever it seizes him, it dashes him down; and he foams and grinds his teeth and becomes rigid. . . . And it has often cast him into the fire and into the water to destroy him. But if you can do anything, please have pity on us and help us. (Mk 9:17b-18a,)

This story's sacred power to instruct our faith is not undone by the realization that the boy's problem was *physiological,* not demonic. For no matter what explanation is employed, the boy, his parents, and their community were faced with a frightening problem. The boy's predicament, therefore, vividly exemplifies the terror of history from which God sent Jesus to free our minds and hearts. By healing the boy through Jesus God was assuring us that the threatening evils in life which can tempt us to despair have no lasting power to harm us. God's saving power can finally heal us from all evil, regardless of whether that evil is explained mythologically or scientifically.

2

Moderate scholarship believes that genuine miracles occur, and that God truly healed people through Jesus to endorse Jesus' Kingdom Message. This conclusion is reasonable because God continues to heal people miraculously in our age through faith in Jesus. But, as already observed in chapter two, moderate scholarship does not think that genuine miracles ever contradict the laws of nature.

A modern thinker recoils at the suggestion that God would interfere with or violate nature's laws. Our God-given power of reason tells us that it is *wrong* for us to act illogically, contradictorily, or uneconomically. We conclude, therefore, that God does not act in such ways.

If God were to interfere with the laws of nature, that would mean that God was acting illogically and contradictorily by destroying the very laws which God is everywhere creating and upholding. Critical reason suggests, therefore, that if miraculous healings genuinely occur, they do not violate the laws of nature. There is probably a way to understand miraculous healings which is fundamentally in harmony with nature.

Any credible explanation of the miraculous should also take into account "the law of parsimony." This law states that hypothetical entities should never be multiplied beyond necessity. In other words, we should always prefer the explanation which allows us to assume the existence of *fewer* hypothetical entities rather than more. For if we humans can see that we should always act with economy and avoid waste or contradiction, it follows that God always acts with economy and logical consistency.

Accordingly, the miraculous healings wrought by God through Jesus should not be understood as unnatural, but as "paranormal" in kind. Paranormal experiences are those which fall outside the expected range of the "normal." They predictably seem strange and uncanny to us. Nevertheless, their occurrence still falls within the range of the "natural," albeit rarely and elusively. When a genuine miracle occurs, God activates some latent potentiality which is not ordinarily operative in our experience. This divinely activated occurrence, however, still belongs to the realm of nature as one of its paranormal possibilities.

If we wish to join the law of parsimony to our attempt to understand miraculous healings, where is the most logical place to begin? We know, to begin with, that the only place in nature where God can act without interfering is in the human spirit which can *freely* open itself to divine influence. God is not interfering with or violating nature when God's action is freely invited or consciously sought. It is probably in the dimension of human spirit, then, that we should begin our search for an understanding of genuinely miraculous healings.

It seems likely that when God produced a miraculous healing through Jesus, God acted through (1) Jesus' willingness to serve God and (2) the free request or hope of the person Jesus healed. The resulting divine influence was mediated through Jesus and paranormally activated and accelerated some latent therapeutic potentiality in the healed person's own nature. God's freely invited intervention resulted in a remission of the healed person's symptoms. And this extraordinary remission was correctly experienced as an act of God wrought through God's prophet, Jesus:

> Fear seized them all; and they glorified God, saying, "A great prophet has arisen among us!" and "God has visited his people!" (Lk 7:16)

Furthermore, by accelerating the remission of pathology, physical or mental, God would not have contradicted any laws of nature. For natural processes themselves can reverse physical or mental pathology. God's power, accordingly, can supernaturally engage and *accelerate* the healed person's own natural capacity to be healed under optimum conditions. Correctly understood, therefore, the miraculous involves the divine activation of some paranormal capacity latent in human nature. Such divine activation never occurs, however, unless human freedom invites that activity.

This contemporary understanding of a miracle clearly differs from the traditional view which assumes a divine contradiction of nature. Traditional insistence that a miracle is something which contradicts the laws of nature, and which only God, therefore, could have caused, is a form of folk hyperbole. This hyperbole is unconsciously meant to insure that God is acknowledged as the cause of a miraculous sign. Those who advocate the traditional definition, however, are unnecessarily overstating their case.

Given the mythological naivete of the past, defending the possibility of miraculous healings will seem unacceptable to some in our skeptical age. Naivete, however, is not the exclusive prerogative of the uneducated. It is true that it would be wrong to return to the oversimplified explanations of the past. But it would also be wrong to presume that we can tie God's hands. Divine action which respects and works through freedom is not the same as interference. If we humans are able to creatively influence and accelerate natural processes, so can God if human freedom opens itself to God with faith and trust.

3

There are several wonder-filled stories in the Gospels which do contradict the laws of nature if we read them literally. In these stories, for example, Jesus walks on water (Mk 6:45-50), changes water into wine (Jn 2:1-10, and feeds a crowd of five thousand by multiplying five loaves and two fishes (Mk 6:34-44).

A critical reading of these and other such stories, however, indicates that they were never meant to be understood literally. Instead, they contain symbolic-midrashic lessons about some aspect of the Christian mystery. The authors of these stories and the communities for which they were written knew that they were theology, not history.

Space and practicality will not allow us to explain all such stories found in the Gospels. Instead, we will examine only one of these stories and leave the others for another day. We will reflect in some detail on this particular story to help the reader see that, from the outset, it was written to teach "theological" lessons about Jesus.

All four of the Gospels contain a story in which Jesus multiplies bread and fish to feed a multitude (Mk 6:30-44; Mt 14:13-21; Lk 9:10-17; Jn 6:1-14). Contemporary scholarship tells us that we should take this story *seriously,* but not literally. It is actually a midrashic reflection on the early church's "eschatological" celebration of the Lord's Supper.

This eschatological celebration of the Lord's Supper recalled Jesus' Resurrection and expected his second coming, but did not yet contain a memorial of his passion. The symbolism in the story of Jesus feeding the multitude is concerned solely with the expectation of *Risen Life* in God's approaching Kingdom; it never suggests the passion of Jesus.

After the passion interpretation of the bread and wine was joined to the Lord's Supper, it became necessary to mention wine with the bread in a manner that pointed to Jesus' death. Since the midrashic story we are considering makes no mention of wine or Jesus' passion, it was probably created by the early church at a time when she still celebrated the purely eschatological form of the Supper.

In the Eucharistic midrash found in the four Gospels, Jesus is presented as the New Moses who feeds God's flock with true manna as he guides us through the desert of this life to the true promised land of God's Kingdom:

> As he went ashore he saw a great throng, and he had compassion on them, because they were like sheep without a shepherd; and he began to teach them many things.
>
> And when it grew late his disciples came to him and said, "This is a desert [*erēmos*], and the hour is now late; send them away to . . . buy themselves something to eat." (Mk 6:34-36a,36c)

The disciples in the story refer to their location as a "desert" in order to suggest a midrashic relation between the saving work of Moses and that of Jesus. Just as Moses mediated salvation from physical evil during the Exodus event, Jesus now mediates spiritual salvation to the New Israel (his church). Translators frequently fail to discern the midrashic symbolism in the story and translate the Greek word for desert (*erēmos*) as "lonely place," or some other literally conceived alternative. Such well-intended but mistaken translations prevent readers from recognizing midrashic connections being taught by the evangelist.

When Jesus is reminded of the multitude's need for food, he marvelously provides them with "a meal" of bread and fish. A critical reading indicates that the mention of the fish is probably secondary. The "two" fish were probably added later (for pastoral reasons to be explained below) to connect the original Eucharistic midrash with the memory of Jesus' appearance to the Twelve while they were at table. On that occasion the disciples were eating a meal of "broiled fish" (Lk 24:41-43; Jn 21:9,13). The Christian teacher who made the addition introduced literary *tension* between the *fish* symbolism of the Easter meal appearance, and the *manna* theme of the original midrash:

> And he said to them, "How many loaves have you? Go and see." And when they had found out, they said, "Five, and two fish" . . . And taking the five loaves and the two fish, he looked up into heaven, and blessed, and broke the loaves and gave them to the disciples to set before

> the people; and he divided the two fish among them all. (Mk 6:38,41-42)

After Jesus feeds the multitude in a manner reminiscent of Moses feeding Israel of old with manna, he directs the disciples to gather the leftover fragments. (In John's account, Jesus adds, "that nothing may be lost." This is surely not meant as a literal expression of concern for fragments of bread. Rather, Jesus' concern is for his disciples who are symbolized by the bread.):

> And they took up twelve baskets of broken pieces. . . . (Mk 12:43)

The statement about "the twelve baskets of broken pieces" is meant to remind us that the loaf of bread which is broken at the Lord's Supper is a symbol of the *unity* of faith and love which should characterize "the twelve tribes" of the New Israel, i.e., the faith community of Jesus. The joyful *fellowship* manifested at the Lord's Supper is a sign of this sacred unity.

Paul the apostle has this same symbolic unity in mind when he says:

> The bread which we break, is it not a participation in the body of Christ? Because there is one loaf of bread, we who are many are [reminded that we are] one body, for we all partake of the one loaf. (1 Cor 10:16b-17)

The Eucharistic prayer found in the early Christian manual called the *Didache* also makes mention of this same sacred unity symbolized by the bread at the Lord's Supper:

> As this broken bread was once scattered over the hills, and then, when gathered, became one loaf, so may your church be gathered from the corners of the earth into your Kingdom. (Did 9:4)

4

Both Mark (8:1-9) and Matthew (15:32-38) contain a second version of the Eucharistic midrash discussed just above. Matthew decided to include this second version which he found in Mark, but Luke chose to exclude it. (We will see below, however, that Luke borrowed some of its midrashic symbolism for use in another narrative.) Mark included the second version of the Eucharistic midrash in his Gospel because this second version contained a variant set of *theological symbols* highly valued by his mission-minded church.

Mark's *first* version of the Eucharistic midrash relates that Jesus "blessed" (*eulogēsen*) the bread which fed the multitude:

> And taking the five loaves and two fish he looked up to heaven, and blessed, and broke the loaves, and gave them to the disciples to set before the people. (Mk 6:41)

The use of the word "blessed" indicates that the story was probably created for a Jewish Christian community whose first language was Aramaic. In Aramaic, one "blessed" (i.e., praised) God for the gift of food (whereas in Greek one "gave thanks"). The story was then translated *literally* into Greek by someone either unfamiliar with customary Greek usage or inflexibly attached to the traditional language of the Aramaic-speaking church.

In addition, the *first* version also says that "five" loaves of bread fed "five thousand" people. This part of the story intends to teach a theological lesson involving numbers. In this instance, the numbers are probably derived from historical memory, not the Old Testament scriptures. Such a lesson can seem uncongenial to our present mode of thinking, but the folk mentality of the ancient Jews and Jewish Christians delighted in lessons which involved symbolic numerology. Such numbers also aided the memory of folk teachers who attached specific lessons (to be recalled and recited) to specific numbers.

Accordingly, the numbers "five" and "five thousand" are probably meant to recall the *third* of the church-founding appearances listed by Paul in 1 Cor 15:3-8. Paul tells us that the Risen Jesus appeared *first* to Peter and *then* to the Twelve; he *next* appeared to more then "five hundred" disciples at one time (probably in Galilee):

> He was raised on the third day in accordance with the scriptures, and . . . he appeared to Cephas [Peter], then to

> the twelve. Then he appeared to more than five hundred disciples at one time, most of whom are still alive, although some have fallen asleep. (1 Cor 15:4b-6)

For the early church, these "five hundred" disciples epitomized the *earliest* faith community of the Risen Jesus called into being by the witnessing of the Twelve. The witnessing of all or some of the Twelve to this large group, Paul tells us, was confirmed by a revelatory appearance of the Risen Jesus himself. We can tell from Paul's testimony that this stunning occurrence profoundly impressed the earliest Christians.

We have already observed that the bread at the Eucharistic meal was perceived as a symbol of Jesus' faith community. And since the multitude fed by Jesus in the Eucharistic midrash also represents his church, an early Jewish Christian teacher probably chose the number "five" from the appearance to the "five hundred" to number the loaves which symbolized the community gathered by the Risen Jesus.

Moreover, Moses was remembered (legendarily) as having led "thousands" of Israelites in the desert. (Num 1:1-46; in reality the desert could not have sustained the multitudes listed in the book of Numbers. The large numbers found therein probably derive from a census taken for tax purposes at the time of Solomon.) The Jewish Christian creator of the story, therefore, probably thought it fitting to increase the size of the symbolic multitude "fed" by Jesus, the New Moses, from "five hundred" to "five thousand." (Luke also uses the number "five thousand" to describe the rapid growth of the early church in Acts 4:4.)

Finally, the *first* of the two feeding stories relates that "twelve baskets" of broken pieces were gathered after the multitude was fed. The number twelve, of course, was associated by Jews with the "twelve tribes" of Israel. Jewish Christians, accordingly, thought of themselves as the "twelve tribes" of the New Israel (Jas 1:1). This, again, suggests that Mark's first feeding story was created to instruct a community of Jewish Christians, probably in Palestine.

5

Although the *second* version of the Eucharistic midrash found in Mark (and Matthew) tells essentially the same story as the first, it, nevertheless, differs from the first in minor but significant ways. The *second* version relates that Jesus "gave thanks" (*eucharistēsas*) over the bread instead of saying that he "blessed" it:

> And he took the seven loaves, and having given thanks he broke them and gave them to his disciples to set before the people. (Mk 8:6)

This change in language from "blessed" to "gave thanks" indicates that the original story was probably revised for use in communities which included Greek-speaking Jewish Christians and increasing numbers of Greek-speaking Gentile converts. As already indicated above, in Greek one "gave thanks" to God for the gift of food, whereas in Aramaic one "blessed" it.

The *second* version again differs from the the first when it tells us that "seven loaves" fed the multitude and "seven baskets" of broken pieces were taken up. The numbers "five" and "twelve" in the original story were probably changed to "seven" in the second to accommodate the story to the instructional needs of increasing numbers of Gentiles in churches outside of Palestine. The choice of the number "seven" was pastoral and midrashic.

Ancient Jewish tradition (based on Gen 10:1-32) believed that there were "seventy" Gentile nations in addition to God's chosen nation, Israel. This same tradition also remembered (aided by Deut 7:1) that "seven" Gentile nations inhabited the promised land (Canaan) before it was conquered by Israel. The numbers "seventy" and (in some circumstances) "seven," therefore, could signify the "Gentiles," i.e., all the nations apart from the chosen nation, Israel. Since "seventy" loaves and baskets of fragments would have proved unwieldy, and "seventy" is a multiple of "seven," the reviser of the original Eucharistic midrash preferred "seven" as a symbol for the Gentiles.

The "seven" loaves and the "seven" baskets of fragments in the revised story signify the many Gentile converts who had entered the Christian faith community. If we again recall that the Eucharistic bread was a symbol of the church, we can see why Jewish Christian missionaries changed the number of loaves and baskets of broken pieces from twelve to "seven." This midrashic alteration was meant to assure Gentile Christians that they too had been part of God's saving purpose from the beginning of salvation history. For God had promised Abraham, "In you all the tribes of the earth shall be blessed" (LXX Gen 12:3; LXX = the Greek Septuagint).

It was probably pastoral concern for the increasing Gentiles in the church that motivated the Jewish Christian teacher who added the "two" fish to the "five" loaves in Mark's *first* Eucharistic midrash. "Five" and "two" are "seven." The reviser expanded the story to provide a midrashic number that could be understood as *foreshadowing* the calling of the Gentiles.

We have already noted that Mark's *second* version of the Eucharistic midrash was not included by Luke in his Gospel. Luke probably found the second version redundant. He decided, therefore, to acknowledge the Gentile converts in his church by other means. To that end, Luke (or his tradition) taught that in addition to commissioning the "Twelve" to assist him with proclaiming the approaching Kingdom to Israel, (9:1-2), Jesus also commissioned "seventy" others, and sent them before him (10:1). The "seventy" other witnesses are meant by Luke to suggest midrashically that Jesus, in accordance with God's saving purpose, intended his message to be carried to *all* (70) *of the nations.*

Luke teaches a similar midrashic lesson in Acts. Since it was primarily the Greek-speaking Jewish Christians who evangelized the Greek-speaking Gentiles, Luke tells us in Acts 6:2-3 that the "Twelve" chose "seven" of these Greek-speaking Jewish Christians (called Hellenists) to oversee that branch of the church.

Finally, the *second* version of the Eucharistic midrash states that a multitude of "four thousand" was fed with the "seven" loaves. Why "four thousand"? The Jewish Christian teacher(s) who revised the story probably wished to signify midrashically (in a manner that aided the teacher's memory) that from the outset God had intended that a multitude of Gentiles would also be gathered into Jesus' faith community from the "four" corners of the earth:

> He will raise an ensign for the nations and will assemble the outcasts of Israel, and gather the dispersed of Judah from the four corners of the earth. (Is 11:12)

6

We find in the *second* version of the Eucharistic midrash in Mark and Matthew one important lesson (Mk 8:2; Mt 15:32) which has no counterpart in the first. In the second version, Jesus, rather than his disciples, tellingly takes the initiative in feeding the crowd:

> I have compassion on the crowd, because they have been with me now *three days,* and have nothing to eat; and if I send them away hungry . . . they will faint *on the way.* (Mk 8:2)

The observation that the crowd had been journeying with Jesus for "three days" should not be taken literally; it is sacramental theology, not history. The two major sacraments in the early church were Baptism and the Lord's Supper. Baptism, the sacrament of Christian initiation, was understood as preparation for the privilege of eating the Lord's Kingdom-anticipating Supper.

Christians in the early church believed (as do Christians today) that in Baptism we are mystically joined to Jesus, and relive with him *the three* most sacred days of his life: Good Friday (when we die with Jesus to sin), Holy Saturday (when we are buried with Jesus in the watery grave of his tomb), and Easter Sunday (when we are raised with Jesus to New Life):

> Do you not know that all of us who have been baptized into Christ have been baptized into his death? We were

> buried with him therefore by baptism into death, so that as Christ was raised from the dead by the glory of the Father, we too might walk in newness of life. (Rom 6:2-4)

Because the baptized were privileged to partake of the Lord's Supper, Jesus alludes to their "three day" baptismal journey as a sacramental preamble to his sacred meal. Everything indicates that it is *the Risen Jesus,* not the earthly Jesus, who we encounter in this (and the other) Eucharistic midrash.

"The way," of course, is *our journey with Jesus* through the desert of this life to the true promised land of God's Kingdom. Mark and Matthew concur with Paul that this mystic journey begins in the mystery of Baptism. But they also remind us that if we hope to complete the journey, we must partake of the sacred Supper which the Risen Lord provides for us while we are "on the way."

7

Before leaving this chapter, we should briefly turn our attention to those extraordinary stories in the Gospels in which Jesus is described as raising the dead. What should we think about those stories? Did Jesus actually raise the ruler's daughter (Mk 5:21-21, 35-43), the widow's son (Lk 7:11-18), and Lazarus (Jn 11:1-44) from true death?

Contemporary standards of reason tell us that it would contradict the laws of nature (and, therefore, be contrary to the creative purpose of God) for someone who had *truly* died to be brought back to life. Contemporary scholarship concludes, therefore, that anyone thought by the early church to have been "raised from the dead" by Jesus was not truly dead. Instead, such a person was probably in a coma judged to be death by the prescientific standards of the ancient world. We know that on many occasions throughout history people have been buried when they were thought to be dead but were actually still alive (in an unconscious state with *drastically* diminished vital signs).

This interpretation of the "raising" stories in the Gospels does not empty them of their power to instruct our faith in God. For even if someone healed by Jesus was thought to be dead, but was actually still alive, the saving significance intended by God when God healed that person through Jesus remains essentially the same. God was signifying through such an event, that no matter what the evils are that threaten us in life, including death, God's gracious love can ultimately save us from all such evils. If we trust in God's goodness as God has taught us to do through Jesus, none of life's terrifying evils have any lasting or final power to harm us.

Questions for Review and Discussion

1. Did Jesus' contemporaries explain serious mental illness scientifically or mythologically? Explain your answer.
2. Mark tell us that Jesus healed a boy who fell to the ground, foamed at the mouth, ground his teeth, and became rigid. What physical illness was this boy probably suffering from, and how did Jesus' contemporaries explain the boy's illness?
3. What evidence indicates that even Jesus' enemies acknowledged that he healed people with astonishing success?
4. What is the traditional definition of a miracle, and why would most contemporary Christian scholars reject that definition?
5. How would contemporary Christian scholarship prefer to explain a miracle?
6. How does the "paranormal" differ from the "normal," and what do they share in common?
7. If God actualized some paranormal possibility in order to provide a miraculous sign, would that action violate the laws of nature? Explain your answer.
8. Does contemporary Christian scholarship think that Jesus restored people who were truly dead to their former natural life? Explain your answer.

9. When the Gospels tell us that Jesus miraculously multiplied loaves and fishes, are they relating history or theology? Explain your answer.
10. How does the second version of the story of Jesus multiplying loaves and fishes differ from the first one? Are these differences historical or theological in nature? Explain your answer.
11. When Jesus observes that the crowd he is about to feed has been with him for "three days," is he relating history or theology? Explain your answer.

Chapter Seven: Jesus' Final Visit to Jerusalem

1

Jesus took his final journey to Jerusalem shortly before the annual Jewish Passover festival. The Gospel accounts of this journey relate that Jesus was enthusiastically welcomed as God's Messiah when he approached Jerusalem in the midst of a crowd of pilgrims. (Tradition has named the day of Jesus' arrival "Palm Sunday.") Moreover, the Gospels all imply that he *intended* and *accepted* this Messianic recognition. The Messianic nature of Jesus' welcome by the crowd is implicit in Mark (11:1-10), but explicit in Matthew (21:1-9), Luke (19:29-40), and John (12:12-16).

Contemporary scholarship informs us, however, that the accounts of Jesus' "triumphal entry" into Jerusalem, have been theologically embellished with a number of midrashic and legendary additions. We should not read these stories, therefore, as ordinary or literal history. Rather, they are *theologically expanded* accounts of an actual event in Jesus' history: his final visit to Jerusalem shortly before Passover. The accounts were expanded to express the early church's understanding of the hidden implications of this final visit when it is remembered in the light of Jesus' death and Resurrection.

In a later chapter we will see that the Gospels contain impressive indications that Jesus did not think of himself as God's Messiah. Nor did he believe that God planned to send a Messiah to Israel. Instead, Jesus looked for the arrival of the end-time king and judge called the Son of Man. After we examine these indications it will become evident that Jesus would not historically have initiated or accepted a Messianic demonstration when he arrived at Jerusalem. We should look, then, for a nonliteral way to understand the triumphal entry stories which we find in the Gospels.

Before we begin our search for an alternate reading of these stories, we should remind ourselves once again that the rejected and crucified Jesus was shockingly contrary to Jewish Messianic expectations. Jesus' disciples had to radically redefine the title Messiah before they could realistically assign it to him. The major apologetic task confronting the apostolic church, therefore, was to present a theologically acceptable defense of her faith in the "spiritual" Messiahship of Jesus.

The church's only hope of presenting an acceptable defense, she realized, lay in a midrashic reading of the sacred scriptures. If she could find enough impressive proof texts which indicated that God had secretly intended to send Israel a lowly, rejected, and suffering Messiah, the Jews should be able to believe in Jesus.

Accordingly, the church searched the scriptures (see Jn 5:39; 7:52) for midrashic foreshadowings of Jesus' unexpected spiritual Messiahship. Any reference to a suffering righteous man, or to a Messiah-king who was nonmilitary and lowly, was presumed to prefigure Jesus. Such a text then became grist for the church's theological mill. A number of references to a suffering righteous man were found (e.g., Ps. 22, Ps 41:9; Ps 69; Is 52:13-53:12), but references to a humble and nonmilitary king were hard to come by. One prized text, however, was found in the writings of Zechariah the prophet.

In the passage we are about to read, Zechariah is assuring the postexilic Jews that the expected Messiah will certainly come as promised. Some of the language used to describe this coming king (thought by Zechariah to be already promised in Gen 49:10-11) is highly unusual. We are told that he will be "humble," will come riding on the "colt" of an ass instead of a war horse, and will bring "peace" instead of warfare and conquest (because God will overwhelm the king's enemies in advance):

> Rejoice greatly, O daughter of Zion! Shout aloud, O daughter of Jerusalem! Lo, your king comes to you . . . humble and riding on an ass, on a colt the foal of an ass.
>
> I will cut off the chariot from Ephraim and the war horse from Jerusalem; and the battle bow shall be cut off, and he shall command peace to the nations. (Zech 9:9-10)

The phrase omitted from the passage just cited (translated from the Hebrew text) describes the coming king as "triumphant and victorious." But the Old Greek text (which the Greek-speaking church probably consulted) describes the coming king as "righteous and able to save." The wording of the Old Greek version would have accorded even more with the church's understanding of Jesus. Zechariah's prophecy, therefore, was eagerly pointed to by the church to advance her claims about the spiritual Messiahship of Jesus.

In order to help preliterate Christians remember the proof texts needed to defend their faith in Jesus, the church wove these texts (or key words from them) into appropriate parts of the remembered history of Jesus. When proof texts were joined to the history of Jesus in this manner, they could more easily be learned and recalled when required for effective witnessing. Consequently, the church joined Zechariah's Messianic text to her memory of Jesus' final visit to Jerusalem. For it was this momentous visit which had triggered the chain of events which led to Jesus' Resurrection and the church's recognition of his spiritual Messiahship.

The early church assumed, of course, that Jesus possessed foreknowledge of everything he had to accomplish during "Holy Week" before the true nature of his Messiahship could be revealed. To express this view, the church described Jesus' final visit to Jerusalem as the triumphant arrival of God's secret Messiah. She accomplished this theological task by joining allusions to or quotations from Zechariah's Messianic prophecy to the story of Jesus' arrival.

Mark provides us with the earliest account of Jesus' triumphant arrival. Both Mark and Luke alude to Zechariah's Messianic prophecy by repeatedly mentioning Zechariah's "colt" (which is the foal of an ass; Zech 9:9b; Luke also alludes to Zechariah's coming "king" in 19:38). But neither Mark nor Luke quote portions of Zechariah's prophecy as do Matthew (21:5) and John (12:15):

> And when they drew near to Jerusalem . . . he sent two of his disciples, and said to them, "Go into the village opposite you, and immediately as you enter it you will find a colt tied, on which no one has ever sat; untie it and bring it. If anyone says to you, 'Why are you doing this?' say, 'The Lord has need of it, and will send it back immediately.'" (Mk 11:1-3)

The Old Greek version describes the ass's colt as "new," and that is why Mark, followed by Luke, has Jesus describe the colt midrashically as one "on which no one has ever sat."

> And they went away, and found a colt tied at the door out in the open street; and they untied it. And those who stood there said to them, "What are you doing, untying the colt?" And they told them what Jesus had said; and they let them go. And they brought the colt to Jesus, and threw their garments upon it, and he sat upon it. (Mk 11:4-7)

The story of the colt's miraculous borrowing is a folk device which creates appropriate wonder and explains the colt's providential availability as a mount for the secret Son of David. In reality, there probably was no colt. It is highly likely that Jesus walked down the Mount of Olives toward Jerusalem along with his disciples and the throng of singing pilgrims they had joined. By relating that Jesus sent his disciples to fetch the "colt" spoken of by Zechariah, the Gospels intend to imply that Jesus foreknows not only his secret Messianic destiny, but also the foreshadowing scriptures which he must fulfill (see Mk 14:49; Lk 24:26-27,44-46).

Describing the disciples as spreading their garments on the colt obtained for Jesus is another midrashic allusion to Jesus' hidden Messiahship soon to be revealed at Easter. In the Old Testament, garments are spread beneath a man who becomes God's anointed king in unusual circumstances:

> Then Elisha the prophet called one of the sons of the prophets and said to him . . . take this flask of oil in your hand, and go up to Ramoth-gilead. And when you arrive, look there for Jehu the son of Jehoshaphat . . . and lead him to an inner chamber. Then take the flask of oil and pour it on his head, and say, 'Thus says the Lord, I anoint you king over Israel.' Then open the door and flee, do not tarry." (2 Kgs 9:1-3)
>
> So the young man, the prophet, went to Ramoth-gilead. And. . . . the young man poured the oil on his head, saying to him, "Thus says the Lord the God of Israel, I anoint you king over the people of the Lord, over Israel. (2 Kgs 9:4,6)
>
> When Jehu came out . . . they said to him, "Is all well? Why did this mad fellow come to you?" . . . . And he said, "Thus and so he spoke to me saying, 'Thus says the Lord, I anoint you king over Israel.'" Then in haste every man of them took his garment, and put it under him on the bare steps, and they blew the trumpet and proclaimed, "Jehu is king." (2 Kgs 9:11-13)

In Mark's account of Jesus' arrival at Jerusalem, Jesus is being presented midrashically as God's hidden Messiah whose glorious reign is mysteriously about to be inaugurated:

> Many spread their garments on the road, and others spread leafy branches which they had cut from the fields. And those who went before and those who followed cried out, "Hosanna! Blessed is he who comes in the name of the Lord! Blessed is the kingdom of our father David which is coming." (Mk 11:8-10)

Mark relates that the crowd of pilgrims preceding and following Jesus as he approached Jerusalem were mysteriously inspired to recognize and honor his secret Messiahship. Consequently, they extolled Jesus as befitted his Messianic dignity and joyfully anticipated the Kingdom which would come in the wake of his final visit to Jerusalem.

The final verses of Mark's account constitute a midrashic crescendo achieved by quoting and alluding to Ps 118. Ps 118 was one of the psalms of praise (the Hallel) traditionally sung by pilgrims as they approached Jerusalem. This psalm asks for God's blessing on the pilgrim who approaches Jerusalem to worship in God's temple (v. 26). It also mentions festal "branches" borne by worshippers as part of a religious ritual enacted in the Jerusalem temple (v. 27). Since the first part of the crowd's acclamation in Mark's Gospel is a direct quotation from the Old Greek version of this psalm, the slightly differing wording of that version will be quoted below:

> Blessed is he who comes in the name of the Lord! We have blessed you from the house of the Lord. The Lord is God, and he has shined upon us. Celebrate the feast with thick branches. (LXX Ps 118:26-27a)

In addition, Ps 118 contains a major proof text highly prized and frequently quoted (Mk 12:10; Mt 21:42; Lk 20:17; Acts 4:11; 1 Pet 2:7) or alluded to (Mk 8:31; Lk 7:30; 9:22; 17:25; 1 Pet 2:4,7) by the early church. The Jews asked how Jesus could be Israel's promised Messiah if the majority of the Jews *and their religious leaders* refused to acknowledge him as such. One of the ways that the early church answered this question was by pointing to a verse in Ps 118 which she believed portended Jesus' rejection by the Jews and their leaders:

> The stone which the builders rejected has become the head of the corner. This is the Lord's doing, and it is marvelous in our eyes. (Ps 118:22-23)

The rejected stone was viewed by the early church as a mystic foreshadowing of the rejected Jesus. The builders who rejected the stone were thought to be prefigurements of the chief priests who seized Jesus and handed him over to the Romans. After the appearances of the Risen Jesus, his disciples discovered the midrashic implications of Zech 9:9-10 and the psalm (118) being sung by the crowd of pilgrims as Jesus approached Jerusalem for his destined final visit:

> His disciples did not understand this at first; but when Jesus was glorified, then they remembered that this had been written of him and had been done to him. (Jn 12:16)

Accordingly, teachers in the early church quoted and alluded to Zechariah's prophecy and Ps 118 when they related their (apologetic) interpretation of Jesus' final visit. They thereby defended the church's faith in Jesus' hidden Messiahship with the authority of scripture and helped her members to recall the proof texts needed when witnessing to skeptical Jews.

It can be disturbing for those who have been taught a literal understanding of the triumphal entry story to learn about the midrashic expansion which it has undergone. We must realize, however, that teachers in the early church had been schooled in a folk tradition which improvised freely when integrating midrashic proof texts into the structure of a remembered event. These teachers assumed that they had not only a right but a duty to explain and defend their faith in Jesus with the aid of customary teaching techniques.

Those who prefer to read the story literally are certainly free to do so. But they must then assume: (1) that Jesus knew in advance that he was God's secret Messiah, and (2) that the folk marvels in the account literally occurred. They must also explain how Jesus acquired his knowledge of God's secret Messianic purpose. Did God dictate this knowledge to Jesus?

Contemporary scholarship rejects the idea of divine dictation as contrary to our experience of God's interaction with human beings. Such dictation would also be contrary to the nonverbal manner in which God communicates with us at our time in history. Nevertheless, those who prefer the nonliteral reading of the entrance story should remember that some people are not troubled by the idea that God dictated information to Jesus. Their right to understand God's Self-revelation in that fashion should be respected even if one disagrees with them.

2

The evidence suggests that before Jesus took his final journey to Jerusalem, he had decided to deliver a prophetic rebuke to the powerful Sadducean priests who governed the temple in Jerusalem. Jesus would have viewed this reprimand as part of his mission to call all of Israel to readiness for the end-time. The rebuke delivered by Jesus took the symbolic form of angrily overturning some of the tables and chairs belonging to the money changers and merchants who were allowed to change coins and sell animals required by worshipers:

> And he entered the temple . . . and he overturned the tables of the money changers and the seats of those who sold pigeons. (Mk 11:15)

We should not assume that Jesus literally attempted to cleanse the entire northern side of the outer court of the temple of all the merchants and money changers allowed to transact business there. Had he tried to do so, the Jewish temple guards, and possibly also Roman soldiers from the adjoining fortress Antonia, would have intervened. Since Jesus' reputation accompanied him, his brief but dramatic action would have been understood by most as an implicit prophetic rebuke of the chief priests who supervised the temple and its sacred precincts. News of this incident would have traveled quickly through Jerusalem.

Jesus' symbolic expression of disapproval was meant to challenge the priests to stop some unacceptable practice which they allowed in the temple area. The Gospels do not specify precisely what practice Jesus objected to, but since the merchants and money changers had pious pilgrims at a disadvantage, they probably charged them flagrantly unfair rates.

We know, for example, that around A.D. 50 Simeon ben Gamaliel, the leader of the Pharisees, had to take strong measures to prevent the dove merchants from charging outrageous prices which the poor could not pay. Charging unfair prices within sight of God's house was probably perceived by Jesus (and many others) as sacrilegious exploitation of the poor. The midrashic words chosen by Mark to justify the cleansing gesture (a joining of Is 56:7 and Jer 7:11) are probably closer to Jesus' actual intention than the differing words found in the Fourth Gospel:

(Mk 11:17)

> And he taught, and said to them, "Is it not written, 'My house shall be called a house of prayer for all the nations'? But you have made it a den of thieves."

(Jn 2:16)

> And he said to those who sold the pigeons, "Take these things away; you shall not make my Father's house a house of trade."

Jesus probably did not object to the mere practices of changing money and selling animals in the temple's outer court. He would have understood that allowing the merchants to sell sacrificial animals already inspected by the priests was a convenience for worshipers. Likewise, it was convenient for Jews who wished to pay the annual temple tax to be able to exchange unacceptable coins for those required to pay the tax. The protest delivered by Jesus was probably against *the unfair rates of exchange* from which the priests received a percentage.

E.P. Sanders has advanced the view that Jesus's action symbolized an attack, not on the greed of the merchants and temple authorities, but against the very temple itself (*Jesus and Judaism,* ch. 1). The overturning of the merchants' tables, Sanders suggests, symbolized *destruction*—the coming destruction of the temple at the end-time, and its replacement by God with a new temple. This interpretation, however, is unconvincing. Jesus' action was directed not against the temple, but against the entrepreneurs (and their priestly abettors) who were violating its sanctity. The overturning of their tables did not signify destruction. Rather, it signified *disapproval.*

Jesus knew that he was taking a great risk when he publicly rebuked the powerful chief priests. The tragic fate of his predecessor, John the Baptizer, was still a recent memory. To incur the wrath of wealthy and privileged members of the establishment, Jesus realized, placed one in grave danger. He concluded, nevertheless, that God's call for faith and rightness of heart should also be directed to the chief priests. The priests understood the tacit message in Jesus' prophetic action; their hostile response is reported in the Gospels:

> And as he was walking in the temple, the chief priests . . . came to him, and they said to him, "By what authority do you do these things, or who gave you this authority to do them?" (Mk 11:27-29)

We may be reasonably certain that the substance of Jesus' reply is authentic, for it assumes that his mission is a continuation of the Baptizer's, and that Jesus' prophetic authority is essentially the same as John's. The early church soon abandoned that view and assigned Jesus the primary role of Messiah and John the secondary role of Jesus' prophetic precursor:

> Jesus said to them, "I will ask you a question; answer me and I will tell you by what authority I do these things. Was the baptism of John from heaven or from men?" (Mk 11:29-30a)

Jesus and many of his Jewish contemporaries believed that John's authority truly derived from God, and they revered John as a prophet. Furthermore, Jesus considered his own mission to be a direct continuation of John's. If the priests, therefore, were willing to acknowledge the charismatic (i.e., Spirit-endowed) authority of John, they should be willing to acknowledge that of Jesus also. But if they were not, then there was no basis for a meaningful discussion.

However, the priests were not willing to grant that John's prophetic activity was divinely authorized. And yet, they were not willing to disagree publicly, for John was widely regarded as a prophet. They chose, therefore, to answer with diplomatic ignorance. (The huddled discussion reported in Mk 31-32 is the church's editorial surmise of what the chief priests must have been thinking when they gave their reply.):

> They answered Jesus, "We do not know." And Jesus said to them, "Neither will I tell you by what authority I do these things." (Mk 11:33)

The chief priests had no intention of ignoring Jesus. They recognized that he, like the Baptizer, was esteemed by many as a prophet, and that his influence over large numbers of ordinary people was a threat to their own authority. Their greatest concern, however, was that Jesus might harbor political ambition. If so, he might ignite a revolutionary movement which would provoke the Romans and lead to political disaster, possibly even the destruction of the temple. The fourth Gospel contains a memory of such priestly concern which is probably close to the mark:

> If we let him go on thus, everyone will believe in him, and the Romans will come and destroy both our holy place and our nation. (Jn 11:48)

Accordingly, the priests decided that Jesus should be seized and questioned. At the very least, he would thereby be humbled for presuming that he could challenge their authority with impunity. And if he proved intractable or seemed to harbor political designs, they would hand him over to the Roman procurator as a potential threat to political stability.

Questions for Review and Discussion

1. At what time of the year did Jesus take his final journey to Jerusalem?
2. What unusual thing do all four Gospels relate that Jesus did just before he arrived in Jerusalem for the final time?
3. Does contemporary biblical scholarship think we should read the story of Jesus' triumphal entry into Jerusalem as literal history or theologically expanded history? Explain your answer.
4. Why was "apologetic" theology so important for the apostolic church, and what was the church's most urgent apologetic task?
5. Why did the apostolic church prize the Messianic prophecy which she found in Zech 9:9-10?

6. Why do some of the Gospels tell us that Jesus' disciples placed their garments on the colt he had directed them to bring to him?
7. Why is Ps 118:22-23 ("the stone that the builders rejected," et cetera) so frequently quoted and alluded to in the New Testament?
8. Why did Jesus probably decide to cleanse the Jerusalem temple with a symbolic gesture?
9. Why should the right of some Christians to read all of the triumphal entry story as *literal history* be respected by those who are less conservative?
10. Why should the right of other Christians to read the triumphal entry story as theologically expanded history be respected by those who are more conservative?

Chapter Eight: Jesus' Last Supper and Betrayal

1

The last time Jesus gathered his disciples to share his Kingdom-anticipating Supper was on the evening of Holy Thursday. But this Last Supper was decidedly different in mood from all the joyful meals which had preceded it. This Last Supper was characterized by an air of solemn sorrow because Jesus announced at its outset that he knew one of the Twelve had agreed to betray him:

> And when it was evening he came with the twelve. And as they were at table eating, Jesus said, "Truly I say to you, one of you will betray me." (Mk 14:17-18a)

Jesus had probably been warned that the chief priests were planning to arrest him covertly with the aid of an informant who was one of the Twelve. The priests wished to seize Jesus by cover of night to avoid stirring up the crowds who had come to Jerusalem for Passover and the Feast of Unleavened Bread:

> And the chief priests and the scribes were seeking how to arrest him by stealth, . . . for they said, "Not during the feast, lest there be a tumult of the people." (Mk 14:1b-2)

The plot to seize and question Jesus was probably conceived and implemented by the chief priests *without* any assistance from the scribes. Mark probably mentioned the scribes with the chief priests because the scribes of the Pharisees later became the major opponents of the church's mission to the synagogue. The evangelists wished to assure Christians that their chief adversaries had also resisted and persecuted Jesus.

Perhaps the person who informed Jesus of the plot did not know that it was *Judas Iscariot* who had agreed to be the traitor:

> Then Judas Iscariot, who was one of the twelve, went to the chief priests in order to betray him to them. (Mk 14:10)

If Jesus' informant did not tell Jesus which of the Twelve was the traitor, it is likely that Jesus would have quickly discerned the traitor's identity. After Jesus revealed his knowledge of the plot, Judas probably would not have been able to make normal eye contact. We should remember that the earliest of the four Gospels, Mark's, does not name Judas as the traitor. Judas, of course, did not agree to betray Jesus for "thirty pieces of silver." He was probably playing for much higher stakes.

We noted earlier that Jesus' choice of Judas as one of the Twelve caused a serious apologetic problem for the early church. The Jews understandably asked how Jesus could be regarded as God's Messiah and premier prophet if Jesus had chosen a traitor like Judas as a trusted disciple. The early church answered by pointing to texts in the Old Testament which she believed prefigured Jesus' betrayal as part of God's *secret Messianic purpose.* (See the apologetic reference to the "bread" from Ps 41:9 in Mk 14:20.)

The narrative in Matthew's Gospel which describes the remorseful Judas throwing thirty pieces of silver "into" (*eis*) the temple (27:3-5) is midrashic theology, not history. Matthew recounted this incident to allude *apologetically* to Zech 11:12-14:

> And they weighed out as my wages thirty shekels of silver. Then the Lord said to me, "Cast it into the treasury"—the lordly price at which I was paid off by them.

> So I took the thirty shekels of silver and cast them into the treasury which is in the house of the Lord. Then I broke my second staff Union, annulling the brotherhood between Judah and Israel.

Matthew thought this text foreshadowed Jesus' betrayal by Judas (whose name appears in Zech 11:14) in exchange for money (the "thirty pieces of silver" mentioned in Zech 11:12-13). By his treacherous deed, Matthew implies, Judas (Judah) annulled the "brotherhood" between himself and "Israel" (i.e., the other members of "the Twelve" who symbolized the tribes of Israel).

Furthermore, Matthew relates that after Judas betrayed Jesus he was filled with remorse and hanged himself (27:3-5). Raymond E. Brown has examined this Judas legend with his usual thoroughness in *The Death of the Messiah.* He convincingly suggests that the story of Judas' suicide was probably added to the Passion narrative by Matthew to liken Judas' betrayal of Jesus to Ahithophel's betrayal of David during Absalom's revolt. (Ahithophel had been David's trusted advisor.):

> Ahithophel said to Absalom, "Let me choose twelve thousand men, and I will set out and pursue David tonight. I will come upon him while he is weary and discouraged, and throw him into a panic; and all the people who are with him will flee. I will stike down the king only, and I will bring all the people back to you as a bride comes home to her husband. (2 Sam 17:1-3)
>
> When Ahithophel saw that his counsel was not followed. . . . he set his house in order and hanged himself. (2 Sam 17:23)

By means of this allusion, Matthew signified apologetically that the betrayal of David by his trusted adviser, Ahithophel, adumbrated the betrayal of David's Son, Jesus, by Judas. Jesus' betrayal, therefore, was divinely foreintended; his choice of Judas as a trusted disciple, therefore, in no way belies his Messianic credentials. Rather, his betrayal mysteriously confirms his Messianic identity.

It is unlikely that Judas, having experienced the teaching, healings, and exorcisms of Jesus, truly wished to see Jesus harmed. Judas (like Peter; see Mk 8:29) probably assumed or hoped that Jesus was the expected Messiah and grew impatient at the cautious, nonpolitical way in which Jesus proclaimed God's approaching Kingdom. Jesus always avoided anything that might be construed as a Messianic demonstration. Yet it would have been apparent to Judas that Jesus could heal people with *extraordinary* success by calling on power from God.

If Jesus was brought to a confrontation with the Jewish authorities, Judas probably surmised, Jesus would have to call upon God's power to extricate himself, and the Jewish leaders would then recognize Jesus' Messianic authority. They would then rally the nation behind him, and the Kingdom of God would arrive sooner. Whatever his motive, Judas tragically miscalculated.

2

We have no way of knowing when Jesus learned about the chief priests' plan to seize him. He could have been informed anytime between the cleansing of the temple and Holy Thursday. The synoptic tradition recalls that Jesus, during his last visit to Jerusalem, recited a parable which anticipated the probability of his death at the hands of the temple authorities. An *unembellished* form of this parable was probably spoken by Jesus after he learned of their plot, perhaps on Holy Thursday, but possibly earlier.

The early church expanded this parable with theological language which implies that Jesus expected to die as Israel's rejected *Messiah.* But the original form of the parable is still detectable and indicates that, instead, Jesus saw his coming death as the tragic fate of God's end-time prophet. To help the reader more easily grasp the likelihood of this reading, the material later added to the original parable has been omitted:

> A man planted a vineyard . . . and let it out to tenants, and went into another country. When the time came, he

> sent a servant to the tenants, to get from them some of the fruit of the vineyard. And they took him and beat him, and sent him away empty-handed.
>
> Again he sent to them another servant, and they wounded him in the head, and treated him shamefully. And he sent another, and him they killed . . .
>
> He had still one other. . . . Finally, he sent him to them . . . But those tenants said to one another, " . . . Come, let us kill him . . . And they took him and killed him, and cast him out of the vineyard. What will the owner of the vineyard do? (Mk 12:1a,2-9a)

In its original form, this parable was an eschatological warning to the chief priests (the tenants) who were plotting to do violence to the last of the prophets (the servants) sent to them seeking the faith and obedience owed to Israel's covenant God (the owner of the vineyard). It was probably Mark who later read the church's understanding of Jesus' secret Messiahship into the original parable by adding *phrases* near its beginning and its end, and *entire verses* after Jesus' concluding question. Mark's additions to the original conclusion are indicated in brackets below:

> He had still one other, [a beloved son]. Finally, he sent him to them [saying, "They will respect my son"]. But those tenants said to one another, ["This is the heir;] come, let us kill him [and the inheritance will be ours]. And they took him and killed him, and cast him out of the vineyard. What will the owner of the vineyard do?
>
> [He will come and destroy the tenants, and give the vineyard to others. Have you not read this scripture:
>
>> The very stone which the builders rejected has become the head of the corner; this was the Lord's doing, and it is marvelous in our eyes?] (Mk 12:6-11)

3

The Gospel of Mark relates that when the Last Supper began, Jesus took a loaf of bread, offered a blessing over it, and broke it in pieces. He then passed the broken pieces to his disciples and spoke a word which assigned special significance to the bread:

> And as they were eating, he took bread, and blessed, and broke it, and gave it to them, and said, "Take; this is my body." (Mk 14:22)

Mark's account of the Supper (c. A.D. 70) gives the impression that the cup of wine was blessed immediately after the bread. But Paul's much earlier account of the Supper (c. A.D. 55) found in 1 Cor 11:23-25 remembers that Jesus blessed the cup "after supper" (11:25). The Pauline text indicates that the Supper was probably eaten *between* the customary blessing of bread at the beginning of a formal Jewish meal and the customary cup of blessing at its conclusion. The tradition cited by Paul is more likely to be historically correct.

By the time Mark wrote his account, his church had placed the bread and cup sayings side by side for the sake of greater liturgical symmetry and solemnity (liturgy means the public worship of a faith community):

> And he took a cup, and when he had given thanks he gave it to them and they all drank of it. And he said to them, "This is my blood of the covenant, which is poured out for many." (Mk 14:23-24)

Contemporary scholarship tells us that the bread and cup sayings found in the Last Supper accounts were *expanded* by the early church in order to express her understanding of the *deeper meaning* and intent of Jesus' original sayings. The word "take" in Mark's bread saying was probably added by the church as a liturgical directive. The words "of the covenant" found in Mark's cup saying are taken from Ex 24:8 where Moses is described as ratifying the Old Covenant with sacrificial blood ("Behold the blood of the covenant"). The words of Moses from Exodus were added to the words of Jesus in Mark's cup saying to liken Jesus to Moses, and to suggest that Jesus has inaugurated a New Covenant by the sacrificial blood of his death.

The additional words in Mark's cup saying, "poured out for many," are an allusion to Is 53:12 where God's servant is said to give his life "for many." These words are meant to imply midrashically that the rejection and sufferings of Jesus were foreshadowed by the sufferings of God's "servant" (Is 53:4-12).

4

It is likely that the *unembellished* bread and cup sayings actually spoken by Jesus were quite brief. Rudolph Bultmann observed that the earliest form of the sayings is found in the Eucharistic tradition cited by Justin the Martyr in his *Apology* to the Roman emperor Antoninus Pius. Justin, in the course of exonerating Christian beliefs and practices, describes the Eucharistic Memorial celebrated by his church c. A.D. 150:

> The apostles in their memoirs, which are called Gospels, have handed down what Jesus ordered them to do; that he took bread and, after giving thanks, said, "Do this in memory of me; this is my body." In like manner, he took also the cup, giving thanks, and said, "This is my blood;" and to them only did he give it. (Apology I, 66:3-4)

In Justin's Eucharistic account, the actual bread and cup sayings are spare ("This is my body;" "This is my blood"). No additional words of interpretation have been joined *directly* to the sayings which he quotes. It is instructive to note that it is precisely the bread and cup words cited by Justin that are present in all four of the New Testament's Last Supper accounts (1 Cor 11:23-25; Mk 14:22-24; Mt 26:26-28; Lk 22:19-20). But the words in these accounts *beyond* those cited by Justin differ considerably from account to account and are midrashic quotations from or allusions to various Old Testament scriptures.

We can easily see why the early church would have expanded the original sayings of Jesus to express her understanding of their deeper significance. But it is highly unlikely that a *number* of words actually spoken by Jesus with reference to the bread and cup would have been *eliminated* in favor of brevity. Any memory cherished by a faith community is usually expanded over time rather than abbreviated. (It is possible that Justin's tradition might have eliminated *one* nontheological term, cup, from the cup saying for the sake of greater liturgical symmetry.)

It is apparent from Justin's *total* explanation of the Eucharist (not quoted above) that the bread and cup sayings he cites have become "words of institution" possessing sacramental and atoning significance for him and his church. But that significance derives from the theological and liturgical *context* in which his tradition has subsequently enshrined the sayings and not from the sayings themselves. We will see below that the sayings probably meant something quite different in their original setting.

5

The words joined to the bread and cup sayings of Jesus by the early church imply that at the Last Supper Jesus "instituted" the sacrament of the Lord's Supper as a memorial of his *vicariously atoning death.* But we learned in chapter one that the vicarious atonement theology in the New Testament represents a later apologetic interpretation of Jesus' tragic death which was not part of Jesus' self-understanding. And the command to keep the memory of Jesus' Supper (1 Cor 11:24b,25b; Lk 22:19b) is an allusion to Ex 13:3,9-10.

Moreover, a careful reading of the evidence indicates that originally the Lord's Supper commemorated Jesus' *Resurrection* and eagerly anticipated his expected return in glory. It was the Risen Jesus who called this Resurrection celebration into being when he appeared to "the Twelve" (1 Cor 15:5), probably while they were at table eating a meal of bread and broiled fish (Lk 24:41-42; Acts 10:41; Jn 21:9-10,12; Ps Mk 16:14a). Accordingly, the church chose Sunday (the day when Jesus' empty tomb was discovered) as the appropriate day to celebrate the Supper.

Nevertheless, even though Jesus did not think of his death as vicarious atonement, and did not intend to institute the sacrament of the Lord's Supper at the Last Supper, that does not justify the conclusion that *all* the words spoken by Jesus over the bread and cup at the Last Supper are later theological inventions. Paul the apostle maintains emphatically that the Last Supper tradition which he taught the Corinthian church derived ultimately "from the Lord":

> For I received *from the Lord* what I also delivered to you, that the Lord Jesus on the night when he was betrayed took bread, and when he had given thanks, he said, "This is my body." (1 Cor 11:23-24a)

It is reasonable to infer, therefore, that underlying the Supper tradition recalled by Paul is an authentic core of words spoken by Jesus himself. Yet, if Jesus did not intend to institute the sacrament of the Lord's Supper at the Last Supper, what did he mean by the brief words which he probably did speak over the bread and cup?

When Jesus made his figurative references to the broken bread (at the beginning of the Supper) and the cup of wine (at its conclusion), he was probably alluding with anxious foreboding to the outcome of his imminent betrayal. The physical act of "breaking" the bread would have suggested the physical force with which his enemies would soon come and seize him to either stone or crucify him.

Jesus probably anticipated that he might be stoned by the hostile priestly authorities (Lev 24:15-16; cp. 1 Kgs 21:13; Acts 7:11,58; Ant. 20:200) for having purportedly "violated" the sanctity of the temple by his angry cleansing gesture. However, it is conceivable that Jesus also saw the possibility of his being crucified by the Romans. We have no way of knowing if he had been warned that the chief priests intended to hand him over to the Roman prefect. In either case, Jesus probably perceived the broken bread ("This is my body") and poured-out wine ("This is my blood") as signs of his approaching death when his body would be broken (or torn) and his lifeblood poured out.

By his brief reference to the broken bread and poured-out wine, Jesus was probably anticipating his tragic prophetic destiny already suggested by the fate of his predecessor, John the Baptizer. This reading is corroborated by the eschatological saying about wine also spoken by Jesus at the Last Supper (probably following the cup saying):

> Truly I say to you, I will not drink again of the fruit of the vine until that day when I drink it new in the kingdom of God. (Mk 14:25)

We observed earlier that it was Jesus' anticipation of *being separated* from his disciples by impending death which prompted him to say he would not drink wine again until he drank it with them at the eschatological Supper in God's approaching Kingdom.

The substance of Jesus' saying in Mk 14:25 is probably authentic because it indicates that Jesus expected to be raised at the General Resurrection when the Kingdom of God arrived as a *collective* phenomenon. This means that Jesus did not anticipate that he would be raised *individually* by God before the world's end. It also means that Jesus was just as surprised as his disciples to learn that God had "raised" him before the Kingdom of God arrived.

In reality, Jesus saw the "Twelve" again, not at the Great Supper to come in the Kingdom, but when he appeared to them in Galilee while they were at table. It was their stunning encounter with the Risen Jesus which led the Twelve to realize that Jesus was encouraging them to return to the celebration of his Kingdom-anticipating Supper with new revelatory certainty. If the early church had created Mk 14:25 for theological reasons, it would not contain the telltale discrepancy just noted.

6

Traditional Jewish repugnance at the thought of drinking blood does not rule out the likelihood that Jesus spoke *figuratively* of wine as his blood at the Last Supper. On the contrary, the very strength of the Jewish blood taboo requires us to conclude that without the authority of an actual saying of Jesus the earliest (Jewish Christian) church would never have preserved, let alone have invented, such a difficult saying. We can tell from the historical implications of Jn 6:53-56,60,66 that the memory and interpretation of Jesus' cup saying caused the early church more problems than it solved:

> So Jesus said to them, "Truly, truly, I say to you, unless you eat the flesh of the Son of Man and drink his blood, you have no life in you . . . " (Jn 6:53)
>
> Many of his disciples, when they heard it, said, "This is a hard saying; who can listen to it?" (Jn 6:60)
>
> After this many of his disciples drew back and no longer went about with him. (Jn 6:66)

It was probably Mark's anxiety about the blood taboo that moved him to relate reassuringly that the disciples had drunk from the cup *before* Jesus spoke the cup word at the Supper (14:23). Also, Mark's assurance that *all* the disciples drank from the cup, as well as Matthew's sternly inclusive directive preceding the cup saying ("Drink from it, *all* of you," 26:27b), were probably meant to dissuade the disaffected from avoiding the cup.

Ancient Israel had decided well before Jesus that in a clearly "figurative" context wine and blood could be likened metaphorically:

Gen 49:10-11

> Binding his foal to the vine and his ass's colt to the choice vine, he washes his garments in the blood of grapes.

Deut 32:14c

> Curds from the herd, and milk from the flock . . . and of the blood of the grape you drank wine.

And if it be objected that the Judaism which emerged after the exile would no longer have tolerated such a comparison, we can point to the very late book of Sirach (c. 130 B.C.) wherein wine is still referred to as "the blood of the grape":

> He reached out his hand to the cup and poured a libation of the blood of the grape. (Sir 50:15b)

It might be further objected that the texts just cited compare wine to blood in general and not to that of any individual. But appealing to this distinction merely confirms that while Jesus' use of the comparison was unusual (as befitted the unusual circumstances), the comparison itself was not unacceptable.

7

The process by which the "Last Supper" came to be regarded as the occasion when the "Lord's Supper" was instituted involved several complex stages. For about the first decade, the Lord's Supper was exclusively a celebration of Jesus' Resurrection and a joyful anticipation of his expected return on Resurrection Day. We noted above that when the Risen Jesus appeared to the "Twelve" while they were at table eating a meal of broiled fish, they understood that he was encouraging them to return to the celebration of his Kingdom-anticipating Supper with new revelatory certainty. For that reason the apostolic church chose Sunday, not Friday, as the appropriate day for celebrating the Risen Lord's Supper.

Eventually, however, in order to encourage the huge influx of Gentile converts to practice appropriate self-control and sobriety at the Lord's Supper (where wine was a sacred symbol of the eschatological joy caused by the foretaste of the Spirit; see 1 Cor 11:17-29), the church decided that the Passion Memorial, which recalled the solemn and sobering memory of Jesus' obedience unto death, should be joined to her joyous weekly memorial of Jesus' Resurrection.

Initially, the memory of the *Last* Supper was commemorated by Jesus' disciples only once a year at the (Jewish Christian) Passover observance. The first Christians were Jews who remembered that Jesus and his disciples had eaten the Last Supper the night before his tragic death on Good Friday. And Good Friday occurred that year either on the day before or the day of Passover (probably the former).

A midrashic connection was quickly perceived by the earliest Jewish Christians between the Passover "lamb" and the servant of God who is led "like a lamb" to the slaughter (Is 53:7). When they commemorated the Passover each year, therefore, they saw the sacrificial lamb whose blood had saved Israel from death in Egypt as prefiguring the death of Jesus. Accordingly, they integrated the solemn memory of the Last Supper which had preceded Jesus' death on or just before Passover into their yearly observance of the Passover ritual.

This annual Jewish Christian Passover observance became the occasion when the brief bread and cup sayings of Jesus at the Last Supper were theologically expanded and given "sacrificial" and "atoning" significance. The bread, wine, and lamb of the Passover ritual were identified with the bread and wine of the Last Supper of Jesus, "the Lamb of God" (Jn 1:29,36). Paul the apostle was probably citing material which originated in the Jewish Christian Passover observance when he declared in 1 Cor 5:7, "Christ our Passover lamb has been sacrificed."

It was, then, this annual Passion memorial which was eventually joined to the eschatological celebration of the Lord's Supper. After this joining, the church began to teach that Jesus had "instituted" the Lord's Supper at the *Last Supper.* By so doing, the church was legitimating her decision to combine the two originally distinct memorials. She was sincerely convinced that her pastoral decision to do so was something Jesus must have foreseen and foreintended at the Last Supper.

The early church's precritical manner of interpreting the Supper's history may strike us as dishonest, but if we understand it correctly, it is not. Her way of interpreting the complex history of Jesus' Supper would have seemed fully legitimate and necessary had we lived in her historical and pastoral circumstances. (For a lengthier explanation of the complex origin of the Lord's Supper see *Exploring the Evolution of the Lord's Supper in the New Testament,* in this series.)

8

When the Last Supper was concluded, Jesus and his disciples went to the garden of Gethsemane on the Mount of Olives to spend the night:

> And they went to a place which was called Gethsemane; and he said to his disciples, "Sit here while I pray." (Mk 14:32)

In the original form of the Gethsemane story known to Mark, Jesus probably left all his disciples to sleep while he prayed a short distance away. Mark, however, expanded the original story by telling us that Jesus took Peter, James, and John with him to watch and pray. But the hour being late and their eyes heavy, they, like the other disciples, fell asleep. This change in the story was made by Mark to illustrate the spiritual blindness of the disciples before Easter:

According to Mark, "Peter, James, and John" had only recently received an extroardinary revelation on the Mount of Transfiguration (Mk 9:2-8). This revelation confirmed the private instruction Jesus had already given them concerning the secret nature of his Messiahship (Mk 8:31; 9:31; 10:33-34). Ironically, Mark suggests, the tragic drama of the Messianic Secret for which Jesus had tried to prepare his disciples (especially Peter, James, and John) was beginning to unfold before their eyes, but Jesus' instruction continued to elude them.

The synoptic tradition relates that Jesus, while in the garden, prayed in a state of distress over his approaching passion. (The Gospel of John, to the contrary, never allows Jesus to suffer any loss of majesty; see Jn 18:1-11.) Mark describes Jesus' agony as follows:

> And he said to them, "My soul is very sorrowful, even to death; remain here and watch." And going a little farther, he fell on the ground and prayed that, if it were possible, the hour might pass from him.
>
> And he said, "Abba, Father, all things are possible to you; remove this cup from me; yet not what I will, but what you will." (Mk 14:34-36)

Contemporary scholarship reminds us, however, that since Jesus probably prayed silently, and even Mark reports that the disciples were asleep (14:37,40-41), we should probably assume that Jesus' prayer in the garden was composed by the early church (probably Mark) and placed on Jesus' lips. The prayer was meant to serve an exemplary and apologetic purpose; it was fashioned with words taken from several sources:

The *first* source was the church's memory of the way Jesus himself had taught her to pray ("Father," "your will be done," "keep us from temptation," "deliver us from evil"). The *second* source was the language of a suffering righteous man in several psalms which the church believed foreshadowed Jesus' Messianic sufferings. The church used these psalms apologetically to defend her faith in a rejected and crucified Messiah; she also wished to suggest that Jesus knew these psalms presaged his secret destiny:

Ps 116:3-4

> The snares of death encompassed me; the pangs of Sheol laid hold on me; I suffered distress and anguish. Then I called on the name of the Lord: O Lord, I beseech you, save my life!"

Ps 116:8,10-11

> For you have delivered my soul from death, my feet from stumbling . . . I kept my faith even when I said, "I am greatly afflicted"; I said in my consternation, "Men are all a vain hope."

Ps 42:5

> Why are you cast down, O my soul, and why are you disquieted within me? Hope in God; for I shall again praise him, my help and my God.

Ps 43:1-2

> Vindicate me, O God, and defend my cause against an ungodly people; from deceitful and unjust men deliver me! For you are the God in whom I take refuge; why do you cast me off? Why do I go mourning because of the oppression of the enemy?

Ps 43:5

> Why are you cast down, O my soul, and why are you disquieted within me? Hope in God; for I shall again praise him, my help and my God.

9

Jesus' prayer in the garden was interrupted, Mark tells us, by the arrival of those sent by the chief priests to arrest him:

> Judas came, one of the twelve, and with him a crowd with swords and clubs from the chief priests and the scribes and the elders. Now the betrayer had given them a sign saying, "The one I shall kiss is the man; seize him and lead him away safely."
>
> And when he came, he went up to him at once, and he said, "Master!" And he kissed him. And they laid hands upon him and seized him. (Mk 14:43b-46)

It was customary in Jesus' society for disciples to greet their teachers with a respectful kiss. Nevertheless, it seems very unlikely that Judas, accompanied as he was by an armed crowd bent on seizing Jesus, would have actually bestowed an affectionate kiss on Jesus. (The Greek indicates that the kiss was given with more than ordinary feeling.) Our suspicion is encouraged by the absence of any mention of the traitor's kiss in the Gospel of John. Judas' "kiss," therefore, was probably added to the memory of Jesus' betrayal to indicate apologetically that Judas' heinous deed was portended in the scriptures as part of God's secret Messianic purpose:

> Profuse are the kisses of an enemy. (Prov 27:6)

Mark's narrative next recounts that someone standing by who was apparently sympathetic to Jesus drew a sword and attempted to defend him:

> But one of those who stood by drew his sword, and struck the slave of the high priest and cut off his ear. (Mk 14:47)

The substance of this report is probably reliable since it lends no discernible theological lesson to the narrative. Early Christian tradition increasingly felt the need to identify Mark's anonymous sword-wielder as one of the disciples. Matthew (26:51) and Luke (22:49-50) later described him as such, and the Fourth Gospel went the final step by identifying the disciple as Peter (Jn 18:10).

A number of explanations have been offered as to why the person who drew his sword was not named in the earliest tradition: (1) This person was not a disciple but a sympathetic bystander whose name was unknown to the church. (2) This person was a disciple who was left unnamed to prevent the authorities, Jewish and Roman, from learning his identity. (3) This person was a disciple but was cloaked in anonymity to prevent the impression that Christians are violent lawbreakers. (4) This person was a disciple but the church no longer remembered his name. (5) This person was invented by the early church to compensate for the failure of the disciples to defend Jesus.

The fifth possibility does not seem likely, for if the church had invented the story for the reason suggested, she surely would have named one of the disciples as the defender of Jesus. The fourth possibility also seems unlikely, for a disciple who had attempted to defend Jesus would have attained a certain measure of celebrity in the earliest church despite the rebukes he later received in Mt 26:52, Lk 22:51, and Jn 18:11. (There is no reprimand of the sword-wielder in Mark's account of the incident.) As to the remaining options, we have no way of knowing which of them might be correct.

Unless the sword-wielder escaped into the night during the confusion of the arrest, it is difficult to imagine that he could have cut off the ear of one of the arresting party without being seized and severely punished. We must consequently reckon with the possibility that an original "cut" inflicted on the ear of the high priest's servant was hyperbolized by a folk historian into the cutting off of an entire ear.

10

Exegetes observe that the words spoken by Jesus to those arresting him seem to be addressed to the temple authorities. It is reasonably certain, however, that the authorities had not come with the crowd which they sent to seize Jesus. This discrepancy indicates that Jesus' words to his apprehenders are theological, not historical. That impression is strengthened by Jesus' suggestion that his tragic fate is *foreshadowed in the scriptures.* The conviction that the history of Jesus was prefigured in the scriptures probably originated with the apologetic concerns of the early church, not Jesus:

> Have you come out as against a robber with swords and clubs to seize me? Day after day I was with you in the temple teaching, and you did not seize me. But let the scriptures be fulfilled. (Mk 14:48-49)

Mark then relates starkly that when the disciples perceived that Jesus had been seized and bound:

> they all abandoned him and fled. (Mk 14:50)

Where did the disciples go in their panic? We are never told. But since the Risen Jesus appeared to them a short time later in Galilee (Mk 16:7; Mt 28:16; Jn 21:1-12), it is reasonable to surmise that they left Jerusalem that very night and hurried back to the relative security of Galilee. All four Gospels, however, relate that Simon Peter overcame his initial fear and followed Jesus into the courtyard of the high priest to learn what would happen to Jesus:

> Peter had followed him at a distance, right into the courtyard of the high priest; and he was sitting with the guards, and warming himself at the fire. (Mk 14:54)

We have to assume, however, that people could not walk into the courtyard of the high priest's residence at will. How did Peter, therefore, manage to gain entrance? Perhaps the Fourth Gospel is reliable when it informs us that a disciple of Jesus who was known to the high priest and his portress vouched for Peter and brought him inside:

> Peter stood outside at the door. So the other disciple, who was known to the high priest, went out and spoke to the maid who kept the door, and brought Peter in. (Jn 18:16)

Once Peter was inside the courtyard, his atypical presence would have invited scrutiny. In addition to his rustic attire, his Galilean accent would have attested that he was a provincial:

> One of the maids of the high priest came and seeing Peter warming himself, she looked at him and said, "You also were with the Nazarene, Jesus." But he denied it saying, "I neither know nor understand what you mean." And he went out into the gateway.
>
> And the maid saw him, and began again to say to the bystanders, "This man is one of them." But again he denied it. (Mk 14:66-69)

Then follows the conclusion of the story of Peter's triple denial of Jesus. It is probable that this account is basically historical, for the early church is not likely to have created a story which presents Peter, the Rock, in such an unfavorable light. We are told that after Peter's third denial, he heard a cock crow and remembered the prediction spoken to him earlier by Jesus, either during (Jn 13:36-38) or shortly after the Last Supper:

> And Jesus said to them, "You will all fall away. . . . Peter said to him, "Even though they all fall away, I will not." And Jesus said to him, "Truly I say to you, this very night, before the cock crows twice, you will deny me three times." (Mk 14:27a,29-30)

The substance of Jesus' prediction is probably authentic but has been expanded in folk fashion with "details remembered after the fact." Jesus, having been forewarned by someone of his impending betrayal, probably told his disciples that he knew they would be frightened and flee when his enemies came for him that night. It was then that Simon Peter would have insisted that, come what may, he would not abandon Jesus.

Jesus probably responded by predicting that Peter also would abandon him before cock crow, i.e., morning. (Only in

Mark's account does Jesus predict that Peter will deny him after the cock crows "twice.") Jesus' prediction was not based on divinely dictated information but on (1) the forewarning he had probably received about his betrayal, (2) his knowledge of human nature in general, and (3) his knowledge of Peter's personality in particular. Jesus' original prediction, therefore, probably took a form much like the following:

> Truly I say to you, this very night, before the cock crows, you also will deny me.

Mark's narrative informs us that the curiosity prompted by Peter's presence in the high priest's courtyard did not abate after the probing by the persistent maid:

> And after a little while again the bystanders said to Peter, "Certainly you are one of them; for you are a Galilean." But he began to invoke a curse on himself and to swear, "I do not know this man of whom you speak."
>
> And immediately the cock crowed a second time. And Peter remembered how Jesus had said to him, "Before the cock crows twice, you will deny me three times." And he broke down and wept. (Mk 14:70b-72)

When Peter heard the cock crow he remembered Jesus' words and experienced deep shame and remorse. When Peter later told how he had cravenly fulfilled Jesus' prediction, the church learned the specific details (three denials by the time of cock crow, or possibly a second cock crow) from Peter. When the church later recounted Peter's story she sincerely, but mistakenly, assumed that Jesus had foreseen the story's specific details when he made his general prediction. (Mark and his church believed that God had revealed the *entire* Messianic Secret to Jesus at his baptism.)

What did Peter do after he recovered from his poignant recollection? The Gospels give us no answer. But they also give no indication that Peter was present the next day at Jesus' crucifixion or burial. It is fair to surmise, therefore, that Peter also left Jerusalem before dawn, if not immediately after his breakdown, and returned in fear and shame to Galilee.

Questions for Review and Discussion

1. Why was the Last Supper which Jesus ate with his disciples decidedly atypical?
2. Why did the chief priests prefer to seize Jesus by night?
3. How did the early church explain Jesus' tragic choice of Judas the traitor?
4. Did Judas literally agree to betray Jesus for "thirty pieces of silver"? Explain your answer.
5. How did the parable of the evil tenants, probably spoken by Jesus during Holy Week, differ from the early church's expanded version?
6. What did Jesus probably mean by the brief bread and cup sayings which he spoke at the Last Supper?
7. What is the chief indication that Jesus did not think his death was required by God as substitutional payment for the sins of all other humans?
8. How do we account historically for the words at the Last Supper which assign vicarious atoning power to Jesus death?
9. How did the observance of the Last Supper differ from the celebration of the Lord's Supper in the "earliest" church?
10. Is it probable that Judas actually betrayed Jesus with an affectionate kiss? Explain your answer.
11. Did Jesus actually suggest to those who arrested him that the scriptures which foreshadowed his betrayal, sufferings, and death were being fulfilled by their actions? Explain your answer.
12. Did Jesus actually predict all the specific details in Mark's account of Peter's denial? Explain your answer.

Chapter Nine: Jesus' Trial and Condemnation

1

JESUS IS REMEMBERED IN THE SYNOPTIC GOSPELS AS HAVING responded on three different occasions to the use made by others of the title Messiah. The first of these occasions is reported by Mark as having taken place at Caesarea Philippi (Mk 8:27): Jesus asked his disciples privately who they thought he was, and Peter replied, "You are the Messiah" (8:29). On the other two occasions, Jesus was asked, first by the Jewish high priest Caiaphas (Mk 14:61), and later by the Roman prefect Pontius Pilate (Mk 15:2), if Jesus thought he was Israel's expected Messiah.

As we proceed we will see that there is an instructive complimentarity between the negative response which Jesus gave to Simon Peter (Get behind me, Satan!) and the noncommital answer which Jesus probably gave to his two interrogators during his passion. It will facilitate our purpose, therefore, if we digress briefly from this chapter's stated agenda and begin with the first of these three incidents, the one involving Simon Peter. Since Mark wrote first, and both Matthew and Luke used and modified his account, we will work with Mark's version of the story:

> [27]And Jesus went on with his disciples to the villages of Caesarea Philippi; and on the way he asked his disciples, "Who do men say that I am?" [28]And they told him, "John the Baptizer; and others say, Elijah; and others one of the prophets." [29]And he asked them, "But who do you say that I am?" Peter answered him, "You are the Messiah."
>
> [30]And he charged them to tell no one about him. [31]And he began to teach them that the Son of Man must suffer many things, and be rejected by the elders and the chief priests and the scribes, and be killed, and after three days rise again. [32]And he said this plainly. And Peter took him and began to rebuke him.
>
> [33]But turning and seeing his disciples, he rebuked Peter, and said, "Get behind me, Satan! For you are not on the side of God, but of men." (Mk 8:27-33)

The traditional exegesis of this narrative reads the text uncritically and concludes that Jesus accepted Peter's confession but ordered Peter and the others to keep his Messiahship a *secret.* Jesus then informed his disciples that he was destined to exercise his Messianic office in a mysterious and unexpected manner: he must accept rejection and death before rising after three days as the exalted Son of Man-Messiah.

Critical scholarship tells us, however, that the account of Jesus' response to Peter's confession which we find in Mark probably has been theologically modified. Jesus' original response to Peter's confession in Mk 8:29 is preserved not in 8:30-31, but in 8:33. For if we move directly from 8:29 to 8:33, we obtain a more logical sequence which better accounts for the vehemence of Jesus' negative response in 8:33. This shorter account accords better with Jesus' refusal to discuss the title with Caiaphas and Pilate. It also eliminates the unlikelihood of Peter having rebuked Jesus. The *original* account of the exchange between Jesus and Peter was probably remembered substantially as follows:

> And he asked them, "But who do you say that I am?" Peter answered him, "You are the Messiah." But turning and seeing his disciples, he rebuked Peter and said, "Get behind me, Satan! For you are not on the side of God, but of men." (Mk 8:29,33)

This more likely recounting indicates that Jesus responded directly to Peter's attribution of Messiahship by harshly rebuking him: "Get behind me, Satan!" (See the temptation to embrace political Messiahship suggested to Jesus by "Satan" in Mt 4:8-10; Lk 4:5-7, and notice Jesus' similar reply, "Begone Satan!") It was probably Mark who added verses 30-32 to the original story in order to use his Messianic Secret theology to explain Jesus' negative response to Peter's answer.

The interpretation just presented seems probable for a number of reasons, but we will consider only two: First, the title Messiah is used by Jesus in the Gospels in six different sayings: Mk 9:41; 12:35 (repeated in Mt 22:42; Lk 20:40); 13:21 (repeated in Mt 24:23); Mt 16:20; 23:10; 24:5. However, in only two of these six sayings (Mk 9:41; Mt 23:10) is the title used with clear approval. And Mark and Matthew probably placed these two sayings on Jesus' lips to express the church's faith in his Messiahship. As already noted in chapter four, Jesus evidently shunned the (military) title Messiah, and preferred the (nonmilitary) title Son of Man.

Second, the teaching in Mk 8:30-31 about the hidden and unexpected nature of Jesus' Messiahship has the characteristics of Mark's Messianic Secret theology. Since Mark joined elements of this theology to a number of other stories in his Gospel, these elements are easily detected and compared by exegetes (e.g. Mk 1:34; 3:11-12; 8:30; 9:9; 9:30-32; 10:32-34; 16:8).

Mark and others in the early church would have been perplexed by the memory that Jesus had responded so *disapprovingly* when Peter confessed his belief in Jesus' Messiahship. For they were convinced that the prophetic promises of a Davidic Messiah had to be fulfilled, and they believed that Jesus was descended from King David (Rom 1:3; Mt 1:1-17; Lk 3:23-38).

They concluded, therefore, that God had revealed the Risen Jesus to them as the promised Davidic Messiah (Acts 2:32-33). Why, then, had Jesus refused to accept the title Messiah from Peter (Mk 8:33) or to discuss it with the high priest (Mt 26:63-64; Lk 22:67-69) or the Roman prefect (Mk 15:2-5; Mt 27:11; Lk 23:3)?

Mark realized, of course, that Jesus had turned out to be a completely unexpected kind of Messiah, a *spiritual* Messiah, not the invincible *military* Messiah of popular expectation. But Mark assumed that Jesus, since he is the greatest of God's prophets, had been secretly informed by God of the hidden nature of his Messiahship.

> Surely the Lord God does nothing, without revealing *his secret* to his servants the prophets. (Amos 3:7)

For this reason, Mark relates that God "opened" the heavens and revealed the Messianic Secret to Jesus on the occasion of his Baptism-anointing by John (see the following midrashic sources of God's revealing voice: Ps 2:7; Gen 22:2; Is 42:1):

> In those days Jesus came from Nazareth of Galilee and was baptized by John in the Jordan. And when he came up out of the water, immediately he saw the heavens torn open and the Spirit descending upon him like a dove; and a voice came from heaven, "You are my beloved Son; with you I am well pleased." (Mk 1:9-11)

Mark assumed, therefore, that Jesus had been secretly anointed as a *spiritual* Messiah and that Jesus knew he was destined in God's hidden purpose to undergo tragic rejection and death (like the mysterious "servant" of God in Is 52:13-53:12 and the suffering righteous one in Ps 22; see Mark 10:45 and 15:24,34). In addition, Mark thought Jesus knew that after his death, he would be raised as the exalted Son of Man alluded to in Dan 7:13-14 and would soon return as God's glorious Son of Man-Messiah to conclude history (Mk 14:62).

(Some scholars object that the "Son of Man" spoken of in Dan 7:13-14 is not an individual but an eschatological figure who represents the Jewish people collectively. But even if that oversimplified opinion were true, it would not have been evident to the Christians in the earliest church who read scripture precritically and midrashed "atomistically," i.e., they ignored the *context* in which they found an appropriate midrashic text.)

It was Mark's judgment, accordingly, that Jesus had responded harshly to Peter at Caesarea Philippi because Jesus knew that Peter expected him to be the *military* Messiah of popular hope rather than the Messiah destined by God for rejection and crucifixion before his exaltation. Jesus must have understood, Mark concluded, that his disciples would not be able to grasp the true nature of his Messiahship until that Secret was *fully* disclosed by the *spiritual* victory of his Resurrection (Mk 9:9-10.) It was for this reason, Mark implied, that Jesus avoided the title Messiah during his public mission.

In effect, Mark and other teachers before him in the early church were compelled by the tragic and unexpected developments in the history of Jesus to *redefine* the title Messiah and make it compatible with that history. Only in this fashion could the title be retained and assigned to the Risen Jesus, to whom they knew it mysteriously belonged. Mark then assumed that the new meaning which he and others had assigned to the title was present in the mind of Jesus throughout Jesus' public mission. Understandably, this "redefining" of the title Messiah by Christians led to fierce debates with the Jews.

The ideas reviewed above should help us see that the teaching of Jesus in Mk 8:30-31 about the secret (8:30) and unexpected (8:31) nature of his Messiahship was probably added to the original story of Peter's confession by Mark. Mark sincerely believed that the ideas he attributed to Jesus in 8:30-31 were the ideas that motivated Jesus when he rebuked Peter.

Contemporary scholarship concludes that Mark's Messianic Secret theology contains a fundamental insight that is correct and profoundly significant for Christian faith. But it also contains an assumption which is historically conditioned and mistaken. His *correct insight* is that God truly had destined Jesus for a mysterious and exalted Messiahship which was contrary to ancient Jewish expectation, and that God's purpose would only be understood after Jesus' death and Resurrection.

Mark's *mistaken assumption* is that Jesus, because he is God's definitive eschatological prophet, knew all about God's secret Messianic purpose for him from the time of his Baptism. In actuality, the only one who understood God's secret Messianic purpose throughout Jesus' public ministry was *God.*

Because of Jesus' total commitment to the will of God, Jesus was certainly open throughout his prophetic ministry to whatever additional office God would eventually call him. The evidence indicates, however, that God did not reveal the Messianic Secret to Jesus till the time of Jesus' Resurrection.

If we are troubled by the view Jesus did not know he was God's Messiah before his Resurrection, we should ask ourselves (with encouragement from William James) what difference it truly makes if Jesus did not learn about his Messianic office until *after* he had faithfully fulfilled its unexpected requirements.

Mark, of course, should not be faulted for having unwittingly woven mistaken assumptions into his sacred history of Jesus. Mark honestly did the best job of explaining the data that he was capable of at his time in history. As for God's view of this matter, God knew that the future, with its inevitable increase in knowledge, would teach us to winnow Mark's mistaken assumptions from his correct insights.

2

The Synoptic Gospels relate that after Jesus was seized on the Mount of Olives, he was formally brought to trial before the high priest's council (Mk 14:53) and then before the Roman prefect, Pontius Pilate (Mk 15:1). On both these occasions, we are told, Jesus was found deserving of death (Mk 14:64; 15:15). The Fourth Gospel agrees that Jesus was tried before the Roman prefect and questioned by the Jewish high priest. It knows nothing, however, of a *formal Jewish trial:*

> So the band of soldiers and their captain . . . seized Jesus and bound him. First they led him to Annas; for he was the father-in-law of Caiaphas, who was high priest that year. (Jn 18:12-13)
>
> The high priest [Annas had formerly been the high priest] then questioned Jesus about his disciples and his teaching. (Jn 18:19)
>
> Annas then sent him bound to Caiaphas the high priest. (Jn 18:24)
>
> Then they led Jesus from the house of Caiaphas to the praetorium. It was early. They themselves did not enter the praetorium, so that they might not be defiled, but might eat the passover. (Jn 18:28)

It is easy to see why the church, for theological reasons, would have expanded Jesus' questioning by the high priest into a formal trial before the religious leaders of the Jewish people, but not the reverse. The development of the private questioning into a formal scrutiny was probably done to conform the history of Jesus more closely to the apologetic proof text in Ps 118:22-23. This highly prized proof text justified the early church's claim that Jesus truly qualified as Israel's promised Messiah even though the religious leaders of the nation had rejected him:

> The stone which the builders rejected
> has become the head of the corner.
> This is the Lord's doing;
> it is marvelous in our eyes.

Even if one decides that Jesus was not formally tried before the high priest and a council of advisers, it remains highly likely that Jesus was privately interrogated by the high priest. The early church, however, probably did not have access to any information about this private questioning. To compensate for the gap in her knowledge, the church would have *inferred* what she thought must have happened on the basis of Jesus' trial before Pilate which took place the next morning.

The church does seem to have gained reliable information about the Roman trial. For even Mark, who has Jesus give a (theological) answer to the high priest quite different (14:51-62a) from the one we find in Matthew (26:63-64) and Luke (22:67-70), feels compelled to agree with them about Jesus' answer to Pilate (Mk 15:2; Mt 27:11; Lk 23:3). Since the church's knowledge of Jesus' response to questions about Messiahship probably derived from his Roman trial, we will reverse the order of events found in the Gospels and begin with Pilate's interrogation of Jesus instead of the high priest's.

All four of the Gospels report that when Pilate asked Jesus if Jesus was the "king" of the Jews (king was the Roman equivalent of Messiah), Jesus responded by *laconically* reminding Pilate that it was Pilate, and not Jesus, who had referred that title to Jesus (Mk 15:2; Mt 27:11; Lk 23:3; Jn 18:37). Jesus' brief and noncommital response to Pilate (*su legeis,* "The words are yours [not mine]," i.e., "You invoked that title [not I]") is exactly the same in all three Synoptic Gospels:

> And as soon as it was morning, the chief priests . . . bound Jesus and led him away and delivered him to Pilate. And Pilate asked him, "Are you the king of the Jews?" And he answered him, "You have said so." (Mk 15:1-2)

The noncommital response is easily overlooked in the Fourth Gospel's theologically expanded dialog between Jesus and Pilate, but its presence is still discernible:

> Pilate entered the praetorium again and called Jesus, and said to him, "Are you the king of the Jews?" . . . Jesus answered him, "My kingship is not of this world. . . . Pilate said to him, "So you are a king?" Jesus answered, "You say [*su legeis*] that I am a king." (Jn 18:33,36-37a)

The substance of Jesus' noncommital response is probably reliable since it disagrees with the later decision of some teachers in the early church to describe Jesus as forthrightly claiming the title Messiah (Mk 14:61-62a; Jn 4:26). We can easily see why a noncommital response was later made affirmative for theological reasons, but it is difficult to justify the opposite having occurred.

In effect, Jesus refused to discuss the title Messiah (or king). He probably avoided the title because he considered it theologically mistaken and in no way related to his proclamation of God's coming Kingdom. To Pilate, however, Jesus' noncommital response probably seemed ominous, and it was probably this perception of Pilate's which finally sealed Jesus' fate. Since Jesus would not *explicitly* deny that he was the "king" of the Jews, Pilate probably suspected him of harboring political aspirations. Jesus, he decided, would have to be executed as a possible threat to Roman authority.

This interpretation is supported by the sign Pilate placed on Jesus' cross to notify and warn the public of Jesus' crime: "The king of the Jews" (Mk 15:26; see also Mt 27:37; Lk 23:38; Jn 19:19). If the church had created the words on the sign for a theological purpose, she would have used the title "Messiah" instead of the Roman equivalent, "king."

Given the bent of all the evangelists to interpret the passion of Jesus in accordance with their own theological preferences, it is impressive and surely significant that they all agree (the Synoptics explicitly, the Fourth Gospel implicitly) about Pilate's question and Jesus' noncommital response. Their agreement about this crucial response strongly supports the essential historicity of Jesus' answer.

3

All four of the Gospels portray Pilate as unwilling (or, in Mark's case, not fully willing) to put Jesus to death because he was convinced of Jesus' innocence:

> And Pilate said to the chief priests and the multitudes, "I find no crime in this man." (Lk 23:4; see Mt 27:23; Jn 18:38; Mk 15:14)

Accordingly, we are told, Pilate tried to appeal to Jewish national pride in order to release Jesus:

> After this he went out to the Jews again, and told them, "I find no crime in him. But you have a custom that I should release one man for you at the Passover; will you have me release for you the king of the Jews?" They cried out again, "Not this man, but Barabbas!" Now Barabbas was a robber. (Jn 18:38b-40)

The Jewish crowd is portrayed as rejecting Pilate's efforts to release Jesus, and, instead, they demand the release of Barabbas, variously described as a robber (Jn 18:40), a notorious prisoner (Mt 27:16), a murderer and insurrectionist (Lk 23:27), and someone arrested in connection with murder and insurrection (Mk 15:7). Pilate, we are told, was intimidated by the mob's loud cries and granted their demand:

> So Pilate, wishing to satisfy the crowd, released for them Barabbas; and having scourged Jesus, he delivered him to be crucified. (Mk 15:15)

Historians assure us that there is no evidence whatsoever that Pilate customarily released a prisoner to the Jews at Passover. Also, the historical information that we possess about Pilate suggests that he would probably not have allowed himself to be coerced by a Jewish crowd into rendering an unwilling verdict. What the evangelists have given us, therefore, is probably a folk addition to the trial story intended to teach a religious lesson about Jesus.

In reality, the early church had practical and theological reasons for deciding to exonerate the Roman prefect and lay the blame for Jesus' death on the leaders of the Jews:

> Now the chief priests and the elders persuaded the people to ask for Barabbas and destroy Jesus. (Mt 27:20)

> So when Pilate saw that he was gaining nothing, but rather that a riot was beginning, he took water and washed his hands before the crowd, saying, "I am innocent of this man's blood, see to it yourselves." (Mt 27:24)

By exonerating the Roman governor (see Deut 21:6-8; Dan 13:46 [in Catholic Bibles; otherwise Sus 46 in the apocrypha), the early church hoped to encourage the view that Jesus was not a criminal and had been executed against Pilate's better judgment. Contrary to Jewish claims, therefore, neither Jesus nor his followers were subverters of established law and order. Also, blaming the Jewish leaders exclusively for Jesus' death enabled the church to point more emphatically to Ps 118 when accounting for Jesus' unexpected fate:

> The stone which the builders rejected has become the head of the corner. This is the the Lord's doing; it is marvelous in our eyes. (Ps 118:22-23)

In order to explain the crowd's desire to have Barabbas freed instead of Jesus, we must become a bit more speculative. Given the lack of any corroborating evidence, it is highly unlikely that this incident actually occurred as reported in the Gospels. It seems more likely that two distinct events were meshed by the early church in folk fashion to make a telling point about Jesus' undeserved execution.

Within living memory, Pilate (or possibly some other Roman governor) had probably released a notorious prisoner named Barabbas in exchange for a bribe or some political advantage. When the church remembered that Barabbas had been released, whereas Jesus had been condemned and cruelly executed, the enormity of the injustice done to Jesus was painfully evident. To vividly illustrate this injustice, the church adapted the story of Barabbas' release and combined it with that of Jesus' execution just before (or possibly on the day of) Passover.

4

Luke reports an unusual interruption of Jesus' trial before Pontius Pilate. We are told by Luke that when Pilate learned that Jesus was a Galilean, he sent Jesus to be questioned by Herod Antipas who happened to be in Jerusalem at the time. There is good reason, however, for suspecting that this story is purely theological in nature, and not historical. Only Luke reports this story; yet, had the other evangelists known of such a striking development, they would certainly have included it in their passion accounts:

> And when he learned that he belonged to Herod's jurisdiction, he sent him over to Herod, who was himself in Jerusalem at that time.
>
> When Herod saw Jesus, he was glad, for he had long desired to see him, because he had heard about him and was hoping to see some sign done by him. So he questioned him at some length; but he gave no answer. The chief priests stood by, vehemently accusing him.
>
> And Herod with his soldiers treated him with contempt and mocked him; then, arraying him with gorgeous apparel, they sent him back to Pilate. (Lk 23:8-11)

The clues necessary for interpreting this story are provided by Luke himself. In the Acts of the Apostles he indicates that the story is apologetic theology based on Ps 2. In this psalm the kings of the earth are described as conspiring against the anointed king of David's line who represents God's Kingly Reign. The desire expressed by the kings to reject God's Anointed was construed by Luke as a midrashic prefigurement of Jesus' rejection by the rulers of this world:

> Sovereign Lord . . . by the mouth of our father David, your holy servant, you said by the Holy Spirit,
>
> "Why do the nations rage,
>   and the peoples imagine vain things?
> The kings of the earth
>   set themselves in array,
> Against the Lord,
>   and against his Anointed."
>   [LXX Ps 2:1-2]
>
> For truly in this city there were gathered together against your holy servant Jesus, whom you anointed, both Herod and Pontius Pilate, with the Gentiles and the peoples of Israel, to do whatever your hand and your purpose had predestined to take place. (Acts 4:25-28)

5

We must now turn our attention to the interrogation of Jesus by the Jewish high priest. In the Synoptic accounts of the interrogation, the high priest asks Jesus specifically if Jesus is the Messiah. And it is very likely that this or a similar question was actually put to Jesus by the high priest. For the high priest would have had to determine if there was a sufficient reason for sending Jesus to Pilate for further questioning and condemnation. Since the church knew that Jesus had responded noncomitally when he was asked this question by Pilate, she probably assumed that Jesus had been asked the same question by the high priest privately and had given the same answer:

> And the high priest stood up and said, "Have you no answer to make? . . . But Jesus was silent. And the high priest said to him, "I adjure you by the living God, tell us if you are the Messiah, the Son of God." Jesus said to him, "You have said so." (Mt 26:62a,63-64a)

The Gospels call attention to Jesus' silence before his interrogators in order to liken him apologetically to the suffering servant of God in Is 53:7 and the suffering righteous man in Ps 38:12-14:

Is 53:7

> He was oppressed, and he was afflicted, yet he opened not his mouth; like a lamb that is led to the slaughter, and like a sheep that before its shearers is dumb, so he opened not his mouth.

Ps 38:12-14

> Those who seek my life lay their snares, those who seek my hurt speak of ruin, and meditate treachery all the day long.
>
> But I am like a deaf man, I do not hear, like a dumb man who does not open his mouth. Yea, I am like a man who does not hear and in whose mouth are no rebukes.

If Jesus actually gave such a noncommital answer to the high priest, it would have seemed just as suspicious to the high priest as it later did to Pilate. It would have been for that reason, therefore, that Jesus (who gathered crowds, preached a coming Kingdom, and had publicly challenged the authority of the priests) was sent to Pilate with the recommendation that Jesus be asked the same question and executed on the basis of his suspect answer.

Matthew (26:64) and Luke (22:70) decided to be consistent and relate that Jesus' reply to the high priest was "essentially" the same as the noncommital answer he was known to have given to Pilate. Only Mark tells us in 14:62 that Jesus answered the high priest's question in an affirmative and unambiguous manner (*egō eimi* = "I am"). But since Jesus is remembered as having given the noncommital response six out of seven times in the Gospels (four times to Pilate, two times to Jewish authorities) it seems likely that the one time he is presented as answering with a forthright affirmation is not history. It is probably Mark's theological interpretation of Jesus' noncommital reply.

The Messianic Secret theology which led Mark to "interpret" Jesus' puzzling response to Peter at Caesarea Philippi also led Mark to "interpret" the noncommital response Jesus was assumed (or remembered) to have made to the high priest. Mark sincerely thought that the remembered unwillingness of Jesus to discuss the title Messiah (or king) was a sign of Jesus' prophetic certainty that his interrogators were incapable of understanding that title's "secret" and "spiritual" meaning.

Jesus' decision to accept his tragic death was understood by Mark as the *beginning* of the process which Jesus knew would lead to his exaltation and the full disclosure of the Messianic Secret. Since Mark wrote his Gospel specifically to explain and defend the hidden and unexpected nature of Jesus' Messiahship, it seemed theologically fitting to Mark to present Jesus as *beginning* to reveal the Secret publicly by a "Messianic" response to the high priest's question. For that reason, the affirmative response which Mark has Jesus give to the high priest is immediately followed by a mysterious midrashic allusion (see Ps 110:1; Dan 7:13-14) to Jesus' imminent exaltation and return in glory as the *fully revealed* Son of Man-Messiah:

> Again the high priest asked him, "Are you the Messiah, the son of the Blessed One?" And Jesus said, "I am; and you will see the the Son of Man sitting at the right hand of Power, and coming with the clouds of heaven." (Mk 14:61-62)

It is important to recognize that Jesus does not *fully* reveal his secret Messianic identity to the high priest. Jesus refers only to his future exaltation and return in glory, not to his preliminary need to be rejected and die before rising (see Mk 8:31; 9:3i; 10:33-34). The portion of his secret destiny that Satan could still try to prevent is left hidden.

Mark thought that his *theological* reading of Jesus' noncommital response was fully justified by (1) the Resurrection of Jesus, (2) by Jesus' Davidic ancestry, and (3) by the midrashic portendings of Jesus' hidden Messiahship which Mark and the early church found in the scriptures. It was assumed by Mark that his interpretation merely indicated externally what Jesus must have been thinking internally when he gave his noncommital answer.

After Jesus asserted his Messiahship to the high priest in Mark's account, the high priest responded with ritual horror:

> And the high priest tore his mantle, and said, "Why do we still need witnesses? You have heard his blasphemy. What is your decision?" And they all condemned him as deserving of death. (Mk 14:63)

In itself, the implied or stated claim to be God's Messiah was not a basis for the charge of blasphemy. The charge, therefore, probably represents the horrified Jewish response to Christian claims that the ignominiously crucified Jesus is the glorious Davidic Messiah promised by God's prophets. To conservative Jews the Christian claim was probably perceived as a "blasphemous" denial of the word of God.

6

Before leaving Jesus' interrogation by the high priest, we should briefly consider the "false" charge concerning the temple that Mark reports was brought against Jesus:

> Now the chief priests and the whole council sought testimony against Jesus to put him to death; but they found none. . . . And some stood up and bore false witness against him saying, "We heard him say, 'I will destroy this temple that is made with hands, and in three days I will build another, not made with hands.'" (Mk 14:55,57-58)

When considering this accusation made against Jesus, we should keep in mind that Mark insists the charge is "false." Furthermore, it is instructive to recall that neither Luke's account of Jesus' interrogation by the chief priests (Lk 22:66-71), nor John's account of Jesus' interrogation by Annas (Jn 18:19-24) *makes any mention* of an accusation involving the temple.

Instead, Luke correctly indicates that the "false" charge against Jesus reported by Mark (and Matthew) actually originated not at the trial of Jesus, but later at Stephen's trial (which Luke was able to relate in the Acts of the Apostles). To help us make this recognition, Luke stresses the similarities between the trial of Stephen and that of Jesus as narrated by Mark:

> Then some . . . arose and disputed with Stephen. But they could not withstand the wisdom and the Spirit with which he spoke. Then they secretly instigated men who said, "We have heard him speak blasphemous words against Moses and God."
>
> And they stirred up the people and the elders and the scribes, and they came upon him and seized him and brought him before the council, and set up false witnesses who said, "This man never ceases to speak words against this holy place and the law; for we have heard him say that Jesus of Nazareth will destroy this place and

> will change the customs which Moses has delivered to us." (Acts 6:9-15)

Stephen, while debating with Greek-speaking Jews over the controversial Messiahship of Jesus, had evidently attempted to convince them that the Risen Jesus is the promised Son of David, and that, as such, he was destined by God to build a mysterious new temple. Moreover, Stephen seems to have asserted that this new temple, the faith community of Jesus, has replaced the Jerusalem temple as God's preferred dwelling place on earth (see Jn 2:19-21; 4:20-24; Acts 7:44-49).

The early church believed herself to be a living temple built by the Risen Jesus, and that Jesus himself is also this new temple's glorious cornerstone. The church's understanding of herself as a living temple built by the Risen Jesus was based on her midrashic reading of the promise God made to David through Nathan the prophet in 2 Sam 7:12-16:

> When your days are fulfilled and you lie down with your fathers, I will raise up your seed after you, who shall come forth from your body, and I will establish his kingdom. *He shall build a house for my name,* and I will establish the throne of his kingdom forever. . . . And your house and your kingdom shall be made sure forever before me; your throne shall be established forever. (2 Sam 7:12-13,16)

In this passage God promised David that one of David's sons would be "raised up" after David's death to build a temple for God. Historically, that son was Solomon. But this same prophecy also promised that one of David's sons would reign on David's throne "forever" (2 Sam 7:13,16). And since David's dynasty was swept from power at the time of the Exile (587 B.C.), the second part of the prophecy had not been fulfilled. (See also the promise of a Davidic builder of a new temple in Zech 6:12-13; the church believed that this text foreshadowed Jesus as the builder of his church.)

The church concluded, therefore, that on a deeper level 2 Sam 7:12-16 mysteriously presaged the Risen Jesus as the Son of David who was "raised up" by God to reign on David's throne "forever." It followed that the Risen Jesus was also destined to be the promised Davidic builder of a *spiritual* temple, his church (Mt 16:18; see also Mk 14:58; Jn 2:18-22). When the Risen Jesus carried out his divinely foreordained task, he made "Peter" the "rock" of this temple-church's foundation (Mt 16:18) by choosing him to be the first Resurrection witness (1 Cor 15:5; Lk 24:34):

> And I tell you, you are Peter [*Petros* = rock], and on this rock I will build my church, and the powers of death will not prevail against it. (Mt 16:18)

Eventually, the apologetic theme of Jesus as the "stone" rejected by the Jewish builders (Mk 12:10-11; Acts 4:11) was joined to the church's "new temple" theology. Jesus was then thought of as the "cornerstone" of his temple-church (1 Pet 2:4-8) in addition to being its Davidic builder. Individual Christians were thought of as "living stones" (1 Pet 2:5) built by Jesus into the temple of the church (1 Cor 3:16-17):

> Come to him, to that living stone, rejected by men but in God's sight chosen and precious; and like living stones be yourselves built into a spiritual house . . . to offer spiritual sacrifices acceptable to God through Jesus Christ. (1 Pet 2:4-5)

Judging by the specifics of the "false" testimony brought against Stephen by his accusers, he also had probably told them of Jesus' prediction that the Jerusalem temple would eventually be destroyed:

> And as he came out of the temple, one of his disciples said to him, "Look, Teacher, what wonderful stones and what wonderful buildings!" And Jesus said to him, "Do you see these great buildings? There will not be left here one stone upon another that will not be thrown down." (Mk 13:1-2)

Jesus, correctly reading the signs of the times, could probably foresee (as could others) that blind political fanaticism on the part of some Jews would lead to an uprising against Rome. When Rome then came to put down the resistance, Jesus realized, Jerusalem and the temple would tragically be destroyed (just as it had been at the time of the exile).

When Stephen informed the Jews that Jesus had predicted the temple's destruction and also that Jesus had been raised on the third day as the Davidic builder of a new temple which has replaced the old temple in God's sight, the Jews were understandably offended. In the angry debates which preceded Stephen's stoning, some of the Jews evidently misconstrued Stephen's teaching about the church as a new temple built by the Risen Jesus and Jesus' prediction of the old temple's destruction. Stephen's irate opponents then garbled his statements into the "false" accusation brought against Stephen (and Jesus) at his "trial":

> And they . . . said, "This man never ceases to speak words against this holy place and the law; for we have heard him say that Jesus of Nazareth will destroy this place and will change the customs which Moses has delivered to us." (Acts 6:12a,13b-15)

This mistaken understanding of Jesus' prediction of the temple's destruction was still circulating among Jews and generating a hostile response when Mark wrote his Gospel. Consequently, Mark introduced the mistaken interpretation into his account of Jesus' "trial" in order to repudiate it as "false" testimony brought against Jesus by some of the Jews (Mk 14:56-58).

(All of the evangelists take measures to clear Jesus of this incendiary charge: Mark, by claiming it is false [14:57-58]; Matthew by claiming Jesus only said, "I am able," not "I will" [26:61]; Luke, by explaining the "false charge" as an erroneous understanding of Stephen's teaching [Acts 6:12-14]; and John by claiming that Jesus spoke of "the temple of his body" [2:21].)

Nevertheless, even though Mark labels the mistaken words ascribed to Jesus as false, we can tell that he probably considered them *in part* to be mysteriously true. (Matthew also understands the words of the charge to be mysteriously true, so much so that he refuses to join Mark in describing them as false; Mt

26:59-61.) For although Mark knew that Jesus had never said that he himself would destroy God's temple, Mark certainly agreed with Stephen that "the Most High does not dwell in houses made with hands" (Acts 7:49), and that Jesus, therefore, had truly *replaced* the Jerusalem temple with the living temple of his church which is "not made with hands":

> And some stood up and bore false witness against him saying, "We heard him say, 'I will destroy this temple that is made with hands, and in three days I will build another, *not made with hands.*'" (Mk 14:58)

Questions for Review and Discussion

1. In the original version of the Caesarea Philippi story (Mk 8:27-33), how did Jesus probably reply when Peter said he thought Jesus was the Messiah?
2. For what reason did Jesus probably reject the title Messiah?
3. Why did Mark think that Jesus had rebuked Peter at Caesarea Philippi?
4. For what three reasons did Mark think that his Messianic Secret theology was correct and necessary?
5. When did Mark think that God had revealed the Messianic Secret to Jesus? What evidence in Mark's Gospel supports your answer?
6. What assumptions of Mark's Messianic Secret theology are true? Explain your answer.
7. What assumption of Mark's Messianic Secret theology is mistaken? Explain your answer.
8. If the high priest asked Jesus if Jesus thought he was the Messiah, did Jesus probably respond affirmatively or noncommitally? How would you justify your answer?
9. What did Mark think Jesus meant by his noncommital response to Pilate? What do you think Jesus meant?

10. When Mark says that Jesus answered the high priest's question affirmatively, is he relating history or theology? Explain your question.
11. Why did Luke omit the "false" saying against the temple in his version of Jesus' trial?
12. For what reasons did the early church believe that Jesus had built a new temple which replaced the old temple?

Chapter Ten: The Crucifixion and Death of Jesus

1

BEFORE THE ROMANS LED JESUS AWAY TO BE CRUCIFIED, they scourged him (Mk 15:15). It was customary for Rome to scourge condemned criminals as part of their punishment. The scourging of Jesus may be judged as historically probable because of Mark's accompanying report about Simon of Cyrene and his sons, Alexander and Rufus.

Evidently Jesus was so weakened by his scourging that Simon was forced to carry the heavy crossbeam for Jesus to the place of execution. It is probable that Alexander and Rufus later became Christians and enjoyed a measure of celebrity because of their father's role in the story of Jesus' crucifixion. It is fair to assume that Mark mentioned them by name in his Gospel because they were known to his church:

> And they compelled a passerby, Simon of Cyrene, who was coming in from the country, the father of Alexander and Rufus, to carry his cross. (Mk 15:21)

The Roman soldiers led Jesus outside one of Jerusalem's gates to a prominent upthrust of rock called Golgotha. On top of this prominence, the Romans had apparently erected permanent vertical beams to which the crossbeams of those to be crucified could be attached. Ordinarily, after condemned criminals had been scourged they were left naked (to better display their bloody trauma as a deterrent) and forced to carry their own crossbeam to the place of execution. However, since the Jews abhorred public nudity, the Romans probably made an exception when executions were carried out at Jerusalem. The Gospels are probably correct, therefore, when they say that the soldiers put Jesus' garments back on him after his scourging and removed them again when he arrived at Golgotha.

Those crucified by Rome were either tied or nailed to the extremities of the crossbeam and the lower part of the vertical beam to which the crossbeam was attached. The Gospels do not directly state that Jesus was nailed to his cross. They nevertheless imply that he was nailed by relating that the Risen Jesus invited his disciples to examine the nail holes in his hands and feet (Lk 24:39a; Jn 20:20,25b,27a).

Mark recounts that *before* the soldiers nailed Jesus to his cross, they offered him sweet wine (*oinos*) mixed with myrrh to help him endure his pain, but he refused:

> And they brought him to the place called Golgotha (which means the place of the skull), and they offered him wine mixed with myrrh, but he did not take it. (Mk 15:22-23)

We are justifiably suspicious when we are told that Jesus is mercifully offered numbing "wine mixed with myrrh" by the soldiers who have just scourged and are about to crucify him. This first offering of wine involves no midrashic reference, but Raymond E. Brown is probably correct when he suggests that it is nevertheless theological in nature: Mark relates that Jesus refused the wine to imply that Jesus intends to drink every drop of the cup of his suffering. This bitter cup was mentioned earlier during Jesus' prayer in Gethsemane:

> Abba, Father, all things are possible to you; remove this cup from me; yet not what I will, but what you will. (Mk 14:36)

Matthew retained Mark's story of the first offering of wine by the soldiers, but he changed Mark's account by substituting "gall" for "myrrh." He probably did so to introduce an apologetic proof text into the first mention of wine. By his midrashic allusion to the suffering righteous man of Ps 69:21a, Matthew meant to teach that the shameful fate of Jesus was divinely fore-intended because foreshadowed in the scriptures.

For the same theological reason, all four of the evangelists make a reference to the *last half* of the same psalm verse (Ps 69:21b): They all relate that Jesus, *while dying on the cross,* was given (Luke says "offered") "vinegar" or "sour wine" (*oxos*) to drink (Mk 15:36a; Mt 27:48; Lk 23:36; Jn 19:29-30; the same word for sour wine is found in the Old Greek version of Ps 69:21b):

> 19 You know my reproach, and my shame and my
> dishonor; my foes are all known to you.
> 20 Insults have broken my heart so that I am
> in despair. I looked for pity, but there was
> none; and for comforters, but found none.
> 21 They gave me *gall* for food, and for my thirst
> they gave me *vinegar* to drink. (Ps 69:19-21)

It is certainly possible that one of the soldiers standing by offered sour wine to alleviate Jesus' terrible thirst. But since this reported action includes an obvious midrashic allusion, it is probable that the report is apologetic theology, not history.

We are told by Mark (15:25) that Jesus was crucified at the "third hour" (nine a.m.), whereas John relates that it was the "sixth hour" (noon). There are no convincing reasons, however, why Mark's account is not esentially reliable. The ancients began dealing with the day's business soon after daylight, and the place of Jesus' execution was just outside one of Jerusalem's gates. John's reckoning of the time of execution was probably determined by his desire to present Jesus as the "Lamb of God" (1:29,36). For the priests began to slaughter the Passover lambs in the Jerusalem temple at noon on Passover eve, and John tells us that it was Passover eve when Jesus was crucified (Jn 19:14).

Mark returns to the hour of the day in 15:33 where he informs us that a portentous darkness covered the land until the ninth hour (3:00 p.m., the time of Jesus' death):

> And when the sixth hour had come there was darkness over the whole land until the ninth hour.

This chronological reference (repeated in Mt 27:45) is probably apologetic theology which alludes to a passage in the prophet Amos. The early church believed this passage presaged the tragic fate suffered by Jesus, God's Messiah-*Son* at the time of the Passover *festival:*

> "And on that day," says the Lord God, "I will make the sun go down at *noon* and darken the earth in broad daylight. I will turn your *feasts* into mourning, and all your songs into lamentation . . . I will make it like the mourning for an only *son,* and the end of it like a bitter day." (Am 8:9-10)

2

Mark, followed by Matthew, relates that just before the dying Jesus was offered sour wine, he cried out to God, praying the first sentence of Ps 22:

> And about the ninth hour Jesus cried with a loud voice, "My God, my God, why have you forsaken me?" (Mk 15:46)

Christian preachers and theologians frequently assert that these words of the dying Jesus indicate that he experienced himself as abandoned by God during his crucifixion. Such an interpretation is understandable and usually well intentioned, but mistaken. There are good reasons for concluding that words from Ps 22 were probably *not* prayed audibly by Jesus from the cross. Rather, they were placed on Jesus' lips by Mark to teach a theological lesson and to serve as a memory device for recalling that lesson.

We have already observed that the major theological task of the apostolic church was the defense of her faith in a crucified, i.e., shockingly unexpected, Messiah. When the church searched the scriptures for midrashic foreshadowings of such a Messiah, she found in Ps 22 a description of the sufferings of a persecuted righteous man which seemed strikingly similar to those of Jesus. This similarity was even greater if one consulted the Old Greek version of Ps 22 (Ps 21 in the Old Greek). The early church was convinced that this psalm prefigured the tragic crucifixion of Jesus.

To help Christians in the early church remember this psalm when defending their faith in a crucified Messiah, Mark built a midrashic reference to it into the story of Jesus' crucifixion by placing the psalm's *first sentence* on the lips of the dying Jesus. This procedure seemed fully legitimate because Mark assumed that Jesus knew he was fulfilling the portendings of this psalm as he died on the cross. Accordingly, when Christians learned the story of Jesus' tragic death, they also learned an impressive proof text for defending their faith in Jesus' disputed Messiahship.

When the first verse of Ps 22 is read in isolation, it can give the impression that the suffering righteous man praying the psalm is in despair. But if one reads the entire psalm carefully it becomes clear that the psalm is a prayer of profound trust and confidence in God, not the prayer of a human who feels abandoned by God. (The reader is urged to read the *entire* psalm and discover that this is emphatically so.)

Such a mistaken impression would not have occurred to the earliest Christians. They would have been familiar with all of Ps 22 and would have understood that its first sentence was an *identifying* sign which pointed to its remaining verses. (When the Gospels were written, the psalms had not yet been numbered). We will examine only those verses of Ps 22 which shed light on its theological use by the early church:

> 1 My God, my God, why have you forsaken me?
> Why are you so far from helping me,
> from the words of my groaning?
> 2 O my God, I cry by day, but you do not answer;
> and by night, but I find no rest.

3 Yet you are holy,
enthroned on the praises of Israel.
4 In you our fathers trusted; they trusted,
and you delivered them.
5 To you they cried, and they were saved;
in you they trusted,
and they were not disappointed.

After the desperate cry for help in the first verse, it is clear that the four verses which follow (2-5) express profound faith and trust in God's saving presence. The next three verses (6-8) are alluded to and sometimes almost directly quoted in the Gospel accounts of those who jeered at the dying Jesus:

6 But I am a worm, and no man; scorned by men,
and despised by the people.
7 All who see me mock at me,
they make mouths at me, they wag their heads;
8 "He committed his cause to the Lord;
let him deliver him, let him rescue him,
for he delights in him."

We will now skip to a series of verses which could easily be imagined as a description of a crucified man. But if we read them critically, it becomes evident that they do not presuppose the situation of someone crucified. Rather, they employ poetic hyperbole to describe the plight of a man pursued by enemies and at the point of exhaustion. This perspiring man is so hot and thirsty from fleeing that he feels his insides are melting and he is near the point of death. His fierce thirst easily suggests that of a crucified man suffering from dehydration:

14 I am poured out like water, and all my bones
are out of joint; my heart is like wax,
it is melted within my breast;
15 my strength is dried up like a potsherd,
and my tongue cleaves to my jaws;
you lay me in the dust of death.

The following three verses (16-18) seemed especially to prefigure the fate of the crucified Jesus in the judgment of the early church. All the Gospels allude to or quote the last of these verses (Mk 15:24; Mt 27:35; Lk 23:34b: Jn 19:23-24):

> 16 Yea, dogs are round about me;
> a company of evildoers encircle me;
> they have pierced my hands and feet—
> 17 I can count all my bones—
> they stare and gloat over me;
> 18 they divide my garments among them,
> and for my clothing they cast lots.

Of the verses just cited, verse 16b calls for special comment. In most translations, the words of this verse suggest the image of Jesus' hands and feet pierced by nails as he dies on the cross. The words in the original Hebrew, however, do not say, "they have pierced my hands and feet." Instead, they express an unusual Hebrew idiom, "like a lion (*ka ari*) my hands and feet," which suggests that the hands and feet of the man praying the psalm are cut and bleeding as if torn by the teeth or claws of a lion (perhaps from falling on sharp stones while trying to evade his enemies).

The original Hebrew of Ps 22:16b, therefore, does not envision a crucified man whose hands and feet have been "pierced" by nails. Why is it, then, that many translators render the Hebrew idiom of this passage with the words "they have pierced"? The answer to this question will require us to review a bit of ancient history.

After Alexander's conquest had spread the use of Greek in the ancient world, the Jews who lived in the diaspora (the region outside of Palestine) translated the Hebrew Scriptures into Greek for use at worship and study. When they came to the difficult idiom in Ps 22:16b, (like a lion my hands and feet) they translated it with the Greek expression, "They pierced (*oruxan*) my hands and feet."

We saw above that when the Greek-speaking Christians in the early church went searching for proof texts, they used the Old Greek version of the Bible. And when they found the Greek version of Ps 22, they understood it (especially the words, "they pierced my hands and feet") to prefigure the crucifixion of Jesus.

They then eagerly appropriated this psalm for apologetic debates, and alluded to or quoted portions of it when narrating the crucifixion of Jesus. The early church's preference for the Old Greek version of Ps 22 continues to influence conservative Christian translators till the present.

It is illuminating to recall that neither Luke nor John joined Mark and Matthew in placing the first sentence of Ps 22 on the lips of the crucified Jesus. They each chose *different* foreshadowing proof texts to place on Jesus' lips, even though Luke probably had the text of Mark in front of him (Lk 23:46; Jn 19:28-30). Such differing editorial choices remind us that the words which the evangelists placed on the dying Jesus' lips are probably theological choices, not historical memories. If the early church had remembered that Jesus actually prayed words from Ps 22 from the cross, it is highly probable that Luke and John also would have related those words instead of preferring other midrashic words.

Although it is likely that Mark is providing theology and not history when he portrays the dying Jesus as audibly praying words from Ps 22, Mark is probably reporting a reliable memory when he (and Matthew) tells us us that Jesus cried out in anguish just before he died:

> And Jesus uttered a loud cry and breathed his last. (Mk 15:37)

A judgment in favor of historicity seems warranted in this case because Jesus' cry just prior to his death suggests no theological purpose of the early church. Instead, the cry is probably a reliable memory of the hideous pain in which Jesus died. The same cannot be said, however, for Mark's account of the centurion's response:

> And when the centurion, who stood facing him, saw that he thus breathed his last, he said, "Truly this man was a Son of God!" (Mk 15:39)

It is highly probable that the centurion's declaration is theology rather than history. The words he utters seem to be an apologetic allusion to the death of the righteous "son of God" spoken of in Wis 2:17-18, 21-22. This righteous son of God was doubtlessly perceived by Mark as a hidden prefigurement of the secret Messianic destiny of Jesus:

> "Let us see if his words are true, and let us test what will happen at the end of his life; for if the righteous man is God's son, he will help him, and will deliver him from the hand of his adversaries." (Wis 2:17-18)
>
> Thus they reasoned, but they were led astray, for their wickedness blinded them, and they did not know the *secret* purposes of God. (Wis 2:21-22a)

The centurion's recognition of Jesus' extraordinary dignity is probably intended by Mark as premonitory of the many Gentiles who will soon come to faith in the crucified and Risen Jesus.

3

Before leaving Jesus' death, we should consider one final matter. The Gospel of John relates that one of the Roman soldiers thrust his spear into Jesus' side to insure that Jesus was dead. When the soldier withdrew his spear, we are told, blood and water flowed from Jesus' side. Although the Fourth Evangelist probably saw sacramental symbolism in the blood and water, it is unlikely that they are merely theological symbols devoid of historicity. The Fourth Evangelist insists emphatically that a trusted eyewitness stands behind his report:

> But one of the soldiers pierced his side with a spear, and at once there came out blood and water. He who saw it has borne witness—his testimony is true, and he knows that he tells the truth—that you also may believe. (Jn 19:34-35)

Who is this mysterious eyewitness appealed to by the Fourth Evangelist? We must, of course, begin by acknowledging that we can never know with complete certainty. But having admitted that, it is our right and duty to seek the best working hypothesis we are capable of.

We may suspect for good reasons that the eyewitness referred to by the Fourth Evangelist is probably the mysterious figure in the Fourth Gospel referred to as "the disciple whom Jesus loved." It was probably this disciple who "was known to the high priest," and who, accordingly, could gain admission for Peter to the high priest's courtyard:

> So the other disciple, who was known to the high priest, went out and spoke to the maid who kept the door, and brought Peter in. (Jn 18:16b)

Since the beloved disciple seems to have been known to and trusted by the high priests' servants, he was probably related by blood to the high priest. It was probably for that reason that this disciple could safely remain in Jerusalem and observe the crucifixion of Jesus. If so, it was he who saw the blood and water flow from Jesus' pierced side.

This probably reliable piece of information, however, comes at the end of a complex and beautiful midrash on the death of Jesus created by the Fourth Evangelist. This midrash presents Jesus as the New Adam through whom God is calling the New Creation into being. To accomplish his theological purpose, the Fourth Evangelist places the mother of Jesus and the beloved disciple beneath the new tree of the cross from which Jesus, the New Adam, has secretly begun to reign as king of the New Creation. The mother of Jesus is a symbol of the church understood as the New Eve, the spiritual bride of Christ and mother of Christians.

The maternal role of the New Eve is suggested when the dying Jesus recommends her to the beloved disciple (who signifies ideal discipleship) as that disciple's "mother":

> When Jesus saw his mother, and the disciple whom he loved standing near, he said to his mother, "Woman, behold, your son." Then he said to the disciple, "Behold, your mother." (Jn 19:26-27a)

Jesus addresses his mother as "woman," to indicate that she is the New Eve for whom the archetypal "woman" in Genesis is the midrashic prototype. We should also recall that the Old Eve was taken as helpmate from the side of the old Adam when God caused him to fall asleep in the garden of Paradise (Gen 2:21-22; see Jn 19:41; 20:15b). Correspondingly, the Fourth Evangelist alludes midrashically to Jesus as the New Adam whose side is opened after he has "fallen asleep" in death (Jn 11:11-14) on the new tree of the cross:

> But when they came to Jesus and saw that he was already dead, they did not break his legs. But one of the soldiers pierced his side with a spear, and at once there came out blood and water. (Jn 19:33-34)

From the pierced side of the New Adam, God is beginning to bring forth the New Eve, symbolized by Mary standing below the new tree of the cross. It is to the New Eve that Jesus, the New Adam "handed over his Spirit" at the moment of his death (Jn 19:30b). The Greek word which the Fourth Evangelist uses for the pierced "side" (*pleura*) of Jesus is the same word used in the Greek Septuagint for one of the "ribs" (*pleurōn*) taken from Adam's side to form Eve.

The blood and water flowing from the side of Jesus represent the two Johannine sacraments through which Jesus calls his church into being by mediating to it the saving gift of the Spirit (Jn 19:30b, "he handed over his Spirit"). The "water" flowing from Jesus' side, accordingly, symbolizes the new "birth" of Baptism:

> Truly, truly, I say to you, unless one is born of water and the Spirit, he cannot enter the Kingdom of God. (Jn 3:5)

This new birth is conferred upon believers by God (Jn 1:13) through Jesus and his bride-church (Jn 20:23). The "blood" flowing from Jesus' side symbolizes the passion-oriented Eucharist with which Jesus the bridegroom-Savior and his bride-church spiritually nourish those born "again" (Jn 3:3) while they are on the "Way" (Jn 14:6) to the "marriage feast" (Jn 2:1; 3:29) of "the Lamb" (Jn 1:29,36; 19:36).

The Eucharistic food is the new fruit of the new tree which gives the new life of the Spirit and frees us from death:

> He who eats my flesh and drinks my blood has eternal life, and I will raise him up at the last day. For my flesh is food indeed, and my blood is drink indeed. (Jn 6:54-55)

This Johannine reflection on the sublime implications of Jesus' Spirit-releasing death (followed by Resurrection) is woven midrashically into the apostolic church's historical memory of that death. As such, it illustrates the wedding of theological interpretation and historical memory which characterizes the Gospels. The sacred union thus achieved gives cause for celebration, for, in the case of self-transcending beings such as ourselves, it is better for inspired poetry to have the last word rather than bare, unadorned historical memory.

Questions for Review and Discussion

1. Who was Simon of Cyrene and why did Mark probably mention that he was the father of "Alexander and Rufus"?
2. Since Rome could either tie or nail criminals to their crosses, what indications are there in the Gospels that Jesus was not tied but nailed to the cross?
3. When Mark says that Jesus prayed the first verse of Ps 21 as he was dying on the cross, is he relating history or theology? Explain your answer.
4. Is the first verse of Ps 22 a cry of despair devoid of all faith and trust in God? Explain your answer.
5. Is the traditional translation of verse 16b of Ps 22 ("they have pierced my hands and feet") describing a crucified man whose hands and feet have been pierced by nails? Explain your answer.
6. For what reason may we suspect that the Gospels of Luke and John do not join Mark in placing Ps 22:1 on the lips of the crucified Jesus?

7. Who do we think the eyewitness might have been who reported that "blood and water" flowed from the pierced side of Jesus?
8. What deeper midrashic meaning did the Fourth Evangelist probably assign to the blood and water flowing from Jesus' pierced side?
9. Do contemporary exegetes think that the mother of Jesus and the beloved disciple were actually standing directly beneath the crucified Jesus? Explain your answer.
10. Why does the Fourth Gospel say that Jesus addressed his mother with the unusual title "woman" as he was dying on the cross?

Chapter Eleven: The Burial and Resurrection of Jesus

1

THE EARLIEST CHRISTIAN TRADITION REMEMBERED THAT JESUS was buried, not by one of the Twelve or some other disciple, but by a Jew named Joseph of Arimathea. This man probably belonged to the circle of wealthy and influential Jews who made up the high priest's council of advisors. Legendary elements eventually gathered around Joseph and turned him into a disciple who buried Jesus out of loyalty and devotion.

This tradition was gradually created by teachers in the early church intent on mitigating the embarrassing memory that Jesus had not been buried by his disciples. Mark is telling us the unvarnished truth when he relates that when Jesus was seized by his enemies, his disciples "all abandoned him and fled" (Mk 14:50).

Although it is true that legendary elements have accrued to Joseph of Arimathea for folk reasons, the memory that he buried Jesus in a nearby tomb is historically reliable. For if the church had created the story of Jesus' burial from whole cloth, she would have attributed that action to someone remembered unambiguously as a disciple of Jesus (probably one of the Twelve).

Mark, who wrote the earliest Gospel, does not claim that Joseph is a disciple; instead, Joseph is described as "a respected member of the council, who was also looking for the Kingdom of God" (Mk 15:43). Luke also refrains from presenting Joseph as a disciple; rather, Luke says that Joseph was "a good and righteous man, who had not consented to their purpose and deed" (Lk 23:50b-51). With Matthew, however, the tide turns; he reassures us in unabashed folk fashion that Joseph "was a disciple of Jesus" (Mt 27:57b). John agrees with Matthew, but strangely qualifies Joseph's discipleship: We are told by John that Joseph "was a disciple of Jesus, but *secretly* for fear of the Jews" (Jn 19:38).

It is very likely that John describes Joseph as a "secret" disciple for theological motives peculiarly his own: Joseph is being likened by John to Jewish Christians who belong to a nearby synagogue. These Jewish Christians fear to acknowledge Jesus publicly lest they be expelled from the synagogue:

> For the Jews had already agreed that if anyone should confess him to be the Messiah, he should be put out of the synagogue. (Jn 9:22)

> Nevertheless many even of the authorities believed in him, but for fear of the Pharisees they did not confess it, lest they should be put out of the synagogue: for they loved the praise of men more than the praise of God. (Jn 12:42-43)

John also surprises us by introducing a Jew named Nicodemus into his account of Jesus' burial. Nicodemus is unknown to the other three evangelists who would have been delighted to be able to relate that the hasty burial of Jesus was dignified with a gift of spices worthy of a king (2 Chr 16:13-14). Nicodemus, however, is no stranger when he appears at Jesus' burial in John's Gospel; he has already appeared in chapter 3:

> Now there was a man of the Pharisees, named Nicodemus, a ruler of the Jews. This man came to Jesus by night. (Jn 3:1-2a)

We are told that Nicodemus comes to Jesus under cover of darkness to suggest that he also is afraid of being ousted from the synagogue from which the Johannine Jewish Christians have recently been expelled. The Fourth Gospel regularly combines the history of (the rejected and suffering) Jesus with the history of the (rejected and suffering) Johannine Christians. The Fourth evangelist writes in this manner to remind the Johannine Christians that they must expect to suffer the same fate as Jesus since they are his disciples in whom he continues his mission:

> As the Father has sent me, so also I send you. (Jn 20:21b)
>
> If the world hates you, know that it has hated me before it hated you. (Jn 15:18)
>
> A servant is not greater than his master. If they persecuted me, they will persecute you. (Jn 15:20)

It is reasonable to infer, therefore, that it was not the historical Jesus whose burial was honored by Nicodemus' generous gift of spices. In reality, Nicodemus' gift was probably lavished upon the burial of a disciple of Jesus from the Johannine community (in whom Jesus continued his mission) who was stoned (Jn 8:59; 10:31-33) when he persisted in returning to a nearby synagogue to witness to Jesus:

> They will put you out of the synagogues; indeed, the hour is coming when whoever kills you will think he is offering service to God. (Jn 16:2)

When the Fourth Gospel, therefore, tells us that Nicodemus was present at Jesus burial, it is probably relating Johannine theology, not history.

2

Next we must examine Joseph of Arimathea's motive for laying Jesus' body in a nearby tomb:

> Joseph of Arimathea, a respected member of the council . . . went to Pilate and asked for the body of Jesus. . . . And when he learned from the centurion that he was dead, he

> granted the body to Joseph. And he bought a linen shroud, and taking him down, wrapped him in a linen shroud, and laid him in a tomb which had been hewn out of rock; and he rolled a stone against the door of the tomb. (Mk 15:43,45-46)

The Gospels (we saw above) suggest that Joseph buried Jesus either out of respect (Mark and Luke) or the devotion of a loyal disciple (Matthew and John). Nevertheless, there are grounds for suspecting that Joseph's motive might not have been friendly. We should recall that (1) the burial was hasty (perfunctory?), (2) the body was probably not washed, and (3) it was not anointed or honored with spices. In addition, (4) several women who were followers of Jesus were looking on (Mk 15:47), but were not assisting with the burial. At the very least this implies that Joseph was not a disciple.

In the Acts of the Apostles, however, Luke attributes a sermon to Paul the apostle in which the burial of Jesus is presented as the last of a series of hostile actions carried out by Jesus' *enemies:*

> Though they could charge him with nothing deserving death, they asked Pilate to have him killed. And when they had fulfilled all that was written of him, they took him down from the tree, and laid him in a tomb. (Acts 13:28-29)

Luke's assertion that Jesus was buried by his enemies is perhaps indirectly confirmed by a statement that we find in John's account of the burial:

> In order to prevent the bodies from remaining on the cross on the sabbath . . . the Jews asked Pilate that their legs might be broken, *and that they might be taken away.* So the soldiers came and broke the legs of the first, and of the other who had been crucified with him. But when they came to Jesus and saw that he was already dead, they did not break his legs. . . .
>
> After this Joseph of Arimathea . . . asked Pilate that he might *take away* the body of Jesus, and Pilate gave him leave. (Jn 19:31b-33,38)

John seems to imply that the Jewish authorities (the high priest and his advisers) took the initiative in burying Jesus and those executed with him. But, if this is true, why would these enemies of Jesus have placed his body in a tomb instead of an ordinary grave for criminals? We may never know for sure, but it is reasonable to suspect that the authorities shrewdly did so to pacify the Jews who regarded Jesus as a prophet.

The high priest and his advisers possibly anticipated that such Jews would be shocked and angry when they learned of Jesus' summary execution and might suspect the involvement of the temple authorities whom Jesus had recently rebuked. But if the Jews sympathetic to Jesus also learned that the Jewish authorities had asked Pilate for Jesus' body and had buried it in a tomb, they might be less inclined to suspect hostile Jewish involvement, and more inclined to attribute Jesus' death exclusively to the Romans.

3

According to Mark, when Joseph of Arimathea wrapped Jesus' body in a shroud and laid it in the tomb, several women who were followers of Jesus were standing nearby as observers:

> Mary Magdalene and Mary the mother of Joses saw where he was laid. (Mk 15:47)

Mary Magdalene and Mary the mother of Joses had already been mentioned by Mark as present among the women "looking on from afar" as Jesus died (Mk 15:40). It is likely that Mark went out of his way to name these women and to report their presence at the burial for an apologetic motive. He probably wished to refute the hostile claim that the women had entered the wrong tomb on Easter morning, one that happened to be empty, and mistakenly concluded that God had raised Jesus from the dead. Mark assures us that the women who found Jesus' tomb empty at Easter were aware of its true location.

That the tomb of Jesus was found empty by a group of women on Easter Sunday is highly probable. If the church had invented the story of the tomb's discovery, those who made the discovery would have been male disciples of Jesus (some of the Twelve) instead of women. For theological reasons, later tradition did bring Peter to view the tomb *on Easter Sunday* (Jn 20:3-6; Lk 24:12). In reality, however, Peter probably visited the tomb only after he had returned from Galilee (Mk 16:7; Mt 28:11) to Jerusalem to witness to the appearances of the Risen Jesus.

Matthew's Gospel relates that after Jesus' burial, the chief priests went to Pilate and asked him to assign Roman soldiers to guard Jesus' tomb. There are, however, good reasons for thinking that Matthew's remarkable story about the guards at the tomb is apologetic theology and not history.

A critical reading of Matthew's story implies that he and his community were probably engaged in bitter controversy with a nearby community of Jews (Mt 28:15). These Jews had rejected Jewish Christian claims about the Resurrection of Jesus which appealed to the empty tomb as confirmation. The tomb of Jesus was empty, the Jews replied, not because God had raised him, but because Jesus' disciples had stolen his body and invented the story of his Resurrection (Mt 27:64).

To counteract the influence of this Jewish accusation, Matthew (or an editor of his work) decided to create an apologetic story which would undermine the accusation's credibility. Matthew strategically divided his apologetic story into three parts (Mt 27:62-66; 28:2-4; 28:11-15). He then placed the first part just before the account of the empty tomb's discovery which he found in Mark (16:1-8) and revised:

> Next day, that is, after the day of Preparation, the chief priests and the Pharisees gathered before Pilate and said, "Sir, we remember how that imposter said, while he was still alive, 'After three days I will rise again.' Therefore, order the sepulchre to be made secure until the third day, lest his disciples go and steal him away, and tell the people, 'He has risen from the dead,' and the last fraud will be worse than the first."
>
> Pilate said to them, "You have a guard of soldiers; go, make it as secure as you can."

> So they went and made the sepulchre secure by sealing the stone and setting a guard. (Mt 27:62-66)

After stationing the soldiers at the tomb, Matthew briefly breaks away from his apologetic story and begins to recount his version of the empty tomb narrative:

> Now after the sabbath, toward the dawn of the first day of the week, Mary Magdalene and the other Mary went to see the sepulcher. (Mt 28:1)

Almost immediately, however, Matthew leaves the two women approaching the tomb and inserts the second part of his apologetic story. The second part describes an apocalyptic earthquake caused by the descent of an angel who rolls the stone away from the tomb. (We should recall the apocalyptic earthquake which accompanied the egress of the saints from their tombs in Mt 27:51-53):

> And behold, there was a great earthquake; for an angel of the Lord descended from heaven and came and rolled back the stone, and sat upon it. His appearance was like lightning and his raiment white as snow. And for fear of him the guards trembled and became like dead men. (Mt 28:2-4)

After his interpolation of the angel's dramatic intervention (which explains how the stone was removed), Matthew returns to the account of the empty tomb's discovery, and the angel "interprets" the empty tomb's meaning for the women who have just arrived:

> But the angel said to the women, "Do not be afraid, for I know that you seek Jesus who was crucified. He is not here; for he has risen, as he said. Come see the place where he lay. Then go quickly and tell his disciples that he has risen from the dead, and behold he is going before you to Galilee. Lo, I have told you." So they departed quickly from the tomb with fear and great joy, and ran to tell the disciples. (Mt 28:5-8)

As the women hasten to fulfill their task, Matthew returns to the guards at the tomb and relates the *third* and final part of his apologetic story:

> While they were going, behold, some of the guard went into the city and told the chief priests all that had taken place. And when they had assembled with the elders and taken counsel, they gave a sum of money to the soldiers and said, "Tell people, 'His disciples came by night and stole him away while we were asleep.' And if this comes to the governor's ears, we will satisfy him and keep you out of trouble."
>
> So they took the money and did as they were directed; and this story has been spread among the Jews to this day. (Mt 28:11-15)

There are a number of good reasons why Matthew's apologetic story is not historically plausible. To begin with, contemporary scholarship does not accept the literal existence of angels. The angel in Matthew's story is an apocalyptic literary device—an *interpreting angel* who explains apocalyptic revelation to humans. In the book of Daniel, apocalyptic mysteries having to do with the end of the world are repeatedly revealed to Daniel through an *interpreting angel* whose function is symbolic and theological (Dan 7:16; 8:15-17; 9:21-23; 10:10-14; 10:18-12:4; 12:5-13).

In addition, the other three Gospels know nothing of the sensational story about the guards at the tomb, which suggests that historically none were really there. Finally, it is not likely that Jewish priests could have persuaded the Roman prefect not to take punitive action if Roman soldiers had failed in their assigned duty. And for that reason the soldiers, even for money, would probably not have been willing to tell a story that advertised their failure.

The story about the guards at the tomb is best understood as an apologetic tactic created to defend Christian faith in Jesus' Resurrection. As such, it has important theological meaning for the Christian faith community. Also, it is a valuable source of historical information about the debate that occurred between

Matthew's community and a nearby community of Jews. Contemporary scholarship advises us, however, that the story should not be consulted as a source of objective historical information about the empty tomb. (The problem of the tomb's emptiness will be examined in chapter twelve.)

4

Now that we have considered the burial of Jesus, we must turn our thoughts to that momentous event which insured that his tomb would be empty on Easter Sunday. As believing Christians whose faith has been confirmed by the gift of God's Spirit, we know that Jesus' tragic death was not the end of his story. God enabled Jesus to pass victoriously through death into Eternal Life and Joy as God's assurance that tragedy, injustice, and death can be transcended.

When the Risen and Spirit-mediating Jesus began appearing to his disciples in possession of New Life, they understood that God had empowered him to defeat death and the powers of darkness (i.e., all the discouraging evils in life which can tempt us to despair). The Risen Jesus is the Light of the world sent by God to free us from our dark fear of "ambiguous" suffering and death. By his victory over fear and death, Jesus has become the Lord of life and death who shows us the way to Eternal Life in God's Kingdom.

We "know" that this Good News is truly from God because we truly experience God confirming it in our hearts with the silent language of divine love, peace, and joy. When we accept the Good News of God's love for us with faith and trust, God endorses our decision by communicating to us the "foretaste" of the Spirit (God's Self-communication as love).

Once our faith in the Risen Jesus has enabled us to taste "the peace of God which surpasses all understanding" (Php 4:7), we will still experience appropriate fear and anxiety in life, but we will never again be held in thrall by the dread of eternal self-loss. Our faith "experience" will have become an unfailing anchor which keeps us ultimately secure during life's terrifying storms.

5

St. Paul is our earliest witness in the New Testament to the appearances of the Risen Jesus. Paul's testimony is especially valuable because he was one of apostles who experienced the Risen Jesus appearing to them and commissioning them as witnesses to his appearances and their sublime meaning. In chapter 15 of 1 Corinthians, Paul has listed in chronological order the appearances of the Risen Jesus that called the church into being and launched her mission of proclaiming the Good News to the world.

This list provided by Paul is especially important because it contains Paul's direct memory of Jesus' revelatory appearance to him. It also includes his memory of the testimony of some of the other apostles (e.g., Peter and probably also James; see Gal 1:18-19; 2:9) about Jesus' appearances to them. The testimony given by Paul to the appearances in this list has been embellished only slightly with theological interpretations (e.g., "Cephas," "according to the scriptures," "fallen asleep"). It is still primarily in the form of directly recalled revelatory experience (prior to its later and inevitable theological expansion). We are, therefore, as close to the original apostolic witnessing as we can get:

> 4He was raised on the third day in accordance with the
> scriptures. 5And . . . he appeared to Cephas and then to
> the twelve. 6Then he appeared to more than five hundred
> disciples at one time, most of whom are still alive,
> though some have fallen asleep. 7Then he appeared to
> James, then to all the apostles. 8Last of all, as to one untimely born, he appeared also to me. (1 Cor 15:4-8)

Paul tells us that the first disciple to whom the Risen Jesus-appeared was "Cephas" (1 Cor 15:5). By "Cephas" Paul means Simon Peter, one of "the Twelve." The unusual name Cephas is the transliteration into Greek (*kephas*) of the Aramaic word for "rock" (*kayfa*). Simon Peter was given the symbolic name

"Rock" because his primary witnessing to the other surviving members of the group called "the Twelve" was understood as the rock of *foundation* on which the earliest community of Christian believers was built (See Mt 7:24-25; 16:18.)

Eventually, teachers in the increasingly Greek-speaking church decided to replace the Aramaic name Cephas with a clearer Greek equivalent, *"Petros,"* formed from the feminine Greek noun for rock, *"petra."* The English name Peter derives (by way of the Latin *Petrus*) from the symbolic Greek name *Petros* assigned to Simon by the earliest church. The account in Matthew's Gospel which states that *Jesus* gave the name "Peter" or "Rock" to Simon at Caesarea Philippi (Mt 16:18) is theological, not historical. It reads back into the earthly mission of Jesus a development which occurred (very soon) after his Resurrection.

We must assume that after Simon Peter experienced the Risen Jesus appearing to and commissioning him (Lk 24:34), he contacted the other remaining members of the group called "the Twelve" and testified to them about his stunning revelatory encounter. After Peter had witnessed to the others, the Risen Jesus himself confirmed Peter's testimony by appearing to the entire group.

A critical reading of the Gospels indicates that the first two church-founding appearances to Peter and the Twelve took place in *Galilee* (Mk 16:7; Mt 28:16; Jn 21:1). However, for theological reasons, Luke and John later moved the appearances from Galilee to Jerusalem, the sacred center of the ancient Jewish world. It is easy to see why the early church would have moved the appearances from Galilee to theologically significant "Jerusalem," but not the other way around.

It is quite possible that those to whom Simon Peter testified had been called to his fisherman's cottage in Capernaum where they and Jesus had frequently stayed before Jesus' death. Plausibly, it was while they were gathered there with Simon Peter eating a meal of bread and "broiled fish" (Lk 24:41-42; Jn 21:9,13) that the *second* of the church-founding appearances took place. One suspects that "broiled fish" was frequently served to guests at the house of Simon the fisherman. This, of course, cannot be proven, but it seems a likely hypothesis in view of Lk 24:41-42 and Jn 21:9,13. (*Nota bene:* only fresh fish is broiled; because of Jerusalem's distance from the sea, salted or dried fish was usually eaten there.)

Paul tells us that after Jesus appeared to Peter and the Twelve he appeared a third time to a much larger group:

> Then he appeared to more than five hundred disciples at one time, most of whom are still alive, although some have fallen asleep. (1 Cor 15:6)

The appearance of the Risen Jesus to more than five hundred disciples at one time is not mentioned anywhere else in the New Testament. This occurrence is possibly included in the reference made by Mark to the appearance of Jesus to "the disciples and Peter" in Galilee (Mk 16:7). However, the explicit mention of Peter makes it more likely that Mark is alluding to the first two church-founding appearances remembered in the concluding verse of the very early creed professed by the Greek-speaking church (1 Cor 15:3-5).

All or some of "the Twelve" had probably gathered this large group in order to testify to the appearances of Jesus. It would seem that when those bearing witness had delivered their testimony, the Risen Jesus again, as in the case of the Twelve, appeared to the entire group in confirmation of the testimony. Such a large group of disciples had probably been followers of Jesus during his Galilean ministry. It is likely that many, if not most, of those belonging to this group later came to Jerusalem with the Twelve to witness to Jesus and to await his anticipated return in glory. (The Resurrection of Jesus was initially understood as the beginning of the end of the world.)

It was probably on the occasion of Paul's visit to Jerusalem to confer with Cephas (Gal 1:18-19) that he also met some of the "more than five hundred brethren" to whom the Risen Jesus had appeared "at one time." This would explain why Paul was able to declare with certainty that most of them were "still alive."

The next person placed by Paul on his list of witnesses is James (1 Cor 15:7), who is called "the Lord's brother" by Paul in Gal 1:18 (probably to distinguish him from James, the son of Zebedee). We learn from Acts and Paul's letter to the Galatians that Jesus' brother James became the leader of the Jerusalem church when Simon Peter was eventually forced to leave that city (Acts 12:1-17). When James assumed the leadership of the mother church in Jerusalem, he also, *ex officio,* became the supervisor (Acts 15:6-21; Gal 2:12) of the worldwide missionary activity which had emanated from that church (Lk 24:47; Acts 1:8; 8:1; 11:19-21).

It was customary, therefore, for all of the apostles returning to Palestine or Syria (Antioch) from a tour of evangelizing to report to James. Even the fiercely independent Paul (Gal 1:11-12,15-17) is described in Acts (21:17-19) as paying such a visit. The oversight of "all the apostles," then, seems to have been a duty especially associated with James. It is quite possible, then, that Reginald Fuller is correct when he suggests (in his *Formation of the Resurrection Narratives*) that the mention of James just before Paul's reference to "all the apostles" has not only chronological but also ecclesiological significance:

> Then he appeared to James, then to all the apostles. (1 Cor 15:7)

Who precisely were "all the apostles" listed by Paul after James in 15:7? Paul speaks of them as if they were a group distinct from the Twelve mentioned earlier in 15:3. Yet, on another occassion Paul indicates that he understands one of the Twelve (Cephas) to be an *apostle* (Gal 1:18-19).

This probably means that Paul considers all of the Twelve to be apostles, but does not think that "all of the apostles" belonged to the group called the Twelve. Certainly Paul was an apostle (Rom 1:1; 1 Cor 1:1; 9:1; 2 Cor 1:1). Barnabas (Acts 14:14; 1 Cor 9:5) and James, the Lord's brother (1 Cor 15:7; Gal 1:19) were probably also apostles (and possibly Romanus and Junius; Rom 16:7). None of the men just mentioned, however, were numbered among the Twelve.

When Paul states that the Risen Jesus appeared to "all the apostles," does he intend us to understand one appearance to the entire group, or does he mean that all the members of this group had experienced an appearance individually or in smaller groups? We cannot say with certainty, but perhaps the latter view has the greater claim to likelihood. For Paul notifies us in 15:6 that Jesus appeared to more than five hundred disciples "at one time" (*ephapax*). But he does not make that qualification in 1 Cor 15:7 when he reports that Jesus appeared to "all the apostles." This suggests that Paul has possibly gathered a number of appearances to apostles other than the Twelve and James into one convenient reference.

"Last of all," Paul tells us, "as to one untimely born, he appeared also to me." Paul's unexpected encounter with the Risen Jesus occurred, we are told in Acts 9:1-8, while Paul was on his way to Damascus to persecute those "belonging to the Way." As Paul understands it, he was the last of those called into the company of the apostles by the Risen Jesus.

This appearance to Paul probably took place between two and three years after the first appearance to Simon Peter. There is obvious disparity between this generally accepted scholarly judgment and the "forty days" mentioned in Acts 1:3:

> To them he presented himself alive after his passion by many proofs, appearing to them during forty days, and speaking of the kingdom of God.

The "forty" days spoken of by Luke, however, are meant as midrashic theology, not history. When Luke says that the Risen Jesus remained on earth for "forty" days before being taken up into heaven, he is suggesting "the Way" in which we must walk to arrive at our heavenly destination (Acts 9:2; 16:17; 18:25-26; 19:23): After we (through Baptism) have died with Jesus to sin on Good Friday and have been raised with him to New Life on Easter Sunday, we must still sojourn through the "forty" years of the desert of this life before we finally arrive at the true promised land of Eternal Life.

Eventually, because of the ambiguity that plagues the transmission of meaning from one cultural milieu to another, the ancient church forgot that Luke's midrashic theology in Acts 1:3

should not be taken literally. She then decided that if Jesus was raised on Easter Sunday, the fortieth day after Easter would have been a Thursday. Christian tradition has *assumed* since that time that Jesus was taken up into heaven on Ascension Thursday.

Ascension Thursday, however, is a theological symbol. It illustrates the church's memory that after a certain time the Risen Jesus stopped appearing to the apostolic church. In reality, the appearance to Paul the apostle (which Paul describes as "last of all" in 1 Cor 15:8) is probably the concluding revelatory occasion which corresponds most closely to the symbol "Ascension Thursday."

6

Now that we have reflected on the witnesses to the Risen Jesus' appearances, we will turn our attention to the appearances themselves. What were they probably like? Again, our best guide is Paul the apostle who speaks from direct experience of the revelatory encounters in question. It is significant that neither Paul nor the author of the earliest Gospel, Mark, provide a narrative account of Jesus' appearances.

Why is it that Paul and Mark provide no narrative details about the appearances? Reginald Fuller has probably provided us with the correct answer: When Paul wrote 1 Corinthians (c. A.D. 55) and Mark wrote his Gospel (c. A.D. 70), descriptions of the appearances had not yet been created, for the earliest church *proclaimed* the appearances of the Risen Jesus (1 Cor 15:3-8; Lk 24:34; Acts 2:32; Mk 16:7), but did not yet *describe* them with narrative detail.

The appearances of Jesus were probably not narrated originally because in actuality they were *brief and stunning* encounters devoid of the narrative details created later to teach specific theological lessons. Instead, the appearances were proclaimed by the apostles as mysterious apocalyptic revelations which signaled the *imminent* end of the world. It took four or five decades and the death of the apostles for the original authority of their brief and urgent proclamation to abate. Only then did theological developments in *narrative* form begin to attach themselves to the early "appearance" traditions.

Since Mark did not possess any appearance "narratives," he decided to conclude his Gospel's passion account by joining to it a theologically expanded story about the discovery of the empty tomb. This story dramatically *proclaimed* the Resurrection of Jesus through the mouth of an angel (16:7). Mark prepared his readers for the angel's climactic announcement by means of five predictions made by Jesus during his final journey to Jerusalem (8:31; 9:9,31; 10:33-34; 14:28). We will return to these predictions in chapter fifteen.

To prepare ourselves to understand Paul's statements about the appearances, we should briefly consider his remarks about the nature of Risen Life. While defending belief in the resurrection of the body in 1 Cor 15, Paul insisted that Risen Life includes a mysterious bodily dimension. But he maintained with equal vigor that the body of Risen Life is not physical, but *spiritual.* Paul made his position clear with the aid of an agricultural metaphor which his contemporaries could easily grasp. He compared the buried body of a Christian who has fallen asleep in Jesus to a planted seed:

> What you sow does not come to life unless it dies. And what you sow is not the body which is to be, but a bare kernel, perhaps of wheat or of some other grain. But God gives it a body as he has chosen, and to each kind of seed its own body. (1 Cor 15:36-38)

Paul is suggesting that before a seed is sown in the earth and germinates, it appears lifeless and insignificant. Judging merely by its exterior, we would conclude that the tiny particle of matter before us has no vital future to speak of. But we know from experience that life is mysteriously present in the heart of the inert seed. And if it is buried in the earth and receives sunlight and water, the very process of the seed's disintegration releases the new, greater, and manifestly living body of the plant which it becomes. We should not fail to notice that there is *con-*

tinuity between the disintegrating seed and the new life that "rises" from its "death."

God, Paul reminds us, is continually bringing life out of death all around us in nature. And in doing so, God brings new and superior bodies out of the death of old and inferior bodies. It then follows, Paul implies, that just as God is able to transform the bodies of disintegrating seeds buried in the earth, God is also able, by the power of the Holy Spirit, to transform our mortal bodies into Risen Life like that of Jesus.

In 1 Cor 15:42-44 Paul takes this implied lesson learned from contemplating the fate of a seed and applies it explicitly to the body of a Christian buried at death. He does so in order to help us understand that the "body" of Risen Life will be "transformed" into a new and higher mode of existence and will no longer be bound by its former physical condition:

> So is it with the resurrection of the dead. What is sown is perishable, what is raised is imperishable. It is sown in dishonor, it is raised in glory. It is sown in weakness, it is raised in power. It is sown a physical body, it is raised a spiritual body. (1 Cor 15:42-44)

Paul explicitly rejects the idea that we will have a "physical" body in Eternal Life. He clearly states in 15:44 that he thinks we will have a "spiritual" body instead. Paul considers *perishability, dishonor,* and *weakness* to be the characteristics of the physical body. It is precisely our fleshly condition and its perishable attributes from which we must be freed if we hope to enter Eternal Life:

> I tell you this, brethren: flesh and blood cannot inherit the Kingdom of God, nor does the perishable inherit the imperishable. (1 Cor 15:50)

How did Paul come by his conviction that in Eternal Life we will have a "spiritual" body, characterized by *imperishability, glory,* and *power,* and not a physical one bound by mortality? It seems reasonable to infer that he based this conclusion on his experience of the Risen Jesus: "The Lord Jesus Christ . . . will change our lowly bodies to be like his glorious body" (Phil 3:21).

Paul knew that the Risen Life of Jesus includes a mysterious "bodily" dimension, for Paul and the other apostles had all experienced the Risen Jesus appearing as "some-body." Yet Paul also knew that there was something extraordinary and atypical about this "bodily" dimension of Jesus' New Life because: (1) ordinarily Jesus was not visible; (2) the occasions when Jesus was experienced as visible were rare and brief; (3) Jesus could appear and disappear at will. Paul realized that *physical* bodies do not behave in that fashion. He probably concluded, therefore, that since the "body" of Risen Life is ordinarily not visible (but may become so on revelatory occasions), its nature must be basically "spiritual" rather than physical.

At this point we should remind ourselves that Paul thinks about the body like an ancient Jew, not an ancient Greek. The Greeks disdained the body as the burdensome prison of the spiritual soul. The Jews thought otherwise; influenced by the oldest Genesis creation story (Gen 2:4b-25), they thought of the body as essential to human participation in God's Eternal Life. But they also thought that the body of Risen Life would be transformed by the power of God's Spirit into an immortal body no longer subject to the physical limitations inflicted on it by Adam's sin.

Furthermore, when Paul uses the word "spiritual" to describe the body of Risen Life, he does not understand it to mean "immaterial" or "nonbodily" as did some schools of ancient Greek philosophy (and later schools influenced by them). For Paul, that which is spiritual is ordinarily invisible, but is not incompatible with an extraordinarily subtle corporeality which can make itself "visible" when appropriate (see Tob 12:15,19 and Mk 12:25). The "spiritual" body of which Paul speaks is a transformed physical body in which the powers of the world to come have been fully released by the Spirit of God:

> If the Spirit of him who raised Jesus from the dead dwells in you, he who raised Christ Jesus from the dead

> will give life to your mortal bodies also through his Spirit which dwells in you. (Rom 8:11)

7

Our attention will now be turned to the problem of how Jesus was able to be seen by the apostles as "appearing." Paul's understanding of Risen Life implies that when Jesus appeared to him, Jesus had a spiritual body, not a physical body. But if the Risen Jesus no longer has a physical body on which physical light can shine, how could Jesus be "seen" by Paul as appearing?

We saw above that it was probably Paul's experience of the appearance and disappearance of the Risen Jesus that convinced Paul that the body of Risen Life is ordinarily invisible but can cause itself to be "seen" in extraordinary circumstances. Can the power of reason find anything in our contemporary experience that sheds light on Paul's conviction?

Did God temporarily recreate the physical appearance of Jesus so that his spiritual body could be seen, and then annihilate that appearance when the revelatory encounter was ended? We have already observed in earlier chapters that contemporary thinkers are repelled by the suggestion that God would interfere with the laws of nature. We also noted that since our God-given power of reason tells us it is *wrong* to act illogically, contradictorily, or uneconomically, we are justified in concluding that God does not act in such ways.

(A reader who has not read section 2 of chapter six might not be able to fully grasp the explanation of Jesus' "Resurrection" appearances which will be presented below. It would not be appropriate, however, to repeat here all that was said there.)

Accordingly, the revelatory appearances of the Risen Jesus should be understood *not* as violations of the laws of nature but as divinely caused manifestations which activate paranormal possibilities latent in nature. Paranormal experiences are those which fall outside the expected range of the "normal" or "ordinary." But even though they are extraordinarily rare and unexpected, they still occur within the range of "natural" possibilities and should not be construed as contradicting nature.

We all know, for example, that "physical" presence and "personal" presence, although normally experienced as conjoined, are not identical. We have all experienced occasions when people were physically present to us but were not "personally" present. For some reason they were not able or willing to give us the "gift" of their personal presence. Personal presence (divine and human) is the most highly prized of all "gifts" because it is freely bestowed out of love and friendship, and can never be compelled or purchased. "If a man offered for love all the wealth of his house, it would be utterly scorned" (The Song 8:7).

Ordinarily we experience personal presence as mediated through *physical* presence, but that is not invariably the case. There seem to be striking paranormal exceptions. Although it is highly unusual, it nevertheless happens that trustworthy people report having experienced an undeniable awareness of someone's personal presence even though that person was physically absent. Sometimes this awareness includes accurate knowledge of what has happened or is happening to a person at a great distance. Such paranormal awareness usually involves a deep and lasting bond of love, more frequently familial.

With the preceding qualifications in mind, the following hypothesis is offered as compatible with the requirements of Christian faith and a scientific world view: The Risen Jesus was probably able to communicate an awareness of his "personal" presence to his disciples in a paranormal way that triggered the release of his physical "appearance" from their memories and projected it onto their experience of his real but invisible presence. This extraordinary communication of Jesus' "presence" enabled the disciples to experience Jesus as both "present" and "appearing" in a stunning revelatory encounter.

Neither logic nor the laws of nature were violated by the resulting vision. It should be noted that the appearance of the Risen Jesus was not purely subjective. It was truly "extramental" in the sense that it was caused by and "clothed" the experienced presence of Jesus who was truly present "outside" the experiencing subject.

The apostolic experience of Jesus appearing "externally" was simultaneously accompanied "internally" by a revelatory communication of God's Holy Spirit (i.e., the divine Self-communication as love). This profoundly numinous experience assured the disciples that God was there and that God's life-creating love was the power which had enabled Jesus to transcend death and appear to them. The manifestly revelatory nature of the encounters assured the disciples that the appearances were not hauntings or hallucinations. (More will be said about the possibility of hallucinations in the final chapter.)

Since the apostles were all precritical thinkers, they were utterly unaware of the paranormal implications of their encounters with the Risen Jesus. And God knew that the accompanying experience of the divine "Self-communication" would lead to their unquestioning acceptance of the appearances as revelatory signs from God. Their acceptance of the revelatory validity of the appearances was the means by which God launched the Christian Message in history as God's answer to humankind's ultimate questions.

It was God's simultaneous communication of the Holy Spirit when the Risen Jesus appeared ("Receive the Holy Spirit." Jn 20:22) which convinced the apostles that God had fully released God's Spirit in Jesus (1 Cor 15:45; 2 Cor 3:17-18) and had empowered Jesus to mediate that Spirit to the world in a definitive new way (Jn 20:19,22; Gal 1:15-17).

Even when Jesus stopped appearing to the apostles, they continued to experience the gift of the Spirit being communicated as divine confirmation when they assembled to celebrate the memory of Jesus' Resurrection (Acts 2:1-4,32-33; 4:31) or proclaimed it to others (Acts 9:17; 10:39-40,44). They understood on these later occasions that the gift of the Spirit was still being mediated through the Risen Jesus (Acts 2:33; Jn 14:26; 7:39), just as the Spirit had been mediated on those earlier occasions when Jesus had "visibly" appeared.

God's Self-communication as love was also experienced as divine *confirmation* of Jesus' teaching that God's love and forgiveness are offered to all who turn away from sin with faith and trust. The disciples, who had only recently abandoned Jesus in cowardly fashion (Mk 14:50), had now personally *experienced* the communication of divine love and forgiveness promised by Jesus. They recognized, consequently, that God was thereby endorsing Jesus' teaching about the offer of divine love and forgiveness to all (Mk 2:5-7), even notorious sinners (Mk 2:15-17; Lk 7:37-50). The disciples also understood that God had assured them through the gift of the Spirit that they too were now empowered to defeat death and reach Eternal Life along with Jesus (Rom 8:11).

8

It seems appropriate at this point to address a question raised by Paul's claim to have "seen" the Risen Jesus. We have no way of knowing whether Paul had ever observed Jesus before Jesus appeared to him. If Paul had ever beheld the earthly Jesus, then Paul possessed a memory which the Risen Lord could activate when he encountered Paul. On the other hand, if Paul had never laid eyes on the earthly Jesus, then, given the explanation of the appearances provided above, how could Paul have "seen" the Risen Jesus? Several possibilities suggest themselves.

(Before we consider these possibilities, we should remind ourselves of the difficulty involved in attempting to answer the question before us. We know very little about Paul's life before his conversion, and the only *specific* information he gives us about his encounter with the Risen Jesus is his insistence that he *had seen* Jesus [1 Cor 9:1] *appearing* to him [1 Cor 15:8]. Any answer suggested, therefore, will necessarily be speculative. Nevertheless, it is incumbent upon us to answer the question we are considering with the best working hypothesis we are capable of. To proceed in this manner is not disingenuous or naive. On the contrary, contemporary physics operates in essentially the same way.)

The first possibility is that Jesus was able to activate Paul's unconscious image of an ideal man and cause it to be projected onto Jesus' invisible presence (at the same time that God conferred the gift of the Spirit). Paul, accordingly, would have "seen" that he had encountered the revelatory (Spirit-mediating) presence of a mysterious man. Jesus then could have "audibly" identified the "perceived" appearance as a revelatory sign of himself. Luke is perhaps close to a remembered account of Paul's actual experience when he relates in Acts 9:5 that Paul asked the encountered Jesus to identify himself ("Who are you?"), and Jesus did so ("I am Jesus.").

Another possibility is that there is something about the very nature of Risen Life that enables it to communicate a visual analogue of its former physical identity. But even in this second case, if Paul had never observed the earthly Jesus, Jesus would still have had to identify himself for Paul. (If this second possibility is correct, it obviates the need for the explanation of the appearances provided above in section 12.) While both of these suggestions are speculative, the second is more speculative and less economical, and, therefore, less likely.

9

Before leaving our discussion of the extraordinary nature of the Resurrection appearances and the divine Self-communication which accompanied them, we should ask if the "commissioning" appearances were accompanied by a "verbal" communication. If the Risen Jesus could cause himself to be briefly "seen" paranormally, then he probably also could have caused himself to be briefly "heard" in the same manner. The pertinent New Testament data are somewhat ambiguous and require us to proceed with caution.

To begin with, the various words attributed to the Risen Jesus in the Gospels and in Acts are strikingly different. They unfailingly reflect the theological vocabularies and concerns of the individual evangelists. We are certainly justified, therefore, if we suspect that these words were created by the early church. And, indeed, critical scholarship indicates that the early church eventually *did* ascribe words to the Risen Lord in order to express her faith in the meaning of his appearances and defend their credibility.

There is, however, one basic theme which is consistently present in the otherwise disparate appearance accounts. The Risen Jesus invariably calls his disciples to be his *witnesses* (Mt 28:10,19-20; Lk 24:34-35,47-48; Jn 20:17-18,21; Acts 1:8). Such impressive unity among otherwise differing sources suggests that beneath the diverse and lengthy theological statements attributed to the Risen Lord in the Gospels, an authentic memory of a *brief* call to bear witness might be preserved.

This assumption seems to find support in the testimony of Paul who says several times that he was called by the Risen Jesus to bear witness specifically to "the Gentiles" (i.e., all "the nations" other than Israel). However, while Paul emphatically asserts that Jesus "appeared" to him (1 Cor 9:1; 15:8), Paul's references to his *commission* do not explicitly state but *imply* that Jesus also "spoke" to him:

> . . . . Jesus Christ our Lord, through whom we have received grace and apostleship to bring about the obedience of faith for the sake of his name among all the nations (Rom 1:4b-5)

Paul also speaks in Galatians of his commission to witness to the Gentiles:

> But when he who had set me apart before I was born, and had called me through his grace, was pleased to reveal his son in me, in order that I might preach him among the Gentiles, I did not confer with flesh and blood, nor did I go up to Jerusalem to those who were apostles before me, but I went away into Arabia; and again I returned to Damascus. (Gal 1:15-17)

After Paul's commission, he went immediately "into Arabia" and began witnessing to "the Gentiles," which suggests a specific (but probably brief) revelatory directive.

If it were not for Paul's testimony, we might be inclined to think that "the call to witness" experienced by the apostles was an inner recognition encouraged nonverbally by the communication of God's Spirit. But it is difficult to see how Paul came by his adamant conviction that he had been sent to preach specifically to "the Gentiles" if his commission did not include a verbal directive (e.g., "Be my witness to the Gentiles."):

> . . . . when they saw that I had been entrusted with the gospel to the uncircumcised, just as Peter had been entrusted with the gospel to the circumcised (for he who worked through Peter for the mission to the circumcised worked through me also for the Gentiles), and when they perceived the grace that was given to me, James and Cephas and John, who were reputed to be pillars, gave to me and Barnabas the right hand of fellowship, that we should go to the Gentiles and they to the circumcised. . . . (Gal 1:7-9)

Because Paul's statements about his commission are not as clear as we would wish, the question we are considering is not easy to decide. But when the issues involved are carefully weighed, it seems more likely that Paul's call to witness to the Gentiles included a brief verbal directive (paranormally activated). And if this was true in the case of Paul, it was probably also true of the "commission" received by the other apostles.

(Those who would like more information about the contemporary understanding of the Resurrection narratives in the Gospels should see *Exploring the Resurrection of Jesus* in this same series. If a more technical treatment of the subject with critical apparatus is desired, see *The Formation of the Resurrection Narratives,* by Reginald Fuller.)

Questions for Review and Discussion

1. Why is it historically probable that Joseph of Arimathea was not a disciple of Jesus?
2. Why is it historically probable that Joseph of Arimathea did bury Jesus?

3. Is it likely that a man named Nicodemus helped bury Jesus and and honored Jesus' death with one hundred pounds of costly spices? Explain your answer.
4. Was Joseph of Arimathea's burial of Jesus necessarily a friendly action of someone who admired Jesus? Explain your answer.
5. Why is Mark's report that a group of women observed Jesus burial probably reliable?
6. Is Matthew's story about the posting of Roman soldiers to guard Jesus' tomb history of theology? Explain your answer.
7. According to Paul the apostle, who was the first disciple to whom the Risen Jesus appeared, and how did this appearance affect that disciple's name? Where does Paul report this first appearance?
8. When the Acts of the Apostles tells us that Jesus was taken up into heaven "forty days" after Easter is it relating history or theology? Explain your answer.
9. What explanation of the Risen Jesus' appearances was provided in this chapter? Is that explanation compatible with a scientific world view? Why does it matter whether our understanding of Jesus Resurrection is compatible with a scientific world view?
10. What additional revelatory experience always accompanied the appearances of the Risen Jesus? Why was this concomitant revelatory experience necessary for faith in Jesus as God's Good News?

Chapter Twelve: Jesus' Empty Tomb

1

THAT THE TOMB OF JESUS WAS FOUND EMPTY BY A GROUP OF women on Easter Sunday is highly probable. If the church had invented the story of the tomb's discovery, those who made the discovery would have been male disciples of Jesus (some of the Twelve) instead of women. For theological reasons, later tradition did bring Peter to view the tomb *on Easter Sunday* (Jn 20:3-6; Lk 24:12). In reality, however, Peter probably visited the tomb only after he had returned from Galilee (Mk 16:7; Mt 28:11) to Jerusalem to witness to the appearances of the Risen Jesus.

The memory of the tomb's discovery by the women was never suppressed, but it was theologically modified fairly soon. The *earliest* interpretation of the tomb's emptiness has been preserved in the Fourth Gospel. This interpretation feared that the enemies of Jesus had stolen his body to further dishonor him:

> They have taken the Lord's body out of the tomb, and we do not know where they have laid him. (Jn 20:2b)

Significantly, the empty tomb's earliest interpretation presupposes that the women *did not encounter an angelic messenger* at the tomb who informed them of Jesus' Resurrection. The original assumption of hostile intervention probably remained unquestioned until the disciples came from Galilee to Jerusalem proclaiming the appearances of the Risen Jesus. It was then that an apocalyptic explanation of the empty tomb was created and placed on the lips of an interpreting angel.

Mark took up the apocalyptically revised story of the tomb's discovery by the women and modified it for use in his Gospel:

> And when the sabbath was past, Mary Magdalene, and Mary the mother of James, and Salome, bought spices, so that they might go and anoint him. And very early on the first day of the week they went to the tomb when the sun had risen. And they were saying to one another, "Who will roll away the stone for us from the door of the tomb?" And looking up, they saw that the stone had been rolled back—it was very large. (Mk 16:1-4)

The memory of the empty tomb's discovery had already been theologically expanded before Mark used and further modified it for use in his Gospel. The rising sun, for example, is obviously intended as a symbol of the Resurrection of Jesus which frees us from our dark fear of death. We are also told that it is the first day of the week to remind us that the Risen Jesus is the beginning of the New Creation promised by the prophets (Is 65:17-18; 66:22; Dan 12:2-4).

Christian teachers were reminded by their reading of Genesis that the old creation had been called into being during a period of seven days, *beginning* with "the first day of the week" when God called "light" out of darkness (Gen 1:3-5). They then concluded that God had raised Jesus as the "light" of the world on Easter Sunday, "the first day" of the week, to signify that the New Creation has *begun* and is hastening toward its completion when the cosmic Sabbath will commence. (See Heb 4:3-5, 9-11 for an example of a Jewish Christian midrash dealing with the eschatological Sabbath.)

Because of the importance of New Creation theology in the earliest church, all four Gospels announce that the empty tomb was discovered on "the first day of the week" at or near the time of *sunrise* (Mk 16:1; Mt 28:1; Lk 24:1; Jn 20:1; 21:4). This announcement is tantamount to proclaiming that the New Creation promised by the prophets has begun with the Resurrection of Jesus.

Some have contended that the empty tomb tradition is quite late and is entirely a theological creation of the church. However, the prominence of "the first day" in the empty tomb story is evidence that the story is an early tradition. If "the first day" midrash which introduces the empty tomb narrative in all four Gospels had not been well established at an early date, the later and far more influential midrash on "the third day" in Hos 6:2 would have totally replaced it (see 1 Cor 15:4; compare Lk 24:1 to 24:7,21,46). The church certainly embellished the tradition of the empty tomb's discovery, but it is highly probable that the *underlying substance* of the tradition is reliable.

The concern of the women about how to move the large stone from the door of the tomb is a legendary touch added by an earlier apocalyptic interpreter of the empty tomb tradition. The women's concern is meant to create dramatic tension and prepare us for the discovery of the stone's "mysterious" removal. In reality, one healthy woman could have rolled the stone away from the door, and we may presume that it was the women themselves who did so on Easter morning.

When the surprised women enter the tomb, they are astonished by a revelatory encounter with an "interpreting" angel. The angel, of course, was added to the tomb tradition by the earliest church as a symbolic means of proclaiming the empty tomb's meaning. The angel, therefore, announces that the tomb is empty because Jesus *has been raised* (the Greek uses the passive voice):

> And entering the tomb, they saw a young man sitting on the right side, dressed in a white robe; and they were amazed. And he said to them, "Do not be amazed; you seek Jesus of Nazareth, who was crucified. He has risen; he is not here; see the place where they laid him. (Mk 16:5-6)

At this point, Mark interrupts the traditional narrative and augments the angel's message to the women:

> But go, tell the disciples and Peter that he is going before you to Galilee; there you will see him, as he told you. (Mk 16:7)

We know that Mark added 16:7 because it explicitly refers to a prediction which Mark had already placed on Jesus' lips in 14:28 ("But after I am raised up, I will go before you to Galilee"). Only someone who had editorially orchestrated the entire Gospel would have been able to arrange such a connection. Mark wished to conclude his Gospel with an angelic declaration *previewing* the appearances of the Risen Jesus to Peter and the other disciples in Galilee. The announcement of these forthcoming appearances was intended by Mark as the final unveiling of the "Messianic Secret" and, hence, as the glorious climax of his Gospel.

(We must remind ourselves that the *earliest* church did not recount the appearances of the Risen Jesus with narrative details. Instead, she "proclaimed" them as conclusive revelatory signs. It was for that reason that Mark, when writing the earliest Gospel, possesed only appearance traditions, and no Resurrection narratives. He innovatively decided, therefore, to "proclaim" the church's faith in the appearances of the Risen Jesus through the interpreting angel which he found in the apocalyptically expanded empty tomb story.)

In the book of Daniel (the first apocalypse, and the only one read to the Jews at the synagogue service), apocalyptic mysteries having to do with the end of the world are repeatedly revealed to Daniel through an *interpreting angel* (Dan 7:16; 8:15-17; 9:21-23). When Daniel receives these awe-inspiring revelations he is consistently overwhelmed with *fear* and *trembling,* and rendered *speechless* (Dan 7:15, 28; 8:17-18, 27; 10:7-11, 15-17). The three women in Mark 16:8 are described as acting in precisely this manner after the interpreting angel discloses the eschatological mystery of Jesus' Resurrection.

> And they went out and fled from the tomb, for trembling and astonishment had come upon them; and they said nothing to anyone, for they were afraid. (Mk 16:8)

The revelation of the empty tomb's meaning by an interpreting angel is an apocalyptic sign that the "end time" has arrived and its mysteries are beginning to unfold. The women's terrified response, therefore, is entirely appropriate and *expected.*

2

From the first Easter Sunday till the present, the empty tomb of Jesus has been a source of speculation and controversy. Many differing explanations of the tombs emptiness have been advanced since the time of its discovery. The explanation which one prefers will depend on the assumptions operating in one's world view. Possible explanations can be suggested ad infinitum. Not everything that is possible, however, is probable. We will examine seven of the better known explanations which have been suggested:

(1) The women went to the wrong tomb on Easter morning. The tomb they entered happened to be empty, and they mistakenly concluded that God had raised Jesus from the dead.

This interpretation was probably known to Mark and his church. Mark seems intent on refuting it when he goes out of his way to relate that two women who were disciples of Jesus were present as observers when the body of Jesus was interred by Joseph of Arimathea:

> And he bought a linen shroud, and taking him down, wrapped him in the linen shroud, and laid him in a tomb which had been hewn out of the rock; and he rolled a stone against the door of the tomb. Mary Magdalene and Mary the mother of Joses saw where he was laid. (Mk 15:46-47)

We saw in chapter eleven that this tradition is probably reliable, for if the early church had created it for apologetic reasons, the confirming witnesses would have been men instead of women.

There is an even weightier consideration that tells against the interpretation being considered: If the women had gone to the wrong tomb and had mistakenly concluded that God had raised Jesus, it would have been easy for the enemies of Jesus to expose such a mistake. They would only have had to go to the right tomb and produce the corpse of Jesus.

(2) The tomb was empty because enemies of Jesus stole his body to deny him a decent burial.

We know from the Fourth Gospel that this interpretation of the empty tomb was probably the original interpretation assigned by the disciples of Jesus in Jerusalem before they heard the apostolic witnessing to his appearances:

> Now on the first day of the week Mary Magdalene came to the tomb early, while it was still dark, and saw that the stone had been taken away from the tomb. So she ran, and went to Simon Peter and the other disciple, the one whom Jesus loved, and said to them, "They have taken the Lord out of the tomb, and we do not know where they have laid him." (Jn 20:2; *see also* 20:16)

This *earliest* stage of the tomb tradition knows nothing of an interpreting angel who reveals the empty tomb's meaning to the women who discovered it. When the Jerusalem disciples eventually heard the apostolic testimony, they changed their original explanation of the tomb's emptiness. They then decided that it was empty because God had taken Jesus through death into Risen Life. (And it was then that the *apocalyptic* interpretation of the tomb's discovery began to develop.)

At that stage, if enemies had stolen Jesus' body to further dishonor him, they would probably have found a way to disclose that fact in order to refute the disciples' claims. There is, however, no indication that anything like this occurred. Instead, the major counterclaim of the Jews was that Jesus' disciples had stolen his body (Mt 27:64).

(3) ***The tomb was empty because the disciples of Jesus stole his body and invented the story of his resurrection in order to vindicate their faith in him.***

We saw above that it was this interpretation which prompted Matthew to create his apologetic counterstory about the guards at the empty tomb. Such an interpretation is unlikely for at least two reasons. First, Jewish tradition at the time of Jesus did not expect the Resurrection of an individual. The apostles knew that the average Jew was predisposed to regard their claims about the *individual* raising of Jesus as preposterous. They had far more to lose than gain by inventing such a story and eventually dying for it. It is difficult to believe, therefore, that the apostles deliberately stole Jesus' body and fabricated their claims that the Risen Jesus appeared to them.

Second, we know from the circumstances of Paul's unusual conversion that he was in no way predisposed to vindicate either a prior state of faith in Jesus or the authority of Jesus. Quite the contrary. Nevertheless, Paul bore witness to the world that he had truly encountered the Risen Jesus. Furthermore, Paul finally sealed his testimony with his blood. Experience teaches that people do not make the kinds of sacrifices made by Paul and the other apostles for the sake of an invented story.

(4) ***Jesus was not truly dead when he was entombed, but in a coma. He later revived, left the tomb and died elsewhere. Because of this unusual development, the women found the tomb empty on Easter morning and mistakenly believed that God had raised Jesus from the dead.***

Some form of this interpretation also seems to have been known to Mark and his church, for Mark seems to be consciously rejecting it in his Gospel:

> Joseph of Arimathea, a respected member of the council, who was also himself looking for the kingdom of God, took courage and went to Pilate, and asked for the body of Jesus. And Pilate wondered if he were already dead; and summoning the centurion, he asked him whether he was dead. And when he learned from the centurion that

> he was dead, he granted the body to Joseph. (Mk 15:43-45)

Mark related the story about Pilate's inquiry (with its *redundant* references to Jesus' death) to reassure the members of his church that, contrary to the claims of some, Jesus was truly dead when buried. Had the Roman centurion in charge of Jesus' execution failed in his duty, his punishment would have been harsh. We may be certain, Mark implies apologetically, that the centurion carried out his orders with enlightened self interest.

Neither Matthew nor Luke relate Mark's apologetic narrative about Pilate's inquiry. The story is absent from their Gospels either because it was missing from their copies of Mark (i.e., had not yet been added to Mark's Gospel by a later editor), or because the churches for which they wrote were not troubled by the claim that Jesus was not dead when entombed. In the latter case, since they experienced no apologetic need for the story, they would have omitted it.

In addition to Mark's reason for rejecting the interpretation being considered, a number of other reasons make it improbable. To begin with, it is difficult to conceive that a crucified man who revived from a coma after being entombed would have been able to remove the large and heavy stone from the tomb's door while still inside the tomb. Even if he somehow managed to do so, he would not have been able to travel far before he either died or found assistance.

If he had died, his crucified corpse would probably have been discovered, reported, and identified. If he had received assistance, this also would probably have led to his identification and would have been reported. A bizarre set of circumstances in which a crucified celebrity left his tomb, but was not found, reported, and eventually identified is possible but not likely. Experience tells us that many things which are possible are not probable.

(5) Jesus was in a coma and not dead when interred. He later revived, left the tomb, and rejoined his disciples. His astonished disciples assumed that God had raised him from

the dead. They then proclaimed his resurrection to the world and pointed to his empty tomb as confirmation of their preaching.

If the scourged and crucified Jesus had managed somehow to leave his tomb and rejoin his disciples, he would have been alarmingly traumatized upon arrival. The notion that his disciples would then have concluded that he had been exalted by God as the Risen Lord is so implausible that it warrants no further comment.

(6) The tomb was empty because God raised and glorified the physical body of Jesus. Since Jesus' glorified physical body was able to pass through locked doors (Jn 20:19), it could also leave the tomb without hindrance.

This is the traditional Christian explanation of the empty tomb. It is based on a naively literal reading of the appearance accounts in the Gospels of Matthew (28:9), Luke (24:39-43), and John (20:20,27). Most exegetes, however, would agree that the physical details in these accounts are secondary and theological in nature. Such details, therefore, are not to be used as reliable sources of information when hypothesizing about the empty tomb. In addition, we noticed earlier that Paul the apostle teaches explicitly that the body of Risen Life is not physical, but spiritual (1 Cor 15:44-46,50).

(7) The tomb was empty because God accelerated the disintegration of Jesus' corpse. God intervened without violating nature to ensure that the appearances of the Risen Jesus would be clear and unambiguous revelatory signs pointing to eternal life.

Since the physical matter of our bodies is not taken through death into Risen Life, then, strictly speaking, the tomb of Jesus did not have to be empty. And yet, in view of the way apocalyptic hope was understood by most Jews in the apostolic age, it was *relatively necessary* for the tomb to be empty. For, guided by the canonical eschatology found in Dan 12:2-3 and Is 26:19, these Jews assumed that the *physical bodies* of the righteous dead would be resurrected in a gloriously transformed state.

If the enemies of Jesus had been able to produce his corpse, the apostolic claim that God raised Jesus from the dead would have been seriously compromised. It is inconceivable, however, that God would launch the Christian Message in history only to have its conclusive meaning contradicted by the production of a corpse. God knew that Jesus' tomb had to be empty if the apostolic witnessing was not to be contradicted by seemingly incompatible evidence.

The only way to guarantee that the revelatory import of Jesus' appearances would not be nullified (at that time in history) was for God to intervene without violating nature and ensure the tomb's emptiness. Precisely what form God's action took, it is impossible to say. But while it is true that we cannot answer the question before us with full certitude, it is also true that we have a duty to search for the best hypothesis we are capable of, given what we presently know.

We know, to begin with, that the only place in nature where God can act without interfering is in the human spirit which can *freely* open itself to divine influence. It is probably in the dimension of human spirit, then, that we should begin our search, and the human spirit most intimately related to Jesus' physical body was that of Jesus himself. With these considerations in mind, the following provisional solution is offered.

God probably acted through Jesus (whose freedom was fully open to the divine purpose) to activate a paranormal force which accelerated the disintegration of Jesus' corpse. This miraculous acceleration guaranteed that the tomb would be empty whether the disciples entered it to mourn Jesus, or the Jews opened it to refute the claim that God had "raised" him. God's action would not have violated creation, because human nature is already graced (or programmed) with the capacity to experience divine influence, respond freely to such influence, and become its instrument.

The result achieved by God's action through Jesus would be akin to the miraculous healings wrought through Jesus' freedom (and the freedom of those he healed) during his earthly ministry. By accelerating either the remission of pathology or the dissolution of Jesus' corpse, God would not have contradicted any laws of nature. Natural processes themselves can reverse physical or mental pathology and can reduce a corpse to dust. Correctly understood, therefore, the miraculous involves the divine activation of some paranormal capacity latent in nature.

By now it is obvious to the reader that the last explanation is the one favored by the author of this book. The reader, however, is obviously free to prefer one of the other six explanations or to create an eighth that better agrees with his or her experience.

Questions for Review and Discussion

1. Why may we be confident that the tradition of the empty tomb's discovery by a group of women on Easter Morning is probably reliable?
2. What was probably the very earliest explanation of the empty tomb provided by the disciples of Jesus? Where can we find evidence for this earliest interpretation in the Gospels?
3. When was the very earliest interpretation of the empty tomb abandoned by the disciples of Jesus?
4. In reality, how was the stone probably removed from the door of the empty tomb?
5. Why do all the Gospels tell us that the empty tomb was discovered on "the first day of the week"?
6. Why did Mark probably report that Pilate sought assurance from a Roman officer that Jesus was truly dead?
7. Why did Matthew join the story of the Roman guards at the tomb to the account of the empty tomb's discovery which he found in Mark?
8. What explanation for the tomb's emptiness was recommended in this book?
9. Would the explanation of the tomb's emptiness recommended in this book entail any violation or contradiction of nature's laws?

10. What are some of the other explanations of the tomb's emptiness listed in this chapter, and why do they seem either probable or improbable to you?

Chapter Thirteen: The Early Church's Messianic Interpretation of Jesus

1

WHEN THE RISEN AND SPIRIT-MEDIATING JESUS BEGAN APPEARING to and commissioning his disciples, they were, of course, stunned into recognition of his revelatory significance for Israel and the world. The unending process of remembering, interpreting, and witnessing to the Christ Event was then launched in history. Suddenly the disciples were confronted with an enormous task: The Risen Jesus had called them to be his witnesses, but what form should their testimony take?

Jesus' disciples were already familiar with the apocalyptic belief that God would "raise" the dead at the end-time. The resurrection of the dead had been an essential part of Jesus' Kingdom message (Mk 12:25; 14:25). The disciples, therefore, reached instinctively for the symbolic idea of resurrection and announced that God had "raised" Jesus as Good News to the world. (When speaking of Jesus' Resurrection, Mark, Matthew, and Luke always state that *God* raised Jesus. Paul uses the same language, except for 1 Thess 4:14. Translators frequently obscure this fact to satisfy the popular assumption [fostered by the Fourth

Gospel and the Nicene and Apostles' creeds] that Jesus raised himself.):

Mk 16:7

He was raised [*ēgerthē*]!

Mt 27:64; 28:7; Jn 2:22; 21:14

He was raised [*ēgerthē*] from the dead!

Lk 24:34

The Lord was raised [*ēgerthē*] indeed and appeared to Simon!

Acts 2:32

This Jesus God raised up [*anestēsen*], and of that we all are witnesses.

Acts 10:40

God raised [*ēgeiren*] him on the third day and made him manifest, not to all the people but to us who were chosen by God as witnesses.

Rom 10:9

If you confess with your lips that Jesus is Lord and believe in your heart that God raised [*ēgeiren*] him from the dead, you will be saved.

1 Cor 15:4

He was raised [*egēgertai*] on the third day in accordance with the scriptures.

The appearances of Jesus were experienced by his disciples as confirmation of his message about the nearness of God's end-time Kingdom. They concluded, therefore, that since the end-time events had mysteriously begun to unfold with the Resurrection of Jesus, the whole world would quickly come to an end and all the dead would be raised and judged with the living.

Jesus' disciples remembered that he had spoken of the exalted Son of Man as the one appointed by God to preside over the end-time (Lk 12:8; Mk 8:38). They decided, therefore, that the Risen Jesus had been revealed to them as that mysterious

Son of Adam, and that Jesus would soon return in glory to judge the living and the dead. Accordingly, the title Son of Man was the first regal title conferred on the Risen Jesus by the church. Luke tells us that around three years after Jesus' Resurrection, it was still the title for Jesus used by Stephen as he witnessed to a hostile crowd of Jews in Jerusalem:

> Now when they heard these things they were enraged. . . . and he said, "Behold, I see the heavens opened, and the Son of Man standing at the right hand of God." (Acts 7:54a,56)

Since the Son of Man was destined to be king of the New Creation, the earliest disciples also spoke of Jesus as "Lord." They addressed him as such when they prayed for his speedy return, at first in Aramaic (*marana tha* = Our Lord, come!; 1 Cor 16:22b; *Didache* 10:6) and soon also in Greek (*erkou kyrie Īēsou* = Come, Lord Jesus!; Rev 22:20b). The Risen One, they believed, had become the Lord of life and death empowered by God to gather God's servants into the New Creation.

Initially, the disciples did not consider giving the title Messiah to Jesus. For they remembered that Jesus had rejected the title at Caesarea Phillipi (Mk 8:27-33) and had refused to discuss it at his trial before Pontius Pilate (Mk 15:2). Furthermore, the ignominious outcome of Jesus' mission was so painfully contrary to Jewish Messianic expectations that to think of him as Messiah seemed impossible.

Nevertheless, as the disciples had more time to reflect on Jesus' tragic fate and its glorious outcome, they began to consider the possibility and even the necessity of giving him the title Messiah. They were historically encouraged to do so for a variety of reasons:

1. Most devout Jews, because of their faith in the words of God's prophets, still expected a Davidic Messiah to be instrumental in bringing definitive salvation to Israel. This hope could take either of two forms:

   a. the traditional expectation of a Golden Age *within* history;

b. some form of two stage apocalyptic hope that looked for an *interim* kingdom before the final establishment of the New Creation (beyond history).

2. These same devout Jews rightly insisted that the many prophetic promises of a Davidic Messiah had to be fulfilled.
3. Jesus' disciples believed that he was descended from David. This meant that, despite his jarring history, Jesus possessed the basic Messianic requirement.
4. Two stage apocalyptic theology eventually assigned *Messianic* titles to the end-time king called the Son of Man (e.g., Enoch 48:10; 52:4; 2 Esdras 7:28; 13:3-4, 51-52). If this development had already begun by the third decade of the first century, it might have suggested to the earliest church that she could join Messianic titles to her belief in Jesus as the Son of Man.
5. The exalted end-time king (and kingdom) promised in Daniel 7:13-14 could be understood midrashically as a hidden foreshadowing of God's "secret" Messianic purpose accomplished *preliminarily* through the exalted Jesus. This interpretation also explained why Jesus was raised *individually* before the General Resurrection.
6. Jesus had sternly rebuked Peter at Caesarea Philippi for assigning him the title Messiah (Mk 8:27-29,33). Yet, Jesus' noncommital response to the title when he was questioned by Pontius Pilate allowed the disciples to wonder: Did Jesus perhaps know that God secretly intended him to be an unexpected spiritual Messiah instead of a military Messiah? Jesus, after all, was put to death as the Jewish Messiah:

    The charge against him read, "The king of the Jews." (Mk 15:27)

Added to the above considerations was the gradual recognition that although Jesus had not invincibly led Israel in military conquest of the nations, he had nevertheless won a much greater victory over the powers of darkness. This spiritual victory, the disciples realized, was God's asssurance to Israel and the nations that they too, through the power of faith and trust, could defeat death and all the other evils encountered in history. Eternal Life and Joy in God's victorious end-time Kingdom had been divinely promised through the crucified and Risen Jesus.

All of these considerations finally led the majority of Jesus' disciples to understand that it was profoundly fitting to proclaim Jesus as God's "Messiah." They realized that they had almost completely redefined the title. But they assumed that this redefinition was a necessary corrective called for by the sacred history of Jesus which had culminated in his Spirit-mediating appearances as Risen Lord.

(Not all the disciples of the Risen Jesus agreed that he should be given the title Messiah. Those disciples, for example, who belonged to the community that produced the "Q Sayings" refused to do so. Jesus is never called Messiah in the Q material. The leaders of the Q community probably remembered that Jesus had rejected the title Messiah and they would not accept its redefinition by other Jewish Christians.)

(It was probably for that reason that Mark refused to use the Q Sayings in his Gospel. Mark wrote his Gospel to defend the secret nature of Jesus' spiritual Messiahship. He would not, therefore, have wished to encourage the theological views of the Q community.)

It goes without saying that the redefinition of the title Messiah by Jewish Christians was vigorously rejected by the Jews. Jewish objections, in turn, required the Jewish Christians to search the scriptures for midrashic proof texts. The authority of scripture was needed to support the Jewish Christian claim that God's "secret" Messianic purpose had all along been quite different from Israel's literally conceived military Messianism. We have already observed in earlier chapters that the more important of these proof texts were woven into the sacred history of Jesus to be used for understanding and defending their faith in his disputed Messiahship.

The Jews, no doubt, demanded to know why God would have concealed the true nature of the Messiah's mission. The church replied (in a culturally conditioned and apologetic fashion) that God had done so in order to prevent Satan from understanding and interfering with God's hidden Messianic purpose. The Messiah's secret mission was to destroy Satan's power over creation by undergoing an atoning death mysteriously presaged in the scriptures (Wis 2:22). The Messiah's death, in turn, made possible the victory of his Resurrection which is God's assurance to humankind of liberation from sin and death.

Through the unexpected triumph of Jesus' Resurrection, the satanic powers that bring darkness and death into the world have been defeated in principle:

> Baptism . . . now saves you . . . through the Resurrection of Jesus Messiah, who has gone into heaven and is at the right hand of God, with angels, authorities, and powers subject to him. (1 Pet 3:21-22)

The subjugation of the demonic powers will be concluded when Jesus returns in glory to defeat death forever and inaugurate the New Creation:

> Then comes the end, when he delivers the Kingdom to God the Father after destroying every rule and every authority and power. (1 Cor 15:24-25)

Paul the apostle was expressing the early church's faith in Jesus' "secretly" achieved victory over the powers of darkness when he declared:

> But we impart a *secret* and *hidden* wisdom of God, which God decreed before the ages for our glorification. None of *the rulers of this age* understood this; for if they had, they would not have crucified *the Lord of glory.* (1 Cor 2:7-8)

2

Mark's Gospel relates a story in which Jesus publicly questioned the traditional notion of Messiahship. It was probably Mark who created this story to teach that Jesus knew the title Messiah would have to be *redefined* to be correctly understood. (Mark sincerely believed that Jesus himself understood God's hidden Messianic purpose in the manner suggested by this story):

> And as Jesus taught in the temple, he said, "How can the scribes say that the Messiah is the son of David? David himself, inspired by the Holy Spirit, declared,
>
> > 'The Lord said to my Lord, sit at my right hand,
> > till I put your enemies under your feet.'
>
> David himself calls him Lord; so how is he his son?" (Mk 12:35-37a)

The question raised by Jesus in this story was not meant by Mark as a denial of the Davidic lineage of the Messiah. Mark provides clear evidence in other places that he believed in the Davidic Sonship of Jesus (see Mk 10:47-48; 11:10). Rather, the story intends to imply that Jesus knew the traditional view of Messiahip was too narrow. The definition, therefore, would have to be broadened to include the secret requirements revealed to Jesus at his baptism-anointing (Mk 1:9-11).

Messiahship, Jesus understood, must include his unexpected suffering as God's atoning "servant" (foreshadowed in Is 53:4-12) and his vindication as the exalted Son of Man-Messiah (adumbrated in Dan 7:13-14). Since this story related by Mark presupposes the apologetic-midrashic concerns of Mark and the early church, it should be understood as theology, not history.

Once the early church decided that she should redefine the title Messiah and give it to Jesus, the door was opened for use of the related Messianic titles "Son of David" and "Son of God" (and a Messianic understanding of the title "Lord"). These titles were gradually assigned to Jesus in stories which had originally lacked them. In the story of blind Bartimaeus, for instance, the title "Son of David" was added to a narrative in which Bartimaeus originally had cried out "Jesus, have mercy on me!":

> And when he heard that it was Jesus of Nazareth, he began to cry out and say, "Jesus, Son of David, have mercy on me!" (Mk 10:47)

Mark probably added the title Son of David to the story to suggest an apologetic lesson about Jesus. The story relates that Jesus was passing through Jericho and, consequently, was nearing Jerusalem for his tragic final visit. Mark wished to remind the church (and her Jewish critics) that the rejection of Jesus at Jerusalem had already been secretly suggested in the history of his father David:

Just as Jesus was destined for betrayal by a trusted friend (Judas) in Jersualem, so his father David had been betrayed by his trusted friend and adviser (Ahithophel) in Jerusalem (2 Sam 15:12; 16:15,20-17:3). Likewise, Jesus was about to be rejected by his people at Jerusalem just as David had been rejected by his people and fled from Jerusalem at the time of Absalom's revolt (2 Sam 15:13-18). The betrayal and rejection of Jesus, therefore, were not valid reasons for rejecting his Messianic identity.

3

When the earliest church redefined Messiahship, she had to hammer out a new understanding of precisely when this reconceived office would be (or had been) bestowed upon Jesus. Before this process was completed, it had passed through five major stages which can be traced in the New Testament:

Stage One: To fully appreciate the church's earliest attempt to explain Jesus' Messiahship, we must recall two basic pieces of information: (a) The church began reinterpreting Messiahship by associating it closely with the Son of Man destined to come in glory at the end of history. (b) There had been nothing regal or Messianic about the actual history of Jesus (judged by traditional expectations).

For these two reasons the church initially surmised that Jesus would not actually assume his royal Messianic office until he returned in manifest majesty as the Son of Man-Messiah. Some exegetes think we hear an echo of this earliest form of Christological speculation in Acts 3:20:

> Repent therefore, and turn again, that your sins may be blotted out. . . . and that he [God] may send the Messiah appointed for you, Jesus, whom heaven must receive until the time for establishing all that God spoke by the mouth of his holy prophets. (Acts 3:19a,20)

Stage Two: Further reflection, however, led others in the early church to conclude that Jesus had already been anointed as God's Messiah and adopted as God's Son at the moment of his *Resurrection.* Paul the apostle agreed with this departure from the purely future understanding of Jesus' Messiahship. The revised view seemed fully justified to Paul because he believed that the extraordinary outpouring of God's Spirit that had transformed Jesus into the Risen Lord *had also anointed Jesus* as God's Messiah:

> If the Spirit of him who raised Jesus from the dead dwells in you, then he who raised *Messiah* Jesus from the dead will also give life to your mortal bodies through his Spirit which dwells in you. (Rom 8:11)

It followed for Paul that the moment of Jesus' passage into Risen Life was also the moment when Jesus was *anointed* with God's Spirit and *adopted* as God's Messiah-Son:

> Paul, a servant of Jesus Messiah, called to be an apostle, set apart for the Good News of God . . . the Good News concerning his Son, who was descended from David according to the flesh and designated Son of God in power according to the Spirit of holiness by his resurrection from the dead. (Rom 1:1-4)

To fully grasp Paul's conviction that Jesus' *anointing* as God's Messiah was synonymous with Jesus' *adoption* as God's Son, we must again recall the pivotal prophecy delivered to David by Nathan the prophet:

> I will raise up your offspring after you, who shall come forth from your body, and I will establish his kingdom. . . . *I will be his father, and he shall be my son.* . . . And your house and your kingdom shall be made sure for ever before me; your throne shall be established forever. (2 Sam 7:12b,14a,16)

In this prophecy God promised to *adopt* David's heir on the day when that heir was *anointed* as David's successor. We saw earlier that God's promise to David was recalled and celebrated in the royal psalm sung on the occasion of a new Davidic king's anointing:

> I will tell of the decree of the Lord: He said to me, "You are my son, *today I have begotten you.*" Ask of me, and I will make the nations your heritage, and the ends of the earth your possession. (Ps 2:7)

The king was *externally* anointed with oil on the day of his adoption as God's Messiah-Son to signify that God had *internally* anointed him with the power of God's Holy Spirit. It was this internal anointing with God's Spirit that empowered the Messiah to exercise his sacred office worthily.

Stage Three: When Mark wrote his Gospel (c. A.D. 70), he had moved well beyond Paul's view that Jesus became God's Messiah when he was raised from the dead. It was clear to Mark that the exorcism of demons had been an astonishing and regular part of Jesus' mission. Mark realized, therefore, that Jesus was able to drive out evil spirits because he was already filled with the power of God's Holy Spirit (Mk 3:22-30).

Since Jesus was manifestly empowered to heal the sick and expel demons from the very beginning of his mission, Mark assumed that God had anointed Jesus with the Holy Spirit and adopted him as God's "Son" at the time of his baptism-anointing by John the Baptizer:

> And when he came up out of the water . . . he saw the heavens torn open and the Spirit descending upon him like a dove; and a voice came from heaven, "You are my beloved Son; with you I am well pleased." (Mk 1:10-11)

It was also on this occasion, Mark assumed, that God had revealed to Jesus the secret nature of the Messianic office to which he had been called.

Stage Four: At a still later stage in the early church's history, the infancy narratives were created. It is evident that when these stories were created the early church had once more revised her estimate of when Jesus was anointed and adopted as God's Messiah-Son. We have already learned in chapter two that Matthew and Luke each recounted a midrashic story which states that Jesus was miraculously conceived by the power of *God's Holy Spirit:*

Mt 1:18

> Behold, an angel of the Lord appeared to him in a dream saying, "Joseph, son of David, do not fear to take Mary your wife, for that which is conceived in her is of the Holy Spirit; she will bear a son, and you shall call his name Jesus, for he shall save his people from their sins."

Lk 1:35

> And the angel said to her, "The Holy Spirit will come upon you, and the power of the Most High will overshadow you; therefore the child to be born will be called holy, The Son of God."

Matthew and Luke both believed that when Jesus was conceived by the Holy Spirit he was also *anointed* by the Spirit and *adopted* as God's Messiah-Son. To verify this conclusion we need only recall the story of the wise men in Matthew's Gospel and the angel's message to the shepherds in Luke's:

Mt 2:2-6

> Behold, wise men from the East came to Jerusalem saying, "Where is he who has been born king of the Jews? For we have seen his star in the east and have come to worship him." When Herod the king heard this he was troubled . . . and he inquired . . . where the Messiah was to be born. They told him, "In Bethelehem of Judea."

Lk 2:10-11

> To you is born this day in the city of David a Savior who is Messiah and Lord. (Lk 2:10-11; see also Mt 2:2-6)

The change in Christological perspective which we find in the Infancy Narratives was the result of the early church's growing understanding that Jesus was destined from the very beginning of his existence to be the hidden Messiah promised by God to Israel.

Stage Five: In the prologue of John' Gospel we arrive at the time-transcending conclusion of the early church's speculation about Jesus' Messiahship. The inspired poetry of the prologue announces that God had intended Jesus to be the Son of Man-Messiah *before time began*. The inauguration of Jesus' Messiahship, therefore, reaches back mysteriously into God's *eternal purpose*.

Johannine theology speculates that when God undertook the work of creation, God consulted the divine "Word." (The divine Word is the Johannine symbol for God's creative knowledge and wisdom). God then foresaw in the divine Word that Adam would sin and bring suffering and death into creation. But God also foreknew through the same divine Word that God had a wise and gracious plan for saving (restoring) creation: God would raise up a New Adam to free creation from the evil inflicted on it by the old Adam.

Moreover, this Son of Adam would be not only a descendant of Adam but also the descendant of David through whom all the promises of salvation made to Israel would be fulfilled. But God chose to conceal the true identity and destiny of the Davidic Messiah. God did so to prevent *the powers of darkness* from comprehending and interfering with God's plan to restore creation.

When, therefore, the time arrived for God to begin the final stage of restoring all things, God's very Word (which contained God's foreknowledge of the hidden divine purpose) joined itself mysteriously to the "flesh" (i.e., human nature) of the descendant of David elected to be the Son of Adam-Messiah. The one so chosen was Jesus of Nazareth. God effected an unparalleled union between God's saving Word and the "flesh" of Jesus to ensure that God's final purpose for creation would be victorious against the powers of darkness.

To fully grasp the prologue's sublime meaning, we must recognize that when it describes God as beginning the work of creation it likens God to a divine architect or master builder consulting a divine master plan (God's Word). The divine Word which contains God's plan for creation is *personified* as a divine agent consulted for the work of creation and finally sent on a temporal mission to ensure the accomplishment of God's saving purpose in Jesus:

> When time began the Word was already there, and the Word was face to face with God, and the Word was God's Word. He was with God in the beginning; all things were made through him, and without him was not anything made that was made. In him was life and the life was the light of humankind. The light shines in the darkness, and the darkness has not overcome it. (Jn 1:1-5)

> And the Word became flesh and pitched his tent among us, full of grace and truth; we have beheld his glory, glory as of the only Son from the Father. . . . And from his fulness we have all received, grace upon grace. For the law was given through Moses; but grace and truth came through Jesus Messiah. (Jn 1:14,16-17)

4

The first four stages of the early church's evolving Christological speculation are "adoptionist" Christologies. They all agree that God *will* or *did* anoint and adopt Jesus as God's Messiah-Son by pouring the Holy Spirit into Jesus' being at a particular moment—his second coming, his Resurrection, his baptism, or his conception. Such a Christological perspective is sometimes referred to as Christology *from below*. Christology from below views the Spirit-anointed humanity of Jesus, David's descendant, as the primary instrument of God's purpose in the Christ event.

It is noteworthy, however, that the fifth stage of the early church's Christological reflection is called "Incarnational" Christology or Christology *from above*. This approach stresses that God's eternal Word descended from on high and became "incarnate" in the "flesh" of Jesus. Christology from above regards the divine Word which joined itself to Jesus as the primary agent in God's Messianic purpose; the human nature of Jesus is secondary. The *Davidic descent* of Jesus, therefore, is not emphasized; instead, the *descent of God's saving Word* into Jesus is assigned primary significance.

Eventually, the Incarnational Christology from above (which dominates the Fourth Gospel) superseded the earlier Christologies from below in the history of the church. This development is understandable when we remember that the Fourth Gospel's emphasis on the Incarnation of God's Word (*logos*) was highly congenial to the Hellenized modes of thought which prevailed in the ancient world. For example, it was probably because Stoic philosophy had ascribed overarching significance to the divine Word or Reason (*logos*) which governs the universe that the Hellenized Jewish philosopher Philo attributed a major role in creation to God's Word or Reason (*logos*); see his *De Opificio Mundi,* 24-25).

When the ancient church formulated her official profession of faith (the Nicene creed), she preferred the grand sweep and explicit divine involvement expressed by the symbolic language of Christology from above: God's eternal Word descended to earth and united with the humanity of Jesus in order to show humans the way to Eternal Life with God. In the descending Christology of the ancient church, therefore, it is primarily God's *Word* in Jesus rather than Jesus who becomes our guide to Eternal Life and Joy.

What should we think about the manifest differences between Christology done from above and that done from below? Are the two approaches contradictory? Was the early church in error during the period when she did Christology from below? The answer to both these questions is "no." The varying approaches to doing Christology created by the early church are salutary reminders that the Christ event is a richly faceted mystery which can be interpreted in a number of different but reconcilable ways. At various times and places in the church's history, various of these basically compatible facets were singled out for emphasis.

Christology from below begins *within history* and emphasizes the humanity of Jesus as the concrete sign through whom God works to give humankind definitive assurance of salvation. Christology from above, on the other hand, begins *beyond history.* It stresses that it is because God's revealing and saving

Word has entered history and dwells in Jesus that Jesus is able to be an efficacious sign of salvation for the world.

Again, Christology from below proclaims the hidden and unexpected Messianic victory of the Risen Jesus over the powers of darkness as God's guarantee of salvation for Israel and the nations. With a decidedly different emphasis, however, Incarnational Christology reminds us that God's eternal plan for finally freeing creation from evil was accomplished by God's eternal Word acting in and through the "flesh" of Jesus.

It is important to recognize that the differing Christological emphases created by the early church are ultimately in accord. Some of the five views listed above include more insight, and some less. But they are all essentially correct faith recognitions that the Risen Jesus is the Messiah-Son of God who mediates God's definitive assurance of salvation to the world.

For it is true that when the mystery of Jesus' "second coming" is finally accomplished, it will be evident to all that he is the Spirit-anointed Messiah who has brought God's plan of salvation to victorious completion. Likewise, when Jesus was "raised" from the dead by God's empowering and anointing Spirit, God revealed to Jesus (and the church) that Jesus had been "adopted" as God's Messiah-Son.

Also, when Jesus was baptized, even if he did not yet know that he had been chosen to be God's "secret" Messiah, God knew that he had been. For God knew that Jesus' freely offered commitment and Davidic descent could be used to accomplish God's hidden Messianic purpose. And when, still earlier, Jesus was conceived, God knew that Jesus was the descendant of David elected by the divine purpose for adoption as God's Messiah-Son.

Finally, it is also true that the hidden Messianic purpose of God which anointed and revealed Jesus at his Resurrection does reach back *beyond time*. For God's saving purpose for creation was eternally foreknown in the divine Word which became flesh in Jesus.

Questions for Review and Discussion

1. What was the first regal title given to the Risen Jesus by his disciples, and why did they think it appropriate to do so?
2. For what two reasons were the disciples of the Risen Jesus initially disinclined to think of him as God's Messiah?
3. What are some of the reasons that gradually led Jesus' disciples to overcome their disinclination to give him the title Messiah?
4. Why did the early church think that God had kept the Messiah's identity and mission a "secret"?
5. Why did Mark probably add the title "Son of David" to the story of blind Bartimaeus healed by Jesus at Jericho?
6. What were the five major stages which the Christological speculation of the early church passed through?
7. How did the *first four* stages of the early church's Christological speculation differ from the *fifth* and final stage?
8. What do biblical scholars mean by the "Adoptionist" Christologies in the New Testament, and why did the early church think that Jesus should be "adopted" by God?
9. What is "Incarnational" Christology and how does it differ from the earlier "Adoptionist" Christologies in the New Testament?
10. How does Christology "from above" differ from Christology "from below"? Which of the two provided the symbolic framework for the Nicene Creed?
11. Why did the ancient (post-apostolic) church eventually favor descending Incarnational Christology over ascending Adoptionist Christology?
12. Are Christologies from above and from below basically compatible or incompatible? Explain your answer.

Chapter Fourteen: The Church's Symbolic Divinization of Jesus

1

AFTER THE EARLY CHURCH HAD ABSORBED THE IMPACT OF THE risen Jesus' Spirit-mediating appearances, she began to reflect on the astonishing revelation which God had given her. The church soon recognized that the knowledge of God's saving purpose disclosed to her through the Risen Jesus reached back beyond time into the mystery of God's eternal purpose. When she began to work out her understanding of God's time-transcending purpose, the church was primarily aided by the symbolic poetry which she found in the Old Testament "wisdom" literature.

The Wisdom literature of the Hebrew and Greek versions of the Old Testament had gradually personified God's Wisdom and had assigned it an instrumental role in the work of creation. (The Greek-speaking majority in the early church used the Greek Old Testament for study and worship.) Before the world was created, the Wisdom literature informs us, "Wisdom" was already in the presence of God:

> With you is wisdom who knows your works and was present when you made the world. (Wis 9:9)

("Wisdom" is a feminine noun in Hebrew and Greek; consequently, personified references to God's Wisdom require feminine pronouns.) Since Wisdom signifies God's creative knowledge, she is described symbolically as a luminous mirror into which God peers for a clear picture of the divine purpose. Before engaging in creative activity, therefore, the divine Architect consults divine Wisdom:

> For she is a reflection of eternal light, a spotless mirror of the working of God, and an image of his goodness. (Wis 7:26)

Accordingly, when God called creation into being, Wisdom was at God's "side" facilitating God's purpose:

> When he established the heavens, I was there,
> when he drew a circle on the face of the deep,
> when he made firm the skies above,
> when he established the fountains of the deep,
>
> when he assigned to the sea its limit, so that
> the waters might not transgress his command,
> when he marked out the foundations of the earth,
> then I was beside him like a master workman.
> (Prov 8:27-30)

In the *Wisdom of Solomon,* God's Wisdom is identified with God's creative Word (of command) in the Genesis creation story:

Gen 1:3,6,8a

> And God *said,* "Let there be light"; and there was light. . . . And God *said,* "Let there be a firmament in the midst of the waters. . . . And God called the firmament Heaven.

Ps 33:6

> By the *word* of the Lord the heavens were made, and all their host by the breath of his mouth.

Wis 9:1-2,4a

> O God of my fathers and Lord of mercy, who have made all things by your *word,* and by your *wisdom* have formed humans to have *dominion* over the creatures you

> have made. . . . Give me the wisdom that sits by your *throne.*
>
> Wis 18:14-15a
>
> For while gentle silence enveloped all things, your all-powerful *word* leaped down from heaven, from the royal *throne,* into the midst of the land that was doomed, a stern warrior carrying the sword of your authentic *command.*

God's Word of Wisdom is spoken of as coming forth from God's mouth (Sir 24:3), sitting by God's throne (Wis 9:4; 18:14), and being sent into the world to instruct humans (Wis 9:9-10; 18:15). Finally, Wisdom is said to have been sent by God to dwell in Israel:

> Then the creator of all things gave me a *command,* and the one who created me assigned a place for my *tent.* And he said, "Make your dwelling in Jacob, and in Israel receive your inheritance." (Sir 24:8)

As the early church reflected on the role of Wisdom in the attainment of God's purpose in creation, she found mysterious midrashic portendings which she believed foreshadowed the mission of Jesus. She concluded that when God consulted divine Wisdom *before* creation, God foresaw Adam's fall. It was then evident to God that the disobedience of Adam would require a New Adam to be God's obedient instrument in freeing the Kingdom of creation from evil. God also foreintended that the election of Israel and the house of David would be essential to the New Adam's final victory over the powers of darkness. Before creation began, therefore, God's secret Messianic purpose was *foreknown* in God's Wisdom.

God's Wisdom, the church believed, was finally "sent" to Israel to accomplish God's conclusive purpose in history through Jesus, the New Adam-Messiah. Jesus, therefore, may be understood, she decided, as the Wisdom of God "incarnate" (i.e., the human to whom God's Wisdom has joined itself in order that God's Reign over creation might be definitively restored).

When the church appropriated the Wisdom symbolism in the Old Testament to explain Jesus and his mission, she went well beyond its limits. Personified Wisdom in the Old Testament was "created" by God prior to the creation of the world (Prov 8:22; Sir 24:8-9). The church, however, decided that it was God's *eternal* and *uncreated* Wisdom who had descended into Jesus. (We should remind ourselves that the presence of God's personified Wisdom in Jesus actually signifies *God's own presence* acting through Jesus in a way that assures the world of salvation.)

2

After the church understood that "the Wisdom of God" was definitively present and acting in Jesus during the Christ event, she began to weave allusions to Wisdom into sayings which she attributed to Jesus:

> The queen of the South will arise at the judgment with the men of this generation and condemn them, for she came from the ends of the the earth to hear the wisdom of Solomon, and behold, something greater than Solomon is here. (Lk 11:31)

In time, the church went further by creating sayings in which Jesus *identified himself* as God's Wisdom incarnate:

> John came neither eating nor drinking, and they say, "He has a demon"; the Son of man came eating and drinking, and they say, "Behold, a glutton and a drunkard, a friend of tax collectors and sinners!" *Yet Wisdom is justified by her deeds.* (Mt 11:18-19)

Only the last sentence in the passage just cited identifies Jesus with Wisdom. The preceding material to which the church joined the Wisdom saying is probably authentic because it presupposes a critical attitude toward Jesus which the church would never have invented. More importantly, it implies a relation of parity between Jesus and John which the church soon denied.

Since sayings which identify Jesus with God's Wisdom express the theological concerns of the early church, it is reasonable to conclude that they were not spoken by Jesus. Such sayings were probably created by charismatic prophet-teachers who addressed the early church in the name of the Risen Jesus (and who found the mystery of Jesus presaged in the wisdom literature).

In the following Matthean saying, for example, the "Risen" Jesus speaks words which paraphrase the instruction delivered to humans by personified Wisdom:

Mt 11:29-30

> Come to me, all you who labor and are heavy laden, and I will give you rest. Take my yoke upon you and learn from me; for I am gentle and lowly of heart, and you will find rest for your souls. For my yoke is easy, and my burden is light.

Sir 24:19,22

> Come to me, all you who desire me, and eat your fill of my produce. . . . Whoever obeys me will not be put to shame, and those who work with my help will not sin.

Sir 51:26-27

> Put your neck under the yoke, and let your souls receive instruction. . . . See with your eyes that I have labored little and found for myself much rest.

3

The early church, in her efforts to point to God's definitive revealing presence in Jesus, sometimes resorted to an extraordinary kind of *hyperbole* (hyperbole is creative exaggeration which calls attention to something subtle which might be overlooked): She sometimes said about Jesus what is properly true only of God, and about God what is literally true only of Jesus. Christian theologians refer to this hyperbolic Christian use of language as "the interchange of attributes" (also called "the interchange of predicates") This symbolic "interchange" has been a characteristic of Christian theology from the apostolic age to the present.

For example, Jesus, even though his humanity is created and temporal, was said by some New Testament authors to have existed with God before the world was created. (We will examine several of these statements below). If taken literally, such statements contradict our experience of the true nature of human finitude, which is intrinsically time-bound and contingent. Nevertheless, as *symbolic* expressions of Christian belief that God's time-transcending purpose for humankind has been revealed within time through Jesus, these hyperbolized statements are permissible and sublimely meaningful. They constitute an extraordinary form of sacred poetry peculiar to Christian discourse.

Well before the Gospels were written, Paul the apostle had figuratively likened Jesus to God's Wisdom by ascribing to Jesus Wisdom's "instrumental" role in the work of creation:

> For us there is one God, the Father, from whom are all things and for whom we exist, and one Lord, Jesus Christ, through whom are all things and through whom we exist. (1 Cor 8:6)

Since God's Wisdom is now mysteriously present in Jesus, Paul concluded, Jesus may be figuratively spoken of as the "mediator" of God's purpose for creation and its restoration. (Flights of apotheosizing were not unusual in the ancient world.) Nevertheless, while Paul, broadly speaking, identified Jesus with the Wisdom of God, he carefully avoided any suggestion of *identity* between God and Jesus ("God was in Christ reconciling the world to himself;" 2 Cor 5:18).

Paul evidently believed that it was because God's Wisdom was present in Jesus that the Risen Jesus had been able to accomplish the preliminary stage of God's wise plan for finally restoring all of creation:

> Creation itself will be set free from its bondage to decay and will obtain the glorious freedom of the children of God. We know that the whole of creation has been groaning together in travail until now; and not only creation, but we ourselves, who have the first fruits of the Spirit,

> groan inwardly as we wait for . . . the redemption of our bodies. (Rom 8:20b-23)

Also, in his *Letter to the Philippians,* Paul quoted an early Christian hymn which celebrates the descent of God's Wisdom into Jesus: Wisdom, the hymn exults, has entered permanently into Jesus the New Adam to enable him to accomplish God's redemptive purpose for creation. Jesus, in turn, by becoming obedient unto death, has freed creation from the curse inflicted on it by the disobedience of the old Adam. And since God's purpose has been attained in Jesus, the hymn continues, Jesus has been exalted into heavenly glory as a sign to all creation that God's conclusive victory over the powers has been won. (Recall that Wisdom is said to be the "image" [or form] of God [Wis 7:26], and that Adam of old conspired with the woman to be "like God;" Gen 3:5,22.):

> Though he was in the form of God, he did not count equality with God a thing to be clung to,
>
> but emptied himself, taking the form of a slave, being born in the likeness of men.
>
> And being found in human form, he humbled himself, and became obedient unto death.
>
> Therefore God has highly exalted him and has bestowed on him the name which is above every name,
>
> that at the name of Jesus every knee should bow, in heaven and on earth and under the earth,
>
> and that every tongue should confess "Jesus Messiah is Lord," to the glory of God the Father. (Phil 2:6-11)

One of Paul's disciples likewise identified Jesus as divine Wisdom in the *Letter to the Colossians.* (Colossians is a deutero-Pauline letter, i.e., it was written by a disciple of Paul, not by Paul himself.) The author of the letter borrowed language from the Wisdom literature in order to present Jesus in the guise of God's creative Wisdom:

> He is the image of the invisible God, the first-born of all creation; for in him all things were created, in heaven and on earth, visible and invisible, whether thrones or do-

> minions or principalities or authorities— all things were created through him and for him. He is before all things, and in him all things hold together. (Col 1:15-16a)

The superiority of Jesus over invisible angelic spirits is emphasized by the author of Colossians to remind the church that Jesus, the New Adam, was destined by God before time began to defeat the fallen angels and to free creation from their power. Such theological symbolism was vital to the early church's task of assuring believers that their lives were no longer subject to the powers of darkness.

Jesus is also said to have existed "before all things" and to hold "all things" in creation together. Again, he is spoken of in this symbolic manner to call attention to the presence of God's Wisdom within him guiding and empowering him to accomplish the restoration of all things. The saving purpose of God foreknown *before* time in the divine Wisdom is now being accomplished *within* time through Jesus.

4

The New Testament's most daring use of wisdom poetry is found in the Gospel of John. We saw in the last chapter that the hymn which begins this Gospel celebrates the belief that God's Eternal Word descended from heaven and became "flesh" in Jesus. When reflecting on the relation between God's eternal purpose and the mission of Jesus, the Johannine church preferred to use the masculine noun "Word" (*logos*) rather than the feminine noun "Wisdom" (*sophia*). The masculine synonym for Wisdom (Wis 9:1-2,4a; 18:14-15a) seemed more appropriate to the author of the Johannine Gospel because the flesh (human nature) into which God's Wisdom "descended" was that of Jesus, God's Messiah-Son:

> When time began the Word was already there, and the Word was face to face with God, and the Word was God's own Word. He was with God in the beginning; all thing were made through him, and without him was not anything made that was made. In him was life, and the

> life was the light of humankind. The light shines in the darkness, and the darkness has not overcome it. (Jn 1:1-5)
>
> And the Word become flesh and pitched his tent among us, full of grace and truth; we have beheld his glory, glory as of the only Son from the Father. . . . And from his fulness we have all received, grace upon grace. For the law was given through Moses; but grace and truth came through Jesus Messiah. (Jn 1:14,16-17)

Whereas the other New Testament authors who point to the presence of God's Wisdom in Jesus do so only on rare occasions, the Fourth Evangelist does so almost continually. We must regularly remind ourselves when reading his Gospel that he is using the "interchange of attributes" to call attention to the unparalleled presence of the Divine Word (God communicating revelatory knowledge) in Jesus.

Jesus, for example, speaks in the passage immediately below as if he had existed with God *before time began.* We must remember, however, that the Fourth Evangelist intends us to understand that God's eternal Word has united with Jesus and now speaks through Jesus. (Presenting Jesus in this fashion ensures that we will not fail to recognize God's definitive revealing presence in Jesus):

> "Your Father Abraham rejoiced that he was to see my day; he saw it and was glad." The Jews then said to him, "You are not yet fifty years old, and have you seen Abraham?" Jesus said to them, "Truly, truly, I say to you, before Abraham was, I am." (Jn 8:56-58)

Even though the Fourth Evangelist delights in pointing to the presence of the Word of God in Jesus, the Fourth Gospel does not identify Jesus with God:

Jn 17:3

> This is eternal life, that they may know you, the *only* true God, *and* him whom you have sent, Jesus Christ.

Jn 14:2

> Believe in God; believe *also* in me.

5

There is a well known passage in John's Gospel which is traditionally assumed to *identify* Jesus as God. This traditional reading, however, must be carefully clarified. The passage in question occurs near the end of the story in which "doubting Thomas" encounters the Risen Jesus.

Exegetes tell us that the story about "doubting Thomas" was created apologetically by the Fourth Evangelist and added later to his Easter account. The story was added to reassure Johannine Christians that the original disciples had truly encountered the Risen Jesus: Even a skeptic like Thomas was finally convinced:

> Now Thomas, one of the twelve, called the Twin, was not with them when Jesus came. So the other disciples told him, "We have seen the Lord." But he said to them, "Unless I see in his hands the print of the nails, and place my finger in the mark of the nails, and place my hand in his side, I will not believe. (Jn 20:24-25)

> Eight days later, the disciples were again in the house, and Thomas was with them. The doors were shut, but Jesus came and stood among them, and said, "Peace be with you." Then he said to Thomas, "Put you finger here and see my hands; and put out your hand and put it in my side; do not be faithless, but believing." Thomas answered him, "My Lord and my God!" Jesus said to him, "Have you believed because you have seen me? Blessed are those who have not seen and yet believe." (Jn 20:26-29)

The intended meaning of Thomas' response to Jesus in 20:28 ("My Lord and my God") will elude us unless we remember the preparatory conversation which Jesus had with Thomas (and Philip) at the Last Supper. Their conversation was initiated when (the divine Word in) Jesus announced that he was about to return (through death) to the Father in order to show us "the way" to reach Eternal Life:

> ". . . And when I go and prepare a place for you, I will come again and will take you to myself, that where I am

> you may be also. And you know the way where I am going." (Jn 14:3-4)

Thomas fails to grasp the meaning of Jesus' words, but his lack of understanding provides Jesus with an opportunity to further instruct him (and the church). The question asked of Jesus by Thomas involves "Johannine irony." Thomas is speaking to Jesus who is the Way, but Thomas does not yet fully "know" Jesus with the eyes of faith. Nor does Thomas yet fully recognize the revealing presence of the Father in Jesus "speaking" a definitive Word of salvation through Jesus:

> Thomas said to him, "Lord, we do not know where you are going; how can we know the way?" Jesus said to him, "I am the way, and the truth, and the life; no one comes to the Father but by me." (Jn 14:5-6)

When the Johannine Jesus says to Thomas, "No one comes to the Father but by me," he does not mean that only those who come to know and believe in Jesus can reach Eternal Life. If that were true, the enormous number of humans who have never had a chance to learn about Jesus (the overwhelming majority) would be excluded from God's gracious love and saving purpose, which is patently absurd.

What the Johannine Jesus is truly telling us is that we cannot come to the Father with *prior certainty* that the Father loves us and will gather us into Eternal Life unless we "know" the definitive assurance which God communicates to the world through the Risen and Spirit-mediating Jesus (Jn 20:22). Also, we cannot have prior knowledge of the "Way" which ensures our safe passage to the Father unless we learn to follow Jesus with faith and trust (Jn 1:37,40,43).

(It is important to recognize that the Fourth Evangelist wrote the dialog between Jesus and Thomas in chapter fourteen of his Gospel during a period of intense conflict with a nearby community of Jews [9:22; 15:18-21; 16:2]. Some of the Jews who belonged to this nearby community secretly believed in Jesus but were afraid to acknowledge him publicly for fear of expulsion from the synagogue [9:22; 12:42]. John's language sometimes intends to warn and embarrass these cryptic Christians into testifying publicly to their faith in Jesus [12:43]).

(This special set of circumstances explains why the Johannine Jesus sometimes insists that one must acknowledge him as God's Messiah if one hopes to attain salvation. This teaching was meant to address the timidity of a particular group of Jewish *Christians* at a specific time and place in history. It must be carefully qualified when read in later and different circumstances. When such historically conditioned language is understood with naive literalness, it unfailingly produces an intolerant fanaticism contrary to the intention of Jesus [13:34-35; 14:12; Mt 5:43-48; 1 Jn 4:16,20-21] and his apostles.)

(Paul the apostle assures us that people who do not know Jesus as God's definitive assurance of salvation can also reach Eternal Life [Rom 2:12-16]. But such people do not possess the same kind and measure of assurance about God's love, forgiveness, and offer of Eternal Life that a disciple of Jesus possesses. This, however, does not mean that God loves Christians more than other people. It means that Christians are privileged to know about God's unconditional love for them and all other people with a definitive kind of revelatory certainty that others do not yet possess.)

Jesus continues by informing Thomas that if Thomas really "knew" (with the eyes of fully informed faith) who Jesus is, he would know that when he encounters Jesus he is also encountering God who is conclusively revealing the divine Self-gift to the world through (the Risen, Spirit-mediating) Jesus. Thomas is finally assured that the time *is at hand* (because Jesus will soon be glorified) when Thomas will "know" with stunning certainty that one who encounters (the Risen) Jesus also encounters the revealing and saving presence of God:

> "If you had known me, you would have known my Father also; henceforth you know him and have seen him." (Jn 14:7)

Philip then compounds Thomas' lack of comprehension by asking Jesus to "show" them the Father (which very thing Jesus has been doing and will do conclusively when he returns as Risen Lord):

> Philip said to him, "Lord, show us the Father, and we shall be satisfied." Jesus said to him, "Have I been with you so long, and yet you do not know me, Philip? He who has seen me has seen the Father; how can you say, 'Show us the Father'? Do you not yet know that I am in the Father and the Father in me? The words that I say to you I do not speak on my own authority; but the Father who dwells in me does his works." (Jn 14:8-10)

We are now prepared to grasp the subtle meaning of Thomas' astonished response to the Risen Jesus in 20:28: When Thomas says, "My Lord," (*ho kurios mou*) he is addressing the Risen Jesus. But when he says, "and my God" (*kai ho theos mou*), Thomas is addressing the definitive revealing presence of the Father whom he now recognizes with full faith awareness to be present in and addressing him through the Risen Jesus (Jn 1:14,18).

6

By now it should be clear to the reader (if it has not been heretofore) that whenever the Christian tradition "apotheosizes" Jesus by calling him God or asserting that he is divine, it is speaking figuratively, not literally. To apotheosize is to speak poetically by attributing divinity to a creature who participates to an extraordinary degree in one or more of God's perfections (beauty, power, wisdom, love). Such statements symbolically employ (even if unconsciously) that peculiarly Christian idiom called "the interchange of attributes."

However, when poets apotheosize Helen of Troy, it is always apparent to those who hear or read their words that they are not assigning literal divinity to a human. Instead, guided by the law of resemblance (every effect resembles its cause), poets are celebrating a divine attribute reflected to an exceptional degree by a creature.

Unfortunately, when preachers and teachers in the Christian tradition attribute divinity to Jesus, it is not always evident that the language being used should be understood nonliterally. If these people are asked about the ambiguity which accompanies their language, they usually reply that their language is expressing a "mystery" which requires faith.

In such a response, however, the word "mystery" actually functions as a synonym for "symbol." When Christians tell us that their language bespeaks "mysteries," they are implicitly (unconsciously) acknowledging that there is necessarily something nonliteral and mysterious about language which speaks of "transempirical" (or inferred) realities.

Such Christians, therefore, are speaking symbolically whether they understand this to be true or not. They frequently, however, become defensive and hostile if they are told that their religious language is necessarily symbolic in nature. Their negative response is usually triggered by popular misunderstanding of the word "symbolic."

People who are not aware that language is necessarily symbolic when used to illustrate transempirical realities usually assume that what is "literally" true is *really* true, and that what is "symbolically" true is *not* really true. This popular misconception explains the resistance frequently generated by the word "symbol." Sincere but misinformed people fear that they would be denying their faith in God's word if they grant that some parts of scripture express symbolic instead of literal truth.

7

It will greatly facilitate our effort to understand traditional Christian statements about the mystery of the Incarnation if we briefly review the important philosophical differences between "divine" and "human" attributes. From the beginning of Christianity to the present, Christians have experienced two intimately related but *distinct* dimensions of reality in Jesus. Both the human nature of Jesus and the divine nature of God are simultaneously present when we encounter Jesus with faith.

Paul the apostle acknowledged this twofold faith awareness when he declared that "God was in Christ reconciling the world to himself" (2 Cor 5:19). Paul "knew" that when he encountered the Risen Jesus (1 Cor 9:1b; 15:8), he had also encountered the revealing presence of God (Gal 1:15-16). But Paul also realized that God's revealing presence "in" Jesus should not be *identified* with Jesus. Paul never calls anyone God but the Creator; he usually calls Jesus the (Risen) Lord or Messiah.

We have seen above that The Gospel of John testifies to this same divine-human duality in Jesus when it announces in the prologue hymn that the "Word" of God became "flesh" in Jesus. When the hymn speaks of the Word of God, it is pointing to God's conclusive revealing presence in Jesus. But when it speaks of the flesh with which the divine Word was united, it is signifying the human nature of Jesus.

THE NATURE OF THE DIVINE WORD (OR GOD'S REVEALING PRESENCE IN JESUS) IS:

1. *Absolute* (God possesses unlimited power to be and in no way depends on any other for the power to be.)
2. *Eternal* (God possesses the power to be in a way that involves no beginning and no end.)
3. *Necessary* (God possesses the power to be in such a way that it is not possible for God not to be.)
4. *Infinite* (God possesses the power to be in absolute and inexhaustible measure.)
5. *Uncreated* (God eternally derives the power to be from God alone and not from any prior cause or source on whom God might be dependent or from whom God might have been derived.)

BY CONTRAST, THE HUMAN NATURE OF JESUS IS:

1. *relative* (humans are bound by limits which make them dependent on God [and parents] for the power to be)

2. *temporal* (humans have a physical beginning and end within space-time)
3. *contingent* (humans are dependent on others—God, parents, and other persons and things—for their initial and continued existence)
4. *finite* (humans possess the power to be in a way that is bound by physical and temporal limits)
5. *created* (humans are called into being by the absolute Being upon whom they ultimately depend for their power to be)

The attributes of God's nature and Jesus' nature are necessarily ontological opposites. If these differing attributes are correctly understood, it is obvious that God cannot cease being God and literally become a created and contingent human being. Likewise, Jesus could not cease being a created human being and "literally" become identical with God. When the Word of God united with the human nature of Jesus, therefore, the nature of God and the nature of Jesus remained distinct and essentially unaltered even though they were intimately united to an unparalleled degree.

By analogy, when bridegroom and bride unite in the ecstasy of their love, they may temporarily feel that all distinctions or barriers between them have been dissolved, and that they have become totally "one." In reality, however, they do not lose their distinct identities. When their rapture subsides, they recognize that their separate identities are still intact and essentially unaltered. *United does not mean identical.*

We have already observed above that the Christian tradition has created a special idiomatic way of speaking about the mystery of the Incarnation called "the interchange of attributes." Once this peculiarly Christian way of speaking about the Incarnation was inaugurated, it remained a permanent part of the Christian tradition and is still with us.

A Christian who employs this symbolic idiom assigns the absolute and uncreated attributes of God to Jesus. Conversely, popular preaching and teaching frequently assign the finite and created attributes of Jesus to God. Christians in past centuries daringly employed such hyperbolic language for a laudable reason. They wished to ensure that those hearing their words (especially the uneducated) would be able to grasp fully that God is truly present in the Risen Jesus communicating definitive assurance of salvation to the world.

While the manner in which the Christian tradition has spoken about the mystery of the Incarnation is understandable and defensible, the time has come when Christian teachers, and especially their official leaders, should state forthrightly and unambiguously that such language is not to be taken literally. Our scientific age insists on critical distinctions about precritical expressons of meaning. When such distinctions are not honestly provided, the Christian Message can easily be rejected as naive and mythological.

8

By the eighth decade of the first century, the church had begun to identify the Messianic title "Son of God" with the divine "Word of God." This development led to a radical transformation of Jesus' "adoptive" Messianic Sonship "from below." From that point forward, Jesus' Sonship was increasingly identified with God's eternal purpose foreknown in the Word, and was soon spoken of as an *eternal* Sonship which descended "from above" (with the Word) into the flesh of Jesus. This stage of evolving Christological language is illustrated by the Fourth Gospel (Jn 1:1,18) and also by the introductory verses of the anonymous *Letter to the Hebrews:*

> God spoke of old to our fathers through the prophets; but in these last days he has spoken to us by a Son, whom he appointed the heir of all things, through whom also he created the world. He reflects the glory of God and bears the very stamp of his nature, upholding the universe by his power. (Heb 1:1-3a)

A superficial reading of this passage might suggest that the author of Hebrews has literally identified Jesus and his exalted

Sonship with the preexistent Word of God. A critical reading of the letter, however, indicates otherwise. For in another part of the same letter (3:2) the author states that:

> Jesus was faithful to the one *who made him.*

This statement is evidence that the language in 1:1-3a is intended figuratively, not literally.

The divine Word was symbolically transformed into the divine Son in order to meet a developing theological need experienced by the subapostolic and postapostolic church. Christian teachers increasingly wished to confer divine dignity on Jesus in order to explain why his vicariously atoning death possessed sufficient value to pay for the sins of all humans. If Jesus were not divine, many feared, he could not have accomplished the mystery of our redemption.

(We saw in chapter one, however, that the idea that Jesus was required by God to pay for the sins of all humans was foreign to Jesus' own thinking. The idea of Jesus' substitutional suffering was created apologetically by the early church to explain the shockingly "unmessianic" and seemingly "accursed" [see Deut 21:22-23] death of Jesus.)

For centuries Christian teachers vigorously asserted the "divinity" of Jesus because of their sincere but mistaken conviction that he had to atone for the sins of the world and could only do so if he were divine. At first this development was resisted by many in the church (especially by Palestinian Jewish Christians who preferred the earlier Christology from below to the later Christology from above), for such a view was contrary to Jesus' self-understanding and could easily lead to belief in two gods.

Nevertheless, the advocates of Jesus' "divinity" prevailed. Asserting the divinity of Jesus proved very popular to the mass of Greek-speaking Gentile converts in the ancient church because (1) it provided hyperbolic certainty that *God was truly present in Jesus* communicating forgiveness and salvation to humankind. (2) It also gave assurance that Jesus possessed sufficient dignity to atone for the sins of the entire world. (3) Presenting Jesus as a divinely "begotten" mediator of creation and salvation (thereby preserving God's "immutability") was highly congenial to Hellenistic thought patterns which were widespread in the ancient world.

The eventual conferring of divine status on Jesus by the ancient church was ironic since the historical Jesus himself would have been alarmed by such a prospect. In Jesus' age, *Palestinian* Jews observed the strictest monotheistic standards in the world. For in the not too distant past, during the cruel persecution (c. 168 B.C.) of Antiochus IV of Syria, they had endured great suffering for their faith in *one* God. The memory of this suffering galvanized their determination to protect their monotheistic faith from all compromise. Devout Palestinian Jews, accordingly, scrupulously avoided calling anyone "God" or "divine" except the Creator.

Since Jews living outside of Palestine had not experienced the terrors of the Syrian persecution, their observance of monotheistic standards was less strict than that of Palestinian Jews. For example, the monotheistic Jewish philosopher Philo who lived in Alexandria (c. A.D. 50) felt free to call the "Word" (logos) through which God had created the world a "second God" (*Quaestiones et Solutiones in Genesin,* II, 62). Such hyperbolic poetry was common in the Hellenistic world, but was totally unacceptable to devout Palestinian (Aramaic-speaking) Jews.

This background enables us to understand Jesus' negative response in Mark's Gospel when a man asked him about gaining Eternal Life:

> And as he was setting out on his journey, a man ran up and *knelt* before him, and asked him, "Good teacher, what must I do to gain eternal life?" And Jesus said to him, "Why do you call me good? No one is good but God alone." (Mk 10:17-18)

The *kneeling* man's hyperadulatory and possibly *adoring* behavior obviously made Jesus uneasy. As a devout Palestinian Jew, Jesus feared that the kneeling man might be attributing *absolute* goodness to him when such goodness belongs only to God. Jesus therefore felt compelled to clarify the situation before he responded to the man's question (Mk 10:19-21). The response which the man's behavior elicited from Jesus is evidence that Jesus did not think that he was God and would not have accepted the kind of honor which is due to God alone.

9

In the centuries that followed the apostolic age, Christians continued to develop the Incarnational symbolism which they found in the New Testament. They developed this symbolism in an effort to better understand the relation between (1) *God,* (2) God's *Word* in Jesus, and (3) the *Spirit* of God mediated to the church through the Risen Jesus.

Eventually the theological reflection of the ancient church produced the doctrine of the Holy Trinity. This doctrine is traditionally understood to mean that God's one divine nature includes *three* divine "persons," the Father, the Son, and the Holy Spirit. However, in the centuries when Trinitarian doctrine was formulated the word "person" as we know and define it did not exist in any language.

Today, the word "person" means an individual who possesses reason and freedom of choice, and who is responsible for his or her actions. But the words used by ancient Christians that have evolved into our word "person" were *prosōpon* (face or actor's mask) in Greek and *persona* (actor's mask) in Latin. Both of these terms were used to name the mask worn by actors in ancient Greek and Roman dramas. Large masks were worn by ancient actors (*dramatis personae* = mask-wearers of the drama) so that members of the audience with poor vision or seated at a distance could identify the characters on stage. The masks were also designed to serve as megaphones. (No one in the ancient world wore corrective lenses or a hearing aid.)

The basic meaning of these ancient terms indicates that the Christians who introduced them into Trinitarian discourse knew that they were speaking in a *figurative* manner. Their choice of these words suggests by analogy that they experienced God's action in the divine drama of the Christ Event as manifesting itself to them through three different *roles:* (1) that of the divine *Father,* (2) that of the divine *Word* "spoken" by the Father, and (3) that of the *Holy Spirit* communicated by the Father. In other words, their faith discerned three distinct Self-manifestations of God in the Christ event:

1. When they experienced God's Self-communication as *divine life,* they named this aspect of God's mysterious Being with the symbol "Father."
2. When they experienced God's Self-communication as *divine knowledge,* they named this aspect of God's mysterious Being with the symbol "Word." (And later, when they thought of Jesus' Sonship as eternally foreknown in and identified with the Word, "Son.")
3. When they experienced God's Self-communication as divine love, they named this aspect of God's mysterious Being with the symbol "Holy Spirit."

The ancient fathers of the church who spoke Greek and Latin understood the basic meaning (face, actor's mask) of the ancient words for God's Self-manifestations in the Christ event. It was for that reason that they sometimes spoke of Jesus as God's "face" so we can see God, and God's "voice" so we can hear God.

At our time in history it would make better sense to speak of the three "Self-manifestations" of God rather than the three "divine persons" in God. The meaning of the various words which we translate as "person" (*prosōpon, persona,* and later, *hypostasis*) has changed so drastically throughout the Christian centuries that the word "person" should be replaced with a word or phrase that does not produce misunderstanding, bafflement, or disbelief.

Trinitarian language actually intends to speak of the apostolic church's experience of God's three distinguishable Self-manifestations during the Christ Event: (1) God's Self-manifestation as the creative source of all life, or *the divine Father;* (2) God's Self-manifestation as conclusive revelatory knowledge given through the Risen Jesus, or *the divine Word;*

and (3) God's Self-manifestation as confirming and sanctifying love, or *the Holy Spirit*. If we were to return to this scripture-derived understanding of God's threefold Self-communication, Trinitarian symbolism would be more intelligible. It could also contribute in a meaningful way to the contemporary faith life of the church instead of producing mystification.

10

Our final concern in this chapter will be to explain briefly the symbolic language found in the church's ancient profession of faith, the Nicene creed. This creed is arranged in three parts, each of which speaks of one of God's three Self-manifestations as experienced in the Christ event.

The reader should recall that the "interchange of attributes" is occurring throughout the second part of the creed which addresses the incarnation of God's Word in Jesus. In this second part, things are said symbolically of the divine Word which are literally true only of the humanity of Jesus. And, conversely, things are said of the humanity of Jesus which are properly true only of the divine Word in Jesus. Much of the language in the second part of the creed is taken directly from the descending Christology of the prologue hymn in the Fourth Gospel:

PART I, THE ETERNAL FATHER

> We believe in one God, the Father, the Almighty, maker of heaven and earth, of all that is seen and unseen.

This section is not difficult to understand. Most people realize that God is being spoken of symbolically as our eternal "Father." In reality, God transcends finite gender distinctions. The creed affirms that God is the Creator of all, including things "unseen," in order to assure us that everything in the universe was created by God and is subject to God's almighty power.

PART II, THE INCARNATION OF GOD'S WORD IN JESUS

> We believe in one Lord, Jesus Christ, the only Son of God, eternally begotten of the Father, God from God,

> Light from Light, true God from true God, one in being with the Father. Through him all things were made.

The reader should be able to recognize that the humanity of Jesus is being symbolically identified with the pre-existent Word through whom God has created the world (Jn 1:1-3). God's Word has come as "Light" into our world to assure us through Jesus that God's saving purpose will finally free us from the powers of darkness (Jn 1:4-5). This symbolic poetry in the second part of the creed is meant to help us grasp that it is God's definitive revealing presence in Jesus which guarantees our salvation:

> For us humans and for our salvation he came down from heaven: by the power of the Holy Spirit he was born of the virgin Mary and became a human.

These words tell us that the divine Word descended into the human nature of Jesus and united with him in order to carry out God's foreintended plan of salvation. (God, of course, does not literally come down from heaven to earth since God is already everywhere.) Jesus' mother is described as a "virgin" to remind us that the church believes she is the mother of David's heir who was called Immanuel (God with us) by Isaiah the prophet. (The mother of Immanuel is spoken of as a "virgin" in the Greek version of Is 7:14):

> For our sake he was crucified under Pontius Pilate; he suffered, died, and was buried. On the third day he rose again in fulfillment of the scriptures; he ascended into heaven and is seated at the right hand of the Father.

This section of the creed speaks as if the divine Word who "came down" from heaven was crucified, buried, and raised. But this symbolic way of speaking is meant to alert us to the presence of God's Word "in Jesus" carrying out God's saving purpose for the world "through Jesus." In reality, it was only the finite humanity of Jesus which underwent crucifixion, burial, and resurrection, not the spiritual reality of the divine Word.

The substance of the very early creed professed by Greek-speaking Christians in the apostolic church is still enshrined in this section of the Nicene creed. Paul the apostle quoted that very early creed in 1 Cor 15:3-5:

> Christ died for our sins in accordance with the scriptures . . . he was buried . . . he was raised on the third day in accordance with the scriptures . . . he appeared to Cephas, then to the twelve.

Gradually, the ancient church modified and expanded the creed prayed by Paul and the early church by placing later expressions of the church's faith before and after it.

The final statement in the second part of the creed expresses the church's belief that the exalted Jesus will return at the end of history to bring God's ultimate justice to the world and ultimate fulfillment to the righteous. This statement is couched in symbolic end-time language, but since it envisions only the exalted humanity of Jesus, it does not employ the interchange of attributes. (The contemporary understanding of symbolic end-time language will be addressed in the final chapter.):

> He will come again in glory to judge the living and the dead, and of his kingdom there will be no end.

PART III, THE GIFT OF THE SPIRIT

As noted above, the third part of the creed personifies the gift of God's Spirit (God's Self-communication as love) now mediated to the church through her faith in Jesus:

> We believe in the Holy Spirit, *the Lord,* the giver of life, who proceeds from the Father and the Son. With the Father and the Son he is worshiped and glorified. He has spoken through the prophets.

It is highly unusual that this part of the creed refers to God's Spirit as "the Lord," for the title Lord is usually reserved for the Risen Jesus in the New Testament. Rarely, if ever, is the reason for this atypical use of the title Lord explained to contemporary Christians.

The appearances of the Risen Jesus to his disciples were always accompanied by a revelatory communication of God's Spirit (he breathed on them and said, "Receive the Holy Spirit" Jn 20:22). To encounter the Risen Jesus appearing "without" was to simultaneously experience God's Self-manifestation as Holy Spirit "within."

Even after Jesus stopped appearing, his disciples still experienced the Gift of God's Spirit being mediated to them when they assembled to celebrate Jesus' Supper or called on him in prayer. The early church remembered that it was through Jesus that God had initially revealed and mediated the gift of the Spirit to her. She concluded, therefore, that whenever she experienced God's Spirit being given to her, it was still being mediated through the Risen Jesus. Her repeated experience of the "Spirit" being given to her through faith in the Risen "Lord" led her to *identify* the two. In the judgment of the early church, the experience of the Spirit was inseparable from the original mediator of the Spirit, the Risen Lord:

> Now the Lord is the Spirit. . . . And we all . . . are being changed into his likeness from one degree of glory to another; for this comes from the Lord who is the Spirit. (2 Cor 3:17-18; see also 1 Cor 15:45)

The ancient church understood that the gift of God's Spirit given to her initially in "Baptism" (which may be conferred "only once") had freed her from sin and empowered her to live a "holy" life of love and service. She also believed that the gift of the Spirit enabled her to be faithful to the essentials of the "apostolic" witnessing, and to fulfill her mission of (lovingly and respectfully) sharing her faith in the Good News with the "whole world."

(In the Nicene creed, the word "catholic" means universal; it therefore includes all branches of the Christian family who are united in loving fellowship. All authentic branches of the Christian church are also faithfully committed to the essentials of the apostolic witnessing in the New Testament.):

> We believe in one holy catholic and apostolic church. We acknowledge one baptism for the forgiveness of sins.

The ancient church concluded her creed by confessing her belief that all the dead will finally be raised to participate with the living in the Final Judgment (already mentioned at the end of the second part). All those judged as righteous will then enjoy Eternal Life in the New Creation:

> We look for the resurrection of the dead and the life of the world to come. Amen.

Questions for Review and Discussion

1. What major role is assigned to God's personified Wisdom in the Old Testament Wisdom literature? How did this role influence the theology of the apostolic church?
2. What does it mean to personify something? Why do humans personify things?
3. Why did the Old Testament Wisdom tradition conclude that God's Word and Wisdom were synonymous? What do the two concepts share in common?
4. Why did some New Testament authors assign the attributes of God's pre-existent Wisdom or Word to Jesus?
5. What do Christian theologians mean when they speak of "the interchange of attributes" in the New Testament and the Christian tradition? Why did the early church think it was desirable for the "attributes" in question to be interchangeable?
6. When doubting Thomas addresses the Risen Jesus with the words "My Lord and my God," is he literally calling Jesus God? What earlier dialog in John's Gospel sheds light on the words Thomas spoke to the Risen Jesus?
7. What important "need" convinced the ancient (post-apostolic) church that she should confer divine status on Jesus? What is ironic about that decision?
8. What is the basic reason why conservative people reject the idea that some words in the Bible might be symbolically true instead of literally true?
9. How do the attributes of God's divine nature differ from those of Jesus' human nature? Why is it important to understand this difference?

10. What was the original meaning of the two earliest terms (Greek = *prosōpon,* Latin = *persona*) used to explain the three distinguishable Self manifestations of God in the Christ Event? Explain your answer and its significance.
11. What would be a more accurate and understandable way of speaking about the three "divine persons" in God at our time in history?
12. What unusual Christian way of using language is present in the second of the Nicene Creed's three parts? Why is it important to recognize the presence of this special way of using language?

Chapter Fifteen: Remaining Questions

The answers to the following questions presuppose that the reader has read the preceding fourteen chapters. If the reader has not done so, the answers will not be fully intelligible.

1. Does the interpretation of Jesus presented in this book destroy genuine Christian faith in Jesus?

Two basic and related issues are raised by the question before us, one involving dialog and the other orthodoxy. We will begin by considering the issue of dialog and then turn to the problem of orthodoxy.

To enter into dialog with the interpretation of Jesus presented in this book will actually strengthen and deepen one's faith understanding of Jesus. Our faith in Jesus as God's Good News will be more meaningful and secure if we learn that it is fully compatible with a scientific world view. Whenever unquestioned assumptions of a mythological or legendary kind are operating unconsciously in our faith understanding, our faith is in some sense vulnerable. For if we were to experience a convincing refutation of a major part of our belief system, there is a possibility that our faith might be abandoned along with our outmoded belief system.

This danger is especially present if those criticizing our belief system are agnostics, atheists, or critical but ill informed believers. Such persons will offer nothing new, positive, and reasonable to replace a discredited belief system. It is beneficial, therefore, to enter into dialog with Christians whose faith understanding agrees with the *essentials* of the apostolic witnessing and is also integrated with a scientific world view. If such Christians convince us that some aspect of our faith understanding is outmoded, they usually do so while advancing a new understanding which can successfully replace the old one.

Even conservative Christians who reject the critical views about Jesus expressed in this book will come away from it with a more secure faith understanding. For unconsciously, if not consciously, they will be reassured by the knowledge that Christians who think critically and scientifically share the essentials of their own faith. If ever their traditional faith understanding ceases to serve them, they will know that there exists a set of Christian answers to critical questions which is fully compatible with the reasonable demands of contemporary science.

As to orthodoxy, all Christians agree that when we encounter the Risen and Spirit-mediating Jesus, we are also encountering God's definitive Self-disclosure. More conservative Christians identify Jesus with God's revealing presence in him, and they insist that the identification is "literal," not symbolic. Less conservative Christians, on the other hand, make critical distinctions about the relation between Jesus and God and refuse to identify the two.

These less conservative distinction-makers agree with Paul the apostle that Christians truly encounter God "in" Christ (2 Cor 5:18). And they also remind us that Paul never asserts that Christ literally "is" God. Paul never calls anyone God but the Creator. To travel with Paul the apostle is to have a very sound theologian for a companion.

Genuine Christian faith does not require us to believe that Jesus is literally God, that he was required by God to pay for our sins, that he was miraculously born of a virgin, or that he was born in Bethlehem. Would Christians refuse to believe that the

Risen and Spirit-mediating Jesus is God's Good News if none of the things just mentioned had ever been said about him?

What is essential for Christian faith is the recognition that God has assured us through the Risen and Spirit-mediating Jesus that we are loved and forgiven, and are being called by God through death into Eternal Life and Joy. About these sacred essentials all Christians of all times and places have agreed. Once again Paul the apostle helps us to discern what is essential:

> If Christ has not been raised, your faith is futile. (1 Cor 15:17a)

2. ***If the explanation of the Gospels given in this book is basically correct, does that mean the church has been reading the Gospels incorrectly for centuries?***

The church's literal reading of the Gospels in past centuries was not incorrect, but, rather, less correct in some respects. A literal reading of scripture is not devoid of truth. The general meaning of the inspired biblical text is usually accessible to any sincere reader or hearer even when the text is understood literally. In precritical centuries, a literal reading of the Gospels caused no serious problems.

A literal reading of the ancient Gospels, however, is unwittingly burdened with a number of naive assumptions from the past that are joined together with the enduring truth in the Gospels (e.g., epilepsy is caused by demons; apologetic stories, mythological elements in stories, or midrashic allusions woven into stories should all be accepted as literal history). When the increasing knowledge of later ages detects and criticizes these naive assumptions, their nonliteral (and nonessential) nature should be readily granted, and they should be explained accordingly.

But all too often, the conservative tendencies of religious people prompt them to cling defensively to the comforting certainties of the past, and they resist necessary change. This mistaken resistance causes the timeless religious truth in the Gospels to be compromised, and their authority is rendered suspect in the eyes of many.

The unwillingness of some conservatives to relinquish the outmoded and nonessential religious ideas of the past is the result of their mistaken identification of past *interpretations* of God (and the world) with the *reality* of God. They sincerely fear that if they deny outmoded biblical assumptions *about* God, they will be denying *God,* and they understandably reject that possibility as intolerable.

In such a situation, the absolute authority of God is mistakenly conferred upon merely relative human expressions about God (and the God-human relationship). This mistaken transfer results in the subtle and insidious form of idolatry called *Bibliolatry* (idolatrous worship of the Bible).

Those who are guilty of Bibliolatry usually assume that God has dictated all of the words in the Bible, and that these words should be identified with God and given divine or absolute authority. Contemporary scholarship, however, emphatically rejects such a view of revelation as oversimplified and mythological.

God does not dictate words to the prophets; rather, God communicates an experience of God's own presence and love. (Most adult Christians "know" from experience that God's Self-communication is undeniably real but *nonverbal.*) Under the impact of God's Self-communication, the prophets are inspired to use language in creative new ways to teach about the reality of God and the God-human relationship. The Bible, therefore, does contain words given to us by God. But God gave us these words indirectly by inspiring a free and intelligent human being to speak words in God's service.

While it is true that the words spoken by the prophets and evangelists are divinely inspired, it is also true that they are culturally *conditioned* and historically *limited.* When expressing their inspired insights into the mystery of God and the God-human relationship, the evangelists included a number of assumptions and teaching devices present in their tradition. These assumptions and conventions were thought to be true or necessary at that time. But later ages, because of increased experience, will find many of them mistaken or no longer adequate without qualification.

When the words which God inspired the evangelists to write are *identified* with God and are given the absolute authority that belongs to God alone, those words soon become the enemy of that spiritual progress which God is calling forth throughout history. All of the words in the Gospels are inspired (i.e., they were written by an author who was moved by an experience of God to teach in God's service), but only those inspired words which speak with enduring validity about God and the God-human relationship are truly "the word of God."

3. Why did ancient Israel's prophets encourage her to expect a military Messiah so contrary to Jesus?

By repeatedly revealing the gift of divine presence and love to the prophets of ancient Israel, God encouraged the prophets to infer and teach that God intended to bless Israel in the *future* with definitive salvation. The prophets correctly understood that a "promise" of sublime blessing to come was implicit in their privileged experience of God's repeated Self-gift. Consequently, they assured Israel that when her response to God's gracious love finally became acceptable, God would surely bestow on her (and, through her, on the nations) an ideal state of justice, peace, and fulfillment (Is 2:2-4; Mic 4:1-4).

(Implicit in such prophetic teaching is a correct but not yet fully developed recognition: We humans must responsibly complete the maturation process before we can finally converge with God and be blessed with participation in God's Eternal Life and Joy.)

God never intended that the promise of "salvation" implicit in the divine Self-communication would be attained by military conquest (although a kind of struggle and conquest are involved). It was the prophets who assumed, in a culturally and historically conditioned fashion, that an ideal and final state of universal peace and justice could only be attained through *military* imposition of God's law on all the nations.

The prophets surmised, therefore, that since God had promised David an unending dynasty (2 Sam 7:11-15), God would surely raise up a Davidic Warrior-Messiah as the instrument through whom universal justice and peace would be imposed on earth. By such means, the prophets concluded, God would restore the Divine Reign over the kingdom of creation.

Initially, Israel thought the salvation God had promised her would come *within* history in the form of a Golden Age, i.e., a time of permanent peace, prosperity, and longevity, presided over by successive kings of David's dynasty. Only later (c. 165 B.C.) did she learn to hope for Everlasting Life in the New Creation which would come after the conclusion of history.

The book of Daniel, in which Israel's new eschatological hope first appeared (c. 165 B.C.), did not suggest that either an heir of David or a military conquest would contribute to the arrival of the New Creation. Nor did it state that the king of the end-time alluded to midrashically as the Son of Adam (Dan 7:13-14) would be a leader of earthly armies. (This is probably one of the reasons why Jesus preferred the title Son of Man to the title Messiah. His privileged experience of God's love convinced him that God's Reign over creation would not be achieved by military violence and bloodshed.)

But we saw in an earlier chapter that the ancient Jews eventually joined the traditional hope for a military Messiah with the new eschatological hope taught by the book of Daniel. This combined future hope found expression in two-stage apocalyptic theology written after the book of Daniel. Jesus was encouraged by his experience of God's love to reject two-stage apocalyptic hope in favor of the nonmilitary hope taught by the book of Daniel. (We have already considered in chapter one the reason why God always intended to send Israel a suffering and tragically rejected Messiah: God's "secret" Messiah was finally revealed to the world as God's answer to the questions raised by the pain, tragedy, and ambiguity which disrupt our existence.)

4. Did Jesus literally speak the three predictions of his death and Resurrection which we find in Mk 8:31, 9:31, 10:33-34?

Jesus probably did predict his death and his Resurrection. But it is very likely that he predicted each of these events in separate sayings, not in one saying. The three predictions we find in Mark are later *combinations* and *expansions* of Jesus' original predictions. It was probably Mark who decided to combine the originally separate sayings and who expanded and multiplied the combined form of the sayings in order to teach his Messianic Secret theology.

We find in Lk 13:31-33 the substance of a genuine prediction made by Jesus about his coming death. We know that the underlying substance of this saying is probably authentic because it speaks of *death* instead of Resurrection as something which Jesus expected in three *figurative* days. Because the empty tomb was discovered on "the third day" (and because Hos 6:2 seemed to foreshadow Jesus' Resurrection on that day), the early Greek-speaking church soon decided that Jesus' remembered reference to three days (which implied a "third day") should be understood as predicting his Resurrection. (Note that the creed Paul quoted in 1 Cor 15:3-5 contains a midrashic reference to "the third day" in Hos 6:2):

> At that very hour some Pharisees came, and said to him, "Get away from here, for Herod wants to kill you." And he said to them, "Go and tell that fox, 'Behold, I cast out demons and perform cures today and tomorrow, and the third day I finish my course. Nevertheless I must go on my way today and tomorrow and the day following, for it cannot be that a prophet should perish away from Jerusalem.'" (Lk 13:31-33)

In the authentic substance of this saying (which Luke has theologically modified), Jesus probably employed two Aramaic idioms. The first speaks of a dangerous or ambiguous event in the not too distant future as coming in *three figurative days* (see Gen 22:4; Ex 19:11; Hos 6:2). This traditional Aramaic (and Hebrew) idiom was probably derived from observing the three days of darkness which conclude each lunar cycle. (The ancients watched the sky at night, not television.)

The second idiom (to go on one's way) is an Aramaic euphemism for *death*. (A euphemism is an agreeable way of speaking about something disagreeable.) Jesus probably anticipated that when he went to Jerusalem to deliver the challenge of his prophetic message and to rebuke the chief priests for the unfair trafficking they allowed in the temple precincts, his action would very likely lead to his rejection and death. (The fate of his predecessor, John the Baptizer, would not have been far from his thoughts.)

Jesus is also remembered in Mark 14:25 as having predicted his Resurrection at the Last Supper:

> Truly, I say to you, I shall not drink again of the fruit of the vine until that day when I drink it new in the kingdom of God. (Mk 14:24-25)

When Jesus came to the Last Supper, he was troubled because he had been warned that one of the Twelve had agreed to betray him. Jesus probably anticipated, therefore, that events which would lead to his death had been set in motion, and he would never again break bread or drink wine with his disciples on earth. However, because of his habitual experience of God's presence and love, Jesus was confident that he would soon be raised at the General Resurrection when the Kingdom of God arrived. He implicitly assured his disciples that he would then be with them again and would drink wine with them at the Great Supper in the New Creation.

We know that the prediction of his Resurrection made by Jesus in Mk 14:25 is probably authentic because it indicates that Jesus expected to be raised at the General Resurrection when the Kingdom of God arrived as a *collective* phenomenon. This means that Jesus did not anticipate that he would be raised *individually* by God before the world ended. In reality, Jesus saw the Twelve again, not at the General Resurrection, but when he appeared to them in Galilee, probably while they were at table. If the early church had created Mk 14:25 for theological reasons, it would not contain this discrepancy.

It seems likely that Mark is the one who took these two remembered predictions of Jesus and joined them into one saying. When Mark combined the predictions for use in his Messianic Secret theology, he then added the "Son of Man" title and one additional prediction. At this stage, the saying became Mk 9:31. (Mk 9:31 is the *least embellished* of the three Markan predictions; it adds only the prediction of betrayal to Jesus' original predictions of death and Resurrection):

> "The Son of man will be delivered into the hands of men, and they will kill him; and when he is killed, after three days he will rise." (Mk 9:31)

Mark produced two additional versions of this saying by adding more details from the passion of Jesus (which Mark assumed Jesus had foreseen; see Mk 8:31). The *most embellished* form of the combined saying was placed on Jesus lips in Mk 10:33-34, just before Jesus arrived at Jerusalem to fulfill his hidden destiny. This form of the saying amounts to a brief summary of the passion which (Mark believed) Jesus knew would precede his Resurrection as the exalted "Son of Man:

> "Behold we are going up to Jerusalem; and the Son of man will be delivered to the chief priests and the scribes, and they will condemn him to death, and deliver him to the Gentiles; and they will mock him, and spit upon him, and scourge him, and kill him; and after three days he will rise." (Mk 10:33-34)

The Markan version of Jesus' predictions of death and Resurrection still understood that Jesus had actually anticipated "death" on the third of three figurative days. For that reason Mark always has Jesus say that the Son of Man will rise "after" three days. But Matthew and Luke later changed Mark's "after" three days to "on" the third day (Mt 16:21; 17:22-23; 20:18-19; Lk 9:22; 18:31-33). It is evident that by the time they wrote their Gospels the original meaning of Jesus' idiomatic reference to death in three figurative days had become blurred. Matthew and

Luke understood the three days of Jesus' metaphor *literally* and related them to Jesus' Resurrection "on the third day."

5. ***How should Christians answer the claim that the appearances of the Risen Jesus reported by Paul and the other apostles were nothing more than hallucinations?***

Hallucinations are the subjective perceiving of sensory phenomena which are not objectively present even though they are judged by the perceiver to be so. These purely subjective experiences can be caused by (1) psychotic states marked by hallucinations, (2) mind-altering drugs, (3) extreme sensory deprivation, or (4) pathological longing for someone deceased or physically distant from the hallucinator.

It should be admitted without hesitation that hallucinations and the appearances of the Risen Jesus have something in common. They both involve the unconscious projection of an image which originates in the memory of the experiencer. However, we saw in chapter eleven (part eight), that the appearances of the Risen Jesus were triggered paranormally by the nonsubjective or extramental communication of his personal presence. The resulting "appearances" of the Risen Jesus were simultaneously accompanied by a communication of God's Spirit (the divine Self-communication as love) which assured the apostles that the "appearing" One was a conclusive *revelatory* sign from God. Hallucinations, on the other hand, are induced by pathology, drugs, or sensory deprivation.

Among the causes of hallucinations, pathological longing for someone deceased seems to be the only one possibly applicable to the apostles' claims to have seen the Risen Jesus. But while it is certain that Jesus' disciples would have grieved over his death, it does not seem likely that large numbers of them would have been susceptible to pathological longing for his continued presence. Most, if not all, of them had families and friends who would have compensated for Jesus' absence.

Far more significantly, however, the appearance reported by Paul is indirect evidence that the appearances were probably not hallucinations. Everything indicates that Paul had never known the earthly Jesus. Paul was not, therefore, grieving or yearning pathologically for Jesus' continued presence. On the contrary, Paul had to make a number of painful reversals of religious, professional, and social commitments because of his unexpected encounter with the Risen Jesus.

But in the last analysis, it is not because of any compelling philosophical or historical arguments that Christians believe the Risen Jesus truly appeared to the apostles and began mediating the "foretaste" of God's Spirit. We believe the apostolic witnessing to the Spirit-mediating appearances of Jesus because we also experience the confirming foretaste of God's Spirit being communicated to us when we hear the Good News of Jesus' Spirit-mediating appearances effectively proclaimed.

6. Was Jesus literally the first human to enter Eternal Life?

Jesus *was* the first human to pass through death and appear as a definitive sign from God that humans can reach Eternal Life. However, Jesus was probably *not* the first human to go through the event of death into Eternal Life.

Contemporary scholarship concludes that all humans since the beginning who have tried to follow their conscience and live a responsible life (as they understood it) have probably been enabled by God to evolve through death into Eternal Life. But humans who were still living within history before God raised Jesus were *unaware* of this outcome. Consequently, they were fearful and uncertain about what lies beyond death. It was precisely to free humans from such fear and uncertainty that God empowered the Risen Jesus to appear to his disciples and to begin mediating the foretaste of the Holy Spirit.

The ancient Israelites who wrote the Genesis creation and fall stories believed that humans had originally been immortal but had lost Everlasting Life through moral failure. Sinful humans, they assumed, were bound by unending death as a consequence of our first parents' failure.

This mythological interpretation of the human condition seemed to the Israelites to make sense of their experience: Their self-transcending design told them that humans were intended by their Creator for unending life and happiness, yet they found themselves bound by universal suffering and death. They concluded, therefore, that something must have gone wrong at the *beginning*. God must have given our first parents a test on which continued immortality depended, and our first parents must have failed the test for themselves and their descendants.

The Israelites correctly understood from their self-transcending design that we humans are destined for unending life. However, they misread their design when they assumed that we were destined to enjoy immortality at the *beginning* of our physical existence instead of after its successful *conclusion*. God worked patiently through historical events and eventually encouraged the ancient Jews (through the prophet who wrote the book of Daniel) to understand that they could "regain" at the *end* the immortality which they thought Adam and Eve had lost for humankind at the *beginning*.

Accordingly, when the ancient Jews began to believe that they could regain immortality at the end of history, they also assumed that the righteous dead were waiting in the upper part of sheol for the coming of God's kingdom (the New Creation). And since the earliest Christians were Jews, most of them held the same view. The early church concluded, therefore, that the righteous dead would have to wait in upper sheol until Jesus returned at the end of history to judge the living and the dead. All the righteous dead would then be raised and, after the final judgment, would be taken by Jesus into the New Creation.

Eventually, early Christian teachers further modified the view which they inherited from ancient Judaism. They taught (as a form of midrashic apologetic) that all deceased humans before Jesus who had believed in God's promise of salvation had to wait in upper sheol until Jesus *satisfied* God's offended justice by dying vicariously for the sins of all humankind.

Contemporary Christian scholarship tells us, however, that the early church discovered the idea of *vicarious* atonement in the "suffering servant poems" in the book of Isaiah (42:1-4; 49:1-6; 50:4-11; 52:13-53:12). Christian Teachers then apologetically used the idea of vicarious atonement to defend their faith in a suffering Messiah who was shockingly contrary to ancient Jewish expectations. They claimed that the tragic rejection of Jesus was midrashically foreshadowed in Isaiah's "suffering servant poems" (especially 52:13-53:12) as part of God's secret Messianic purpose.

The authentic parables and sayings of Jesus, however, contain no suggestion that Jesus thought he had to suffer vicariously for the sins of all humans before God would forgive them. Instead, Jesus declared that God's unconditional love and forgiveness are graciously offered *now* to all who believe and turn away from destructive behavior.

Although Jesus knew his message angered many "religious" people in his society, he nevertheless assured those who believed in his prophetic message (Mk 2:5-7), even notorious sinners (Lk 7:47-49), that their sins were forgiven. Jesus did not tell sinners, "Your sins *will be forgiven* after I die and pay for them." Rather, he assured them in the present tense, "Your sins *are forgiven*" (because God is unconditionally loving and merciful toward all, even God's most prodigal children).

Since we now realize that Jesus did not have to pay for the sins of humans before they could be forgiven and loved by God, there is no reason for concluding that they had to wait in a mythological place of detention until Jesus redeemed them. Accordingly, when contemporary theology reflects on the implications of our self-transcending design in the light of Resurrection faith, it concludes that humans have been destined from the outset to transcend death and arrive at unending participation in God's Eternal Life. In reality, there is no need for a mythologically conceived delay.

Karl Rahner reminds us (*Theological Investigations,* vol. 4) that the only eschatological condition about which God has revealed something specific is the Resurrection, i.e., our ability to attain Everlasting Life beyond death along with Jesus. All the other eschatological teaching in the New Testament represents historically limited speculation. We, therefore, have not only a right but a duty to revise such precritical speculation when advances in knowledge require it.

7. Do the righteous dead have to wait for Jesus to return and raise them on Resurrection day before they can reach Eternal Life?

As indicated just above, contemporary Christian scholars think that responsible humans who have completed the maturation process with faith and trust in God's goodness have probably been evolving through death into Eternal Life from the very beginning. This conclusion means that God's children have been coming home to God from the time of the first humans till the present. But no one living within space-time knew this with conclusive certainty until God "raised" the Spirit-mediating Jesus as God's Good News. God assures us through Jesus and the foretaste of the Spirit that we can all come home to God. (Even on earth, "home is the place where, when you have to go there, they have to take you in.")

8. Will Jesus literally come on the clouds of heaven at the end of history to judge the living and the dead?

In the view of contemporary Christian scholarship, the eschatological symbolism in the New Testament which speaks of the second coming of Jesus as final Judge should be taken *very seriously,* but not literally. Second coming symbolism correctly intends to remind us that all of our lives (and all of human history) are moving inexorably toward a solemn conclusion.

This conclusion will necessarily include a mysterious *ultimate justice* which will right all wrongs and finally correct all the injustice committed throughout history. The symbols of Christian eschatology are also meant to assure us that *ultimate fulfillment* is truly attainable by all who open themselves to that promised gift with faith and trust in God.

But the state of final justice and fulfillment which this symbolism intends to assure us of can be achieved without requiring Jesus to *literally* return with an army of angels at the end of history. When the last human to complete the maturation process and evolve through death into Eternal Life has done so, that person will be with Jesus and all other humans who have reached that sublime goal. The final state of fulfillment for humans promised by eschatological symbolism will then have been achieved. And it is the attainability of this ultimate justice and final joy beyond the terror of history which is essentially being promised by the "second coming" symbolism in the New Testament.

These insights lead us to conclude that when the very last human to reach Eternal Life at the end of history does so, and is gathered into God's love along with Jesus and all of God's saints, the *essential equivalent* of what eschatological symbolism has taught us to expect at the "second coming" will have been achieved. In effect, the "second coming" of Jesus to gather all of God's faith-filled children into Eternal Life will then have taken place.

Therefore, when contemporary Christians anticipate the second coming of Jesus at his Supper, we are not anticipating his *literal* return on the clouds of heaven. Instead, we are reminded by such eschatological symbolism that all of our lives are subject to God's ultimate justice, and that we can attain ultimate fulfillment along with the Risen Jesus if we guide our lives by truth, justice and love *which serves* (See Mt 25:31-46).

9. Since the apostles believed and taught that the world would end in their lifetime, does the world's continuing existence indicate that the eschatological teaching in the New Testament is mistaken?

The eschatological teaching in the New Testament which warns that the world will end in the lifetime of the apostles (Mk 1:14-15; 9:1; Mt 10:23; 1 Thess 4:15-17; 1 Cor 15:51-52) is not mistaken. On the contrary, this teaching remains permanently true in a profoundly meaningful way for the entire Christian faith community. The sense in which this teaching is true, however, presupposes a willingness to understand its language in a *nonliteral* way. It is obvious that the entire world did not end in the lifetime of the apostles. And yet, the individual world of every person who lived during the apostolic age *did come to an end.*

Jesus and his apostles were evidently inspired by God to accept the eschatological hope expressed in the book of Daniel and the preaching of John the Baptizer. God encouraged them to proclaim a message of eschatological hope and warning to the world even though God knew that their understanding of the timing involved would suffer from their historically limited assumptions. Jesus himself refused to predict the time of the end (Mk 13:32). Yet, one gets the impression that he suspected the Kingdom would arrive in the lifetime of some of his contemporaries (Mk 1:14).

The apostles understood that the essential substance of Jesus' end-time teaching was confirmed when God "raised" Jesus from the dead and empowered him to begin mediating the foretaste of God's Spirit. When the Risen Jesus began appearing to his apostles, they concluded that the world was already beginning to end because the resurrection of the dead had already begun with Jesus' appearances. Accordingly, they thought the Risen Jesus would quickly return in glory to conclude history and gather the righteous into God's Kingdom. They mistakenly announced, therefore, that the whole world would "literally" end in their lifetime.

However, despite their mistaken assumptions about the time when the whole world will end, the end-time teaching of Jesus and his apostles remains an essential and profoundly true part of God's saving purpose in history. For God knew that when Jesus did not return in the lifetime of the apostles, the church would have to reconsider the apostolic declaration of the world's impending end. She would then be forced to realize (with the help of Ps 90:4) that eschatological language should be construed in a *nonliteral* manner:

> First of all you must understand this, that scoffers will come in the last days with scoffing, following their own passions and saying, "Where is the promise of his coming? For ever since the fathers fell asleep, all things have continued as they were from the beginning of creation." (2 Pet 3:3-5)
>
> But do not ignore this one fact, beloved, that with the Lord one day is as a thousand years, and a thousand years as one day. The Lord is not slow about his promise as some count slowness, but is forbearing toward you, not wishing that any should perish, but that all should reach repentance. (2 Pet 3:8-9)

The nonliteral mode of understanding eschatological symbolism remains valid for every generation of faithful Christians till the end of time. For while it is true that the *entire* world did not end in the lifetime of the apostles, we noted above that the *individual* world of every person in the apostolic age *did come to an end.* Likewise, the individual world of all presently living persons is rapidly moving toward its conclusion irrespective of whether we will still be alive when the whole world ends. God's Word, therefore, contains a divinely intended warning that our allotted time in this world is short, and that, all too soon, we will have to give an account of our stewardship.

Accordingly, the Kingdom of God and the Final Judgment which precedes it are *always drawing near.* Each successive generation must prepare to submit to God's Final Judgment in order to enter God's *always-approaching Kingdom.* For this reason the Christian tradition teaches that there is a "particular Judgment" which precedes the "General Judgment." And we have already seen in the answer to the preceding question that the "General Judgment" is a powerful eschatological symbol for the *unfailing* triumph of God's Justice and Goodness at the end of human history:

> Then I saw thrones, and seated on them were those to whom judgment had been committed. Also I saw the souls of those who had been beheaded for their testimony to Jesus and for the word of God. . . . They came to life and reigned with Christ a thousand years. . . . This is the first resurrection. Blessed and holy is he who shares in the first resurrection! Over such the second death has no power.

10. Did the earthly Jesus know everything that God knows?

Traditional Christian theology assumed that Jesus always knew everything that God knows. It sincerely made this assumption for several "precritical" reasons. (1) The Fourth Gospel says that the Word of God became incarnate in Jesus. And we have already seen in chapters thirteen and fourteen that the divine "Word" is a symbol for God's creative knowledge and wisdom. Accordingly, early Christian theology decided that since the divine Word had joined itself to Jesus' flesh, Jesus, while on earth, must have known everything that God knows. (2) Jesus is presented in the Gospels as possessing foreknowledge of the future (e.g., Jerusalem's destruction, Judas' betrayal, Peter's denial, the availability of an ass for his triumphal entry into Jerusalem, and his own death and Resurrection); he must, therefore, have had access to God's knowledge.

Contemporary scholarship, however, makes a clear distinction between the human knowledge of Jesus and the knowledge of the divine Word (i.e., God's revealing presence) present in him. Jesus possessed extraordinary knowledge about the reality of God and the God-human relationship. But his knowledge about everything else was ordinary. (We saw in chapter six, for example, that Jesus, like everyone else in his society, probably assumed that epilepsy was caused by evil spirits.) When the reality of "God's Word" united with the "flesh" of Jesus in the mystery of the Incarnation, the nature of God (including God's knowledge) remained entirely distinct from the reality of Jesus' human nature. United does not mean identical.

Moreover, many contemporary theologians would agree with the process philosophers that God's foreknowledge of free human actions is relative, not absolute. This view asserts that God has a highly probable statistical foreknowledge of our free future actions, but not absolute foreknowledge. If God possessed absolute foreknowledge of our future actions, then our actions would be absolutely predetermined, and we would not truly be free. (Conservative theologians would not agree with the process philosophers and theologians about this matter.)

Also, when we reflect on Jesus' foreknowlege of the future, we should do so with the help of Ockham's razor (i.e., the law of parsimony = we should always prefer a simpler to a more complicated hypothesis). If we do so, we can shave away the precritical assumptions present in past interpretations of Jesus' predictions. If we do not assume that Jesus knew everything that God knows because of the presence of God's Word in him, we are free to look for a simpler, more economical explanation of his predictions:

(1) Jesus could see that the political fanatics in his society were determined to instigate a revolt against Rome. He also realized that the might of Rome would crush such a revolt and destroy Jerusalem in the process. Jeremiah the prophet had earlier been able to foresee the similar consequences of the revolt against Babylonia. We should remind ourselves that Jesus was probably not the only one who could foresee the likelihood of coming disaster.

(2) We observed earlier in chapter eight that Jesus was probably forewarned by some sympathetic person who had learned that one of the Twelve planned to betray him.

(3) In chapter nine we noted that Peter's denial was something Jesus could foresee as probable because of his knowledge of Peter's personality. Jesus realized that when his enemies actually came to seize him, Peter would be just as frightened as the other disciples and would flee to avoid capture and possible death. Additional details learned "after the fact" were joined to Jesus original prediction by the early church.

(4) The miraculous availability of the ass at Bethphage on Palm Sunday was explained in chapter seven as midrashic theology (not history).

(5) Jesus' predictions of his death and Resurrection have already been explained in the answer to question four in this chapter.

11. Why does the Apostles' Creed say that Jesus "descended into hell"?

In order to grasp the answer to this question we should begin by reminding ourselves that the word in Hebrew that corresponds to the English word "hell" is "sheol." Before the book of Daniel introduced the eschatological promise of Everlasting Life in the New Creation, the ancient Jews believed that everyone who died and went to sheol was in the same condition and would remain there forever. The only difference was that wicked people were thought to go there sooner and good people only after the reward of a long life on earth. ("Honor your father and your mother that your days may be long in the land which the Lord your God gives you"; Ex 20:12.)

But after the book of Daniel introduced eschatological hope, the Jews decided that sheol had to be divided into two distinct parts. The righteous, they believed, were waiting in *upper* sheol and the wicked in *lower* sheol until the world ended and the Final Judgment occurred. After the Judgment, the righteous would enter the New Creation, but the wicked would be cast back into lower sheol to suffer everlasting punishment. Until the end of history, therefore, all the dead would have to wait in sheol until they were raised on Judgment Day.

When the early church reflected on the assurance of Salvation which God had revealed to her through the Risen Jesus, she correctly discerned that this salvation was also extended to all good human beings who had lived and died before Jesus. She *assumed,* therefore, that between Good Friday (when Jesus died) and Easter Sunday (when she believed God had raised him), the soul of Jesus had descended into upper sheol to await his Resurrection and to announce the Good News of salvation to the righteous dead waiting there. (We find an obscure variation on this kind of speculation in 1 Peter 3:18-20.)

By means of this symbolic theology the church reminded herself that the assurance of salvation from sin and death revealed to humankind through Jesus reached back through time to the very beginning of the human race. All humans, therefore, have access to the gracious love and forgiveness of God which enable us to reach Eternal Life in God's Kingdom.

12. Since the electrical impulses required for consciousness are derived from the material body, how do Christians answer the objection that there can be no conscious life after the body's physical dissolution at death?

It is true that the electrical impulses required for spiritual (i.e., rational, self-transcending) consciousness are derived from the material body. But, as indicated in chapter two, matter and energy are convertible ($E = mc^2$). Energy is the ultra-subtle and invisible form of matter, and matter is a concentrated and visible form of energy. We have also learned from Life philosophy that human spirit (i.e., the power of unlimited self-transcendence) is the most complex form of energy released by the evolutionary process.

This means that our spiritual center (traditionally called the spiritual soul) which can anticipate transcending our physical body's dissolution is actually *a subtle form of matter.* This subtle form of matter can be thought of as a "spiritual body" which is the subtle precipitate of our physical body's dissolution. As such, it is the subtle material source of the electrical impulses required for transformed consciousness beyond death. Given this monistic interpretation of human spirit (which frees our understanding of the body/soul relationship from ancient Greek dualism), there is no compelling reason why human consciousness cannot transcend death. And there are impressive indications in our self-transcending design that it probably does.

Contemporary physics suggests that the structure of the matter and energy which constitute our universe may involve ten dimensions. (When these ten dimensions are assumed, the related mathematical computations produce no unwanted infinities.) Four of these dimensions are present in our experience of *macroscopic* phenomena. The other six dimensions are *submicroscopic* in nature and are characterized by "negative" mathematical infinity (which reverses the laws that govern "positive" mathematical infinity). Some or all of these submicroscopic dimensions are involved in the astonishing world of fractal geometry in which increasingly smaller variations of "irregular" designs keep receding infinitely into ultramicroscopic depths.

It is probably in an ultramicroscopic realm akin to the more remote reaches of fractal geometry that the divine programming is located which governs the evolution of energy and matter. This realm has been equipped with the unlimited number of possible designs and contingency plans required for the unfolding of increasingly complex forms of life. If favorable circumstances arise, these latent designs emerge from evolutionary potentiality.

Paramount among these latent designs is the eventual emergence of the subtle spiritual body which transcends our physical dissolution. This spiritual body, in turn, is programmed to release unendingly the subtle electrical impulses required for our new mode of consciousness in Eternal Life. The arrival of our personal consciousness at full participation in God's creative Life is the divinely orchestrated consummation of the "anthropic principle" which undergirds the evolution of life in our universe.

13. Does belief in Eternal Life and unending consciousness after death contradict the law of entropy which says that all things in the universe will eventually run out of the undissipated energy necessary for work (or continued activity)?

In the physical dimension, energy always tends toward maximum entropy or heat death. (Entropy is the decline in ordered or undissipated energy available to do work in any physical system.) There are indications in our experience, however, that the law of entropy is transcended in the dimension of spirit.

We have already observed that spiritual energy is the most complex form of energy released by the evolutionary process. (Spirit is the power of unlimited self-transcendence; i.e., the power to engage in creative discovery with mathematical infinity.) Our self-transcending design implies that human spirit has been programmed to lock into "permanence" when it emerges from the evolutionary process. This conclusion cannot be experimentally verified but it can be *experientially* verified when we reflect on our astonishing ability to think about "permanence."

Human spirit possesses the power to think about permanence even though nothing in our universe is truly permanent. The ability to think about permanence was probably programmed into our spiritual design to enable us to creatively anticipate our death-transcending destiny. This recognition allows us to conclude reasonably that the spiritual body which transcends physical dissolution also transcends the law of entropy. The spiritual energy which makes conscious activity possible beyond death is no longer limited by physical laws. Spiritual energy is permanently *recycled* instead of being degraded and does not arrive at maximum entropy.

Questions for Review and Discussion

1. Does the interpretation of Jesus presented in this book destroy genuine Christian faith in Jesus? Explain your answer.
2. If the explanation of the Gospels given in this book is basically correct, does that mean the church has been reading the Gospels incorrectly for centuries? Explain your answer.
3. Why did ancient Israel's prophets encourage her to expect a military Messiah so contrary to Jesus?
4. Did Jesus literally speak the three predictions of his death and Resurrection which we find in Mk 8:31, 9:31, 10:33-34? Explain your answer.
5. How should Christians answer the claim that the appearances of the Risen Jesus reported by Paul and the other apostles were nothing more than hallucinations?
6. Was Jesus literally the first human to enter Eternal Life? Explain your answer.
7. Do the righteous dead have to wait for Jesus to return and raise them on Resurrection day before they can reach Eternal Life?
8. Will Jesus literally come on the clouds of heaven at the end of history to judge the living and the dead? Explain your answer.
9. Since the apostles believed and taught that the world would end in their lifetime, does the world's continuing existence indicate that the eschatological teaching in the New Testament is mistaken? Explain your answer.
10. Did Jesus know everything that God knows? How does contemporary biblical scholarship explain Jesus' prediction of Jerusalem's destruction, Judas' betrayal, and Peter's denial?
11. Why does the Apostles' Creed say that Jesus "descended into hell"?
12. Since the electrical impulses required for consciousness are derived from the material body, how do Christians answer

the objection that there can be no conscious life after the physical body's dissolution at death? Explain your answer.

13. Does belief in Eternal Life and unending consciousness after death contradict the law of entropy which says that all things in the universe will eventually run out of the undissipated energy necessary for work (or continued activity)? Explain your answer.